Beer Lover's Oregon

Beer Lover's Oregon

First Edition

Logan Thompson

gpp

Guilford, Connecticut

All the information in this guidebook is subject to change.
We recommend that you call ahead to obtain current information
before traveling.

Copyright © 2013 Morris Book Publishing, LLC

All photos by the author.

Editor: Kevin Sirois
Project Editor: Meredith Dias
Layout Artist: Casey Shain
Text Design: Sheryl P. Kober
Maps: Alena Joy Pearce © Morris Book Publishing, LLC

ISBN 978-0-7627-8373-1

Printed in the United States of America
10 9 8 7 6 5 4 3 2 1

Contents

About the Author

Logan Thompson has lived for most of his life in the suburbs of Portland, Oregon, where he fell in love with craft beer and the amazing culture surrounding it. He is owner of BlogAboutBeer.com, a popular blog focused on helping people discover and appreciate quality beer. Logan is an amateur homebrewer who enjoys eating ridiculously spicy foods and pairing them with hoppy Northwest brews.

Acknowledgments

Writing this book was a bit of a commitment. I did a lot of traveling around the state visiting breweries and beer bars. I want to thank my beautiful wife, Renee, for putting up with me, especially because she was pregnant with our second daughter literally the entire time I was working on the book. I also want to thank my friend Sean and his family for helping me in my beer travels and doing the tough job of sampling so many Oregon beers with me.

This book also wouldn't have been possible without the help of so many great brewers, brewery and bar owners and employees, and the numerous people who work so hard in the craft beer industry in Oregon. Thanks!

Introduction

If you love beer, you could call Oregon paradise. For years the state has been known to love and celebrate its amazing beer culture. Oregon has an abundance of breweries, brewpubs, bars, and restaurants that understand that beer should have flavor, and needs to be appreciated and respected.

I've lived in the Portland area the majority of my life, and for those of you like me, it's easy to take for granted just how amazing of an area Oregon is for those who love beer. Not only is there an abundance of delicious craft beer, the brewers in Oregon are some of the most creative in the country as they push the limits on beer styles and aren't afraid to try new things with their beers.

What's so great about the state is that I truly believe there is a beer here for everyone, even those who claim they don't like beer. You can find sour beers, fruit beers, Belgian-style beers, barrel-aged beers, chocolate beers, and, of course, plenty of beers bursting with hops and everything in between. If you don't like beer, use this book to try something new. I'm sure you'll be able to find a beer in the state that you'll enjoy. For those who are already lovers of beer, use this as a guide to branch out and experience all that the state has to offer.

Oregon is home to so many great breweries and is continuing to grow. Some people may say that we are reaching a saturation of breweries in the area, but I believe the more the merrier. As more craft beer enters the market, more people are able to experience the greatness that makes up craft beer.

So sit down, grab an Oregon beer, and read about the great breweries, brewpubs, beer bars, restaurants, and beer festivals in the state. Cheers!

How to Use This Guide

The beer scene in Oregon is growing at a rapid pace. In this guide you'll find a listing of breweries, brewpubs, and a handful of beer bars broken down by areas of the state. Although it's a comprehensive listing of breweries, no doubt more breweries will open after the printing of this book, making it an even greater state to live in or visit if you're a beer lover.

The establishments listed in *Beer Lover's Oregon* are organized alphabetically within the following cities and regions: Portland, Portland Suburbs, The Coast & Western Oregon, Columbia River Gorge & Mt. Hood, Willamette Valley, Southern Oregon, Central Oregon, and Eastern Oregon.

It's important to note that the breweries in this book are production breweries, those that bottle, keg, and can most of their beer for sale and distribution to bars, restaurants, and liquor stores. Some have a taproom on site where you can sample their product. Each brewery listed in this book includes a **Beer Lover's Pick,** a look at one of their best or most interesting beers being produced, along with tasting notes. The brewpub listings are made up of establishments that sell the majority of the beer they brew on the premises at their own restaurant and bar.

After the brewery, brewpub, and beer bar listings, you'll find sections on:

Beer Festivals: A look at some of the largest and most interesting beer festivals in the state that allow you to sample quite a large selection of beers from multiple breweries.

BYOB: Brew Your Own Beer: Oregon is one of the best states to be a homebrewer because of its great access to some amazing shops and fresh ingredients. Here you can find a handful of shops around the state to help you get started brewing, along with some clone recipes for those already familiar with brewing.

In the Kitchen: Beer is great on its own, but it can also make an amazing ingredient in food. In this section you'll find recipes you can make at home utilizing beer from around Oregon.

Pub Crawls: If you're visiting a city and want to make the most of your time, check out these itineraries of some great pub crawls. Grab some friends and some good comfortable shoes to walk in, and head out for a beer lover's adventure using these trip suggestions.

Glossary of Terms

ABV: Alcohol by volume—the percentage of alcohol in a beer. A typical domestic beer is a little less than 5 percent ABV.

Ale: Beer brewed with top fermenting yeast. Quicker to brew than lagers, and most every craft beer is a style of ale. Popular styles of ales include pale ales, amber ales, stouts, and porters.

Altbier: A German style of ale, typically brown in color, smooth, and fruity.

Barleywine: Not a wine at all but a high-ABV ale that originated in England and is typically sweet. American versions often have large amounts of hops.

Barrel of beer: Production of beer is measured in barrels. A barrel equals 31 gallons.

Beer: An alcoholic beverage brewed with malt, water, hops, and yeast.

Beer bar: A bar that focuses on carrying craft or fine imported beers.

Bitter: An English bitter is an English-style ale, more hoppy than an English mild, but less hoppy than an IPA.

Bock: A German-style lager, typically stronger than the typical lager.

Bomber: Most beers are packaged in 12-ounce bottles. Bombers are 22-ounce bottles.

Brewpub: Typically a restaurant, but sometimes a bar, that brews its own beers on premises.

Cask: Also known as real ales, cask ales are naturally carbonated and are usually served with a hand pump rather than forced out with carbon dioxide or nitrogen.

Clone beer: A clone beer is a homebrew recipe based on a commercial beer.

Contract brewery: A company that does not have its own brewery and pays someone else to brew and bottle its beer.

Craft beer: High-quality, flavorful beer made by small breweries.

Double: Two meanings. Most often meant as a higher-alcohol version of a beer, most typically used in reference to a double, or imperial, IPA. Can also be used as an American translation of a Belgian *dubbel,* a style of Belgian ale.

ESB: Extra-special bitter. A traditional malt-heavy English pub ale with low bitterness, usually served on cask.

Gastropub: A beer-centric bar or pub that exhibits the same amount of care selecting its foods as it does its beers.

Growler: A half-gallon jug of beer. Many brewpubs sell growlers of their beers to go.

Gypsy brewer: A company that does not own its own brewery, but rents space at an existing brewery to brew it themselves.

Hops: Hops are flowers used in beers to produce aroma, bitterness, and flavor. Nearly every beer in the world has hops.

IBU: International bittering units, which are used to measure how bitter a beer is.

Imperial: A higher-alcohol version of a regular-strength beer.

IPA: India Pale Ale. A popular style of ale created in England that has taken a decidedly American twist over the years. Often bitter, thanks to more hops used than in other styles of beer.

Kolsch: A light, refreshing German-style ale.

Lager: Beer brewed with bottom-fermenting yeast. Takes longer and is harder to brew than ales. Popular styles of lagers include black lagers, Doppelbocks, Pilsners, and Vienna lagers.

Malt: Typically barley malt, but sometimes wheat malt. Malt provides the fermentable sugar in beers. The more fermentable sugar, the higher the ABV in a beer. Without malt, a beer would be too bitter from the hops.

Microbrewery: A brewery that brews less than 15,000 barrels of beer a year.

Nanobrewery: A brewery that brews four barrels of beer per batch or less.

Nitro draft: Most beers that are served on draft using kegs pressurized with carbon dioxide. Occasionally, particularly with stouts, nitrogen is used, which helps create a creamier body.

Pilsner: A style of German or Czechoslovakian lager, usually light in color. Most mass-produced beers are based on this style.

Porter: A dark ale, similar to the stout but with fewer roasted characters.

Pounders: 16-ounce cans.

Quad: A strong Belgian-style ale, typically sweet and high in alcohol.

Regional brewery: A brewery that brews up to 6 million barrels of beer a year.

Russian imperial stout: A stout is a dark, heavy beer. A Russian imperial stout is a higher-alcohol, thicker-bodied version of regular stouts.

Saison: Also known as a Belgian or French farmhouse ale. It can be fruity, and it can also be peppery. Usually refreshing.

Seasonal: A beer that is brewed only at a certain time of year to coincide with the seasons.

Session beer: A low-alcohol beer, one you can have several of in one long drinking "session."

Stout: A dark beer brewed with roasted malts.

Strong ale: A style of ale that is typically both hoppy and malty and can be aged for years.

Tap takeover: An event where a bar or pub hosts a brewery and has several of its beers on tap.

Triple (Tripel): A Belgian-style ale, typically lighter in color than a Dubbel but higher in alcohol.

Wheat beer: Beers, such as Hefeweizens and Witbiers, are brewed using wheat malt along with barley malt.

Yeast: The living organism in beer that causes the sugars to ferment and become alcohol.

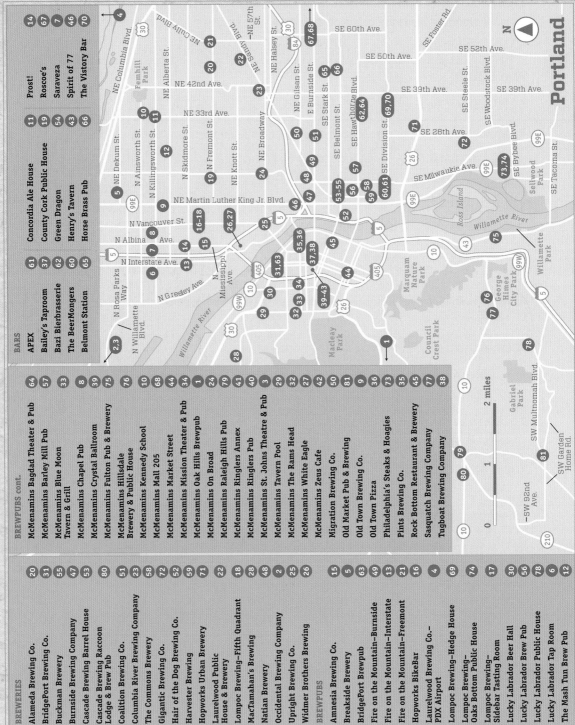

Portland

N

BREWERIES

20	Alameda Brewing Co.
31	BridgePort Brewing Co.
55	Buckman Brewery
47	Burnside Brewing Company
53	Cascade Brewing Barrel House
80	Cascade Brewing Raccoon Lodge & Brew Pub
51	Coalition Brewing Co.
23	Columbia River Brewing Company
58	The Commons Brewery
72	Gigantic Brewing Co.
52	Hair of the Dog Brewing Co.
59	Harvester Brewing
71	Hopworks Urban Brewery
22	Laurelwood Public House & Brewery
18	Lompoc Brewing–Fifth Quadrant
28	MacTarnahan's Brewing
48	Natian Brewery
2	Occidental Brewing Company
25	Upright Brewing Co.
26	Widmer Brothers Brewing

BREWPUBS

15	Amnesia Brewing Co.
5	Breakside Brewery
63	BridgePort Brewpub
49	Fire on the Mountain–Burnside
13	Fire on the Mountain–Interstate
21	Fire on the Mountain–Freemont
16	Hopworks BikeBar
4	Laurelwood Brewing Co.–PDX Airport
69	Lompoc Brewing–Hedge House
74	Lompoc Brewing–Oaks Bottom Public House
17	Lompoc Brewing–Sidebar Tasting Room
30	Lucky Labrador Beer Hall
56	Lucky Labrador Brew Pub
78	Lucky Labrador Public House
6	Lucky Labrador Tap Room
12	The Mash Tun Brew Pub

BREWPUBS cont.

64	McMenamins Bagdad Theater & Pub
57	McMenamins Barley Mill Pub
33	McMenamins Blue Moon Tavern & Grill
8	McMenamins Chapel Pub
39	McMenamins Crystal Ballroom
80	McMenamins Fulton Pub & Brewery
75	McMenamins Hillsdale Brewery & Public House
76	McMenamins Kennedy School
10	McMenamins Mall 205
68	McMenamins Market Street
44	McMenamins Mission Theater & Pub
34	McMenamins Oak Hills Brewpub
1	McMenamins On Broad
24	McMenamins Raleigh Hills Pub
79	McMenamins Ringlers Annex
41	McMenamins Ringlers Pub
40	McMenamins St. Johns Theatre & Pub
3	McMenamins Tavern Pool
29	McMenamins The Rams Head
32	McMenamins White Eagle
27	McMenamins Zeus Cafe
50	Migration Brewing Co.
81	Old Market Pub & Brewing
9	Old Town Brewing Co.
36	Old Town Pizza
73	Philadelphia's Steaks & Hoagies
35	Pints Brewing Co.
45	Rock Bottom Restaurant & Brewery
77	Sasquatch Brewing Company
38	Tugboat Brewing Company

BARS

61	APEX
37	Bailey's Taproom
62	Bazi Bierbrasserie
60	The BeerMongers
65	Belmont Station
11	Concordia Ale House
19	County Cork Public House
54	Green Dragon
43	Henry's Tavern
66	Horse Brass Pub
14	Prost!
67	Roscoe's
7	Saraveza
46	Spirit of 77
70	The Vistory Bar

0   1   2 miles

Portland

It's no secret that Portland is a city that loves its beer. With this love comes a massive selection of quality breweries, brewpubs, beer bars, bottle shops, and restaurants that take great pride in serving some of the finest beers found in the country. From breweries that started at the beginning of the craft beer revolution, such as Widmer, BridgePort, and MacTarnahans (Portland Brewing Company as of January 2013), to the recent explosion of smaller breweries popping up around the city, you could call Portland a beer lover's paradise.

It's not just the quantity of breweries in the city that make it what it is, but the specialization that each brings to the beer scene. For the consumer, this means it's easy to find a beer to fit pretty much any taste. If sour beers are your thing, Cascade Brewing has you covered. If you prefer European-style ales, The Commons Brewery offers a great selection. Those who like rare or experimental styles can check out Hair of the Dog, Breakside Brewery, or Buckman Brewery. Whatever your tastes, there is a beer just for you in Portland.

Breweries

ALAMEDA BREWING COMPANY

4765 NE Fremont St., Portland, OR 97213; (503) 460-9025; AlamedaBrewing.com; @alamedabrewing

Founded: 1996 **Founder:** Matt Schumacher **Brewer:** Carston Haney **Flagship Beer:** Klickitat Pale Ale **Year-round Beers:** Black Bear XX Stout, El Torero Organic IPA, Yellow Wolf Imperial IPA, Irvington Porter, Siskiyou Golden Ale, Klickitat Pale Ale **Seasonals/Special Releases:** Papa Noel's Olde Ale, My Bloody Valentine, St. Brigid Irish Red, Bad Bunny Cream Ale, Huckleberry Hound IPA, Barn Owl Imperial Brown Ale **Tours:** No **Taproom:** Yes

Part brewery, part brewpub, Alameda Brewing Co. has been a staple in Portland since the mid-'90s. Located in Northeast Portland, Alameda caters well to the local neighborhood through their brewpub as well as supplying the city and surrounding states with both year-round and seasonal beers. With distribution limited to the northwestern US, Alameda's 20-barrel brewery pumps out 22-ounce bottles of the house brews, and the 5-barrel brewhouse located behind the bar in the brewpub helps turn out quality beers available on draft. With 6 house beers and a handful of seasonals, Alameda focuses on crafting solid beers that don't disappoint. Their **Yellow Wolf Imperial IPA** is very hops forward yet is complex enough that it doesn't overpower the beer like many imperial IPAs tend to do. **Klickitat Pale Ale,** which is the brewery's flagship beer, is a favorite to many and is definitely worth a drink, as it packs a finely created marriage of malts and Cascade hops.

Walking into the brewpub, you are met with a powerful smell of hops, because their brewing equipment is situated conveniently by the front door. The industrial ambience makes Alameda a great place to relax with friends after work, enjoy a pint, and devour some great food. The menu fits the Portland scene well with a variety of Northwest-inspired fare including seafood, sandwiches, and other traditional brewpub items. For the fish lover, make sure to try the steelhead gyros or the Greek seafood linguini. The whiskey barbecue baby back ribs never disappoint. If meat isn't your thing, they offer a veggie burger made with the brewer's spent grain, peppers, and onions that goes great with pretty much any beer on the menu.

Black Bear XX Stout
Style: Foreign-Style Stout
ABV: 6.8 percent
Availability: Year-Round

Black Bear XX Stout has won multiple medals at the Great American Beer Festival and it's easy to see why. With a color that's about as dark as you can get a beer, this stout is surprisingly smooth and creamy, yet not too heavy. Notes of chocolate, coffee, dark berries, and a hint of spicy rye shine through, making it great for pairing with both chocolate desserts and grilled meats. The black bear on the label looks like he may be in the mafia, so you'd better not mess with him and just order the stout.

Portland

BRIDGEPORT BREWING COMPANY

1318 NW Northrup St., Portland, OR 97209; (503) 241-7179; BridgePortBrew.com; @bridgeportbrew

Founded: 1984 **Founders:** Dick and Nancy Ponzi **Brewer:** Jeff Edgerton **Flagship Beer:** Bridgeport India Pale Ale **Year-round Beers:** BridgePort India Pale Ale, Cafe Negro Coffee Infused Porter, Blue Heron Pale Ale, Kingpin, Hop Czar **Seasonals/Special Releases:** Summer Squeeze, Ebenezer, Dark Rain, Old Knucklehead, Witch Hunt **Tours:** By appointment **Taproom:** Yes

BridgePort Brewing Co., which claims to be Oregon's oldest craft brewery, has been a leader in the Oregon beer scene since being founded in 1984. Founded as the Columbia River Brewery, the brewery changed its name to BridgePort

Brewing Company two years later around the time their brewpub first opened. One of their first beers, **Blue Heron Pale Ale,** was the first in Portland to be bottled by a craft brewery. Eleven years after Richard and Nancy Ponzi first opened the doors to their brewery, it was sold to the Gambrinus Company, the parent company of Spoetzl Brewery in Shiner, Texas, and Trumer Brauerei Brewery in Berkeley, California, among others.

When Gambrinus took over the brewery in 1995, they replaced the lineup of beers with classic English ales, which lasted roughly 15 years. Once again the brewery recently decided to change the lineup for a major rebranding by replacing their ESB, Stout, Porter, and Ropewalk with **Cafe Negro Coffee Infused Porter, Kingpin,** and **Hop Czar.** Their **BridgePort IPA** and Blue Heron continue to be their best sellers.

Beer Lover's Pick

BridgePort India Pale Ale
Style: American IPA
ABV: 5.5 percent
Availability: Year-round
The BridgePort IPA isn't your typical West Coast–style IPA. It's not incredibly assertive and could almost come across as a pale ale. Regardless, it's a great beer with a lot of character. It's a hazy golden color with a decent off-white head that quickly fades. Fruit, pine, and a touch of biscuit fill the nose. The flavor is a slightly stronger version of the smell with the addition of citrusy hops. The texture is creamy and light, making it a great gateway IPA for those new to the style.

If you want to enjoy some of their beer while you eat, they offer a brewpub in Portland's Pearl District. The brewpub is located in the Portland Cordage Company Building, which was built in 1887 and features rustic brick walls, aged wood, and a warm atmosphere that is perfect for relaxing and drinking a good beer. The brewpub offers BridgePort's line of beers with some special seasonals available only on draft. The menu offers pizzas named after Portland bridges, burgers, salads, and an array of other entrees. Their house-smoked pulled pork sandwich is a great choice to pair with their IPA, as the barbecue sauce plays well with the nice hoppy character of the beer.

BUCKMAN BREWERY

909 SE Yamhill St., Portland, OR 97214; (503) 517-0660; BuckmanBrewery.com; @buckmanbrewery
Founded: 2010 **Founder:** Jack Joyce **Brewer:** Danny Connors **Flagship Beer:** None
Year-round Beers: Chamomellow,Ginger **Seasonals/Special Releases:** Black Saison, Dark Hemp, Assam Tea Ale, Apple Beer, Parnold Almer, Side Dish, Jasmine Green Tea Mead, Fruit Cake **Tours:** Yes, M–F at 4 p.m. **Taproom:** Yes, located at the Green Dragon

Buckman Botanical Brewery, also known as Buckman Brewery or Buckman Village Brewery, is all about making beer untraditionally. Located inside the Green Dragon, one of Rogue's beer bars in Portland, Buckman has reduced the amount of hops they add to their beers and replaced them with botanicals such as chamomile,

jasmine green tea, citrus, fresh ginger, and hemp. With a beer lineup that is bound to convert some tea drinkers into beer lovers, they proudly brew up recipes that are completely unique. From their **Side Dish,** made with marshmallow roots and sweet potatoes, to their **Ginger,** a beer made with ginger, each beer is specially infused with their botanical brewing philosophy. One of their most popular beers is **Chamomellow,** a unique and light beer made with chamomile that is all tea-flavored upfront, followed by a smooth honey sweetness.

The name Buckman Brewery pays homage to the Buckman neighborhood in southeast Portland where they brew. Space inside the brewhouse is shared with both the Oregon Brew Crew's small one-barrel brew system, which is used to make home-brews, as well as a distiller inside of the Green Dragon. If you visit, it's the only place in the country where you can drink and see two breweries and a distillery in action at the same time. While Buckman's beer isn't distributed heavily, they have permanent taps set up at the Green Dragon along with a few other restaurants around the area. Buckman beers are also found at many other Rogue Ales locations, as they are the parent company of the small brewery. Their beer is offered in kegs, 40-ounce bottles, and growlers, which can be bought inside of the Green Dragon. Each weekday you can take a tour of the Buckman Brewery at 4 p.m. and learn about their brewing process, hear from their brewmaster, and check out their 15-barrel system.

Beer Lover's Pick

Black Saison
Style: Saison
ABV: 5.5 percent
Availability: Year-round

The Black Saison is an interesting beer that should be tried just for its uniqueness. To call it a saison almost seems unfair. It's a very dark black beer with minimal head that dissipates very quickly. Dig your nose in it and you can make out some faint aromas of sweet milk chocolate, fruit, herbs, and a touch of Belgian yeast. Take a sip and you will wonder why it's called a saison. Mild chocolate flavors and sweet tea flavors give way to a touch of spice that lingers. It's an incredibly light and session-able beer that gets better with each taste.

BURNSIDE BREWING COMPANY

701 E. Burnside, Portland, OR 97214; (503) 946-8151; BurnsideBrewCo.com;
@burnsidebrewco
Founded: 2010 **Founders:** Jason McAdam, Jay Gilbert, and Adam Cassie **Brewer:**
Jason McAdam **Flagship Beer:** Burnside IPA **Year-round Beers:** IPA, Alter Ego
Imperial IPA, Oatmeal Pale Ale, Stock Ale, Stout, Sweet Heat **Seasonals/Special
Releases:** Burnside Alt, Gratzer, Oyster Strong Ale, Meridian Rye, The Fruity Monk,
Berliner-Weisse, Permafrost, Nuggets With Attitude Fresh Hop **Tours:** No **Taproom:** Yes

Over the past few years a new wave of breweries has entered the Oregon beer
scene that blends traditional brewing techniques with innovative and interesting ideas that end up producing some truly creative beers. Burnside Brewing
Company, which launched at the end of 2010, has taken both their production

Beer Lover's Pick

Burnside Stock Ale
Style: ESB
ABV: 5.8 percent
Availability: Year-round
Often American breweries will
add extra hops to Americanize
traditional English-style beers.
With the Burnside Stock Ale they
did a fantastic job at brewing
a beer true to its original ESB
style. The copper and amber beer
is malt forward with a toasted
biscuit and caramel flavor that
playfully lets the herbal yet
fruity hops know who's boss.
This is the type of beer that
makes you want to sit in an old
tavern and knock these back all
afternoon while mingling with
the regulars.

Portland

brewery and brewpub and turned them into unique experiences. When it comes to brewing, head brewmaster Jason McAdam isn't afraid to try new ideas and take risks. The result is a lineup of beers that have a great balance of traditional, true-to-form styles and those made with ingredients not typically associated with beer. One of Burnside's most interesting beers is **Sweet Heat,** a wheat ale made with apricot puree and scotch bonnet peppers that's light and fruity with a subtle hint of heat from the peppers. They have chosen to keep all of their beers unfiltered.

Each of the beers they make is created with food pairing in mind, as food plays a significant role in their company. With the same creativity that is put into beer, the brewpub menu is not your typical burger-and-fries pub food (although they do offer a burger seared in duck fat). Lovers of many kinds of meats will enjoy choosing from dishes consisting of elk, boar, pork, lamb, beef, seafood, and duck. If you visit, try the Cohiba. It's duck confit wrapped in collard greens, making it look like a cigar, and is served in an ashtray.

Burnside Brewery isn't in the nicest part of town, but it's a shining light in the neighborhood. They've taken an industrial-looking building and crafted a space that's open with a friendly feel to it. Cracked concrete floors, wood beams, high ceilings, and an open kitchen behind the bar give it a personality of its own, making it a great place to grab dinner and some tasty brews with friends.

CASCADE BREWING

939 SE Belmont St., Portland, OR 97214; (503) 265-8603; CascadeBrewing.com; @cascadebrewing

Founded: 1998 **Founder:** Art Larrance **Brewer:** Ron Gansberg **Flagship Beer:** Kriek and Apricot **Year-round Beers:** The Vine, Sang Noir, Portland Ale, Red Eye Rye, Cascade IPA, Kriek, Apricot **Seasonals/Special Releases:** Vlad the Imp Aler, Bourbonic Plague, Sang Royal, Sang Rouge, Cuvee Du Jongleur, and many more **Tours:** No **Taproom:** Yes

In a region known for producing extremely hoppy beers, brewmaster Ron Gansberg of Cascade Brewing set out to carve a niche that would set the brewery apart from the hops race other Oregon beer makers were in. Using his background in winemaking and years of brewing experience at BridgePort Brewing in Portland, Gansberg has helped make Cascade one of the best sour beer–producing breweries in the US. Since they introduced sour beers in 2007, they've won multiple awards at the Great American Brewer's Festival for **Bourbonic Plague, Kriek,** and **Vlad the Imp Aler** and have received a lot of national recognition for these same beers.

With beers containing all kinds of fruits, such as apples, raspberries, apricots, strawberries, blueberries, cherries, and grapes, as well as a variety of other ingredients, both beer and wine fans will find a brew that fits their mood. Although sour and fruit beers are their specialty, they also produce a handful of IPAs, saisons, and other styles. Each of their beers is aged in oak barrels, and you can always get two beers straight from the barrel at their Barrel House. All brewing is done at the Raccoon Lodge & Brewpub location, which is where they started, although they have an aging room at the Cascade Brewing Barrel House.

The brewpub at Raccoon Lodge has more of the suburban-restaurant atmosphere, as it's located in the Raleigh Hills neighborhood. With a menu filled with typical pub food, the beer is what makes this place shine. Their second and newer location, Cascade Brewing Barrel House, is located in southeast Portland and has much more

Beer Lover's Pick

Sang Noir
Style: Wild Ale
ABV: 9.5 percent
Availability: Seasonal
When sour ales are done right, they are a masterpiece. Sang Noir should be considered a masterpiece. A blend of red and double red beers comes together and is aged in bourbon and Pinot Noir barrels for 12 to 24 months. It is then blended with aged Bing and Sour Pie cherries, giving it a fruity yet very tart flavor. Between the barrel aging and the fruit, so many flavors and aromas come into play that you'll spend some considerable time mapping them out. You may pucker your face, but this beer is so worth it.

of a city vibe. With 18 constantly rotating beers on tap, it's a great location to meet up with friends. Their food menu is small with a selection of salads, sandwiches, and small plates, each listed with a beer to pair with it.

COALITION BREWING COMPANY

2724 SE Ankeny, Portland, OR 97214; (503) 894-8080; CoalitionBrewing.com; @coalitionbrewin

Founded: 2010 **Founders:** Kiley Hoyt and Elan Walsky **Brewer:** Bruce MacPhee
Flagship Beers: Wu Cream Ale and Two Dogs IPA **Year-round Beers:** Two Dogs IPA, King Kitty Red, Bump's Bitter ESB, Mr. Pig's Pale, Hanso Stout, Wu Cream Ale, Loving Cup Maple Porter **Seasonals/Special Releases:** Wheat the People **Tours:** No **Taproom:** Yes

While many breweries are started by avid homebrewers, a few such as Coalition Brewing have made it part of who they are. Started in 2010 by two home-brewers who just happened to meet, the brewery produces a core of easy-to-drink traditional Northwest-inspired beers. The brewery itself is situated across the street from their pub and includes a 10-barrel brewing system along with a 10-gallon pilot system. They regularly have local homebrewers come in to brew on the pilot system through what they call the Coalator Program. Brewers can fill out an application and work with their head brewer to create a few batches of their own beer, which will then be available in the pub right next to their house brews.

Their house brews don't stray too far from your typical brewery offerings, but each is a solid beer. The lineup includes a pale ale, IPA, red ale, ESB, cream ale, stout, and a maple porter, one of their most interesting beers offered year-round. The **Loving Cup Maple Porter** is a well-balanced beer with coffee and caramel aromas, and a touch of cocoa and maple syrup in the taste. It's definitely worth a try. Their **Two Dogs IPA** is a little tamer than other Northwest IPAs in the bitterness department. It's easy drinking without the huge punch to the face many other breweries offer in this classic Northwest style. While they are currently offering only a handful of their beers in 22-ounce bottles, you can fill up growlers in the pub or find their beers on draft at multiple Portland-area establishments.

The pub is located across the street from the brewery in a space that's just big enough for a couple of wooden tables and a bar. There is a large rollup door that

Beer Lover's Pick

King Kitty Red
Style: Amber Ale
ABV: 5.75 percent
Availability: Year-round
Named after the neighborhood cat, Leo, King Kitty Red has a tough side. It's a red ale with a Northwest flair brewed with four different hop varieties. The color is a beautiful deep amber, the nose is all caramel and toasted malts, and the flavor is pure deliciousness with a somewhat sweet and grainy malt, finishing with a touch of bitterness. With a flavor that lingers, it's a beer that you can take your time and enjoy. Try it with their chicken wings for a meal that's fit for a king.

opens up the pub to the outdoor sidewalk seating area. A back patio is also available on those nice days, and shares space with the neighboring Grilled Cheese Grill. While you're able to get food at either the Grilled Cheese Grill or the pub, the pub menu is somewhat limited. The menu consists of options such as nachos, chili bowl, Frito pie, chicken and sausage gumbo, chicken wings, crab cakes, or a pulled pork sandwich.

COLUMBIA RIVER BREWING COMPANY
1728 NE 40th Ave., Portland, OR 97212; (503) 943-6157; ColumbiaRiverBrewpub.com
Founded: 2010 **Founder:** Rick Burkhardt **Brewer:** Rick Burkhardt **Flagship Beers:** Hop Heaven IPA, War Elephant IPA, Stumblers Stout **Year-round Beers:** War Elephant Double IPA, CRB Pale Ale, CRB ESB, Hop Heaven, Sandy Blonde, Stumbler's Stout, Rose City Wheat, Trippel Vision **Seasonals/Special Releases:** Paddlers Porter, Drunken Elf, Wee Heavy, Dubbel Vision, HollyWood Hefe **Tours:** No **Taproom:** Yes

With so many breweries in Portland, what happens to the space and brew systems of those that move on or relocate? In the case of the Laurelwood Pizza Company, Laurelwood Brewing's original pub located on NE 40th and Sandy Boulevard in the Hollywood district, it was converted to a brand-new brewery called Columbia River Brewing Company. For owner Rick Burkhardt, the brewpub was a chance to take his 30 years of brewing experience and create something special. Taking over the space, Columbia River Brewing's owners have set out to make a name for themselves by creating great beers and transforming the location into their own. Walking in, you feel almost like you're in a lodge, with wooden tables, beams, and rafters filling the space. One of the best parts of the pub is the large windows looking into the brewhouse, allowing you to take a look at the shiny kettles and watch the brewers work their magic. The place is very family friendly, so it makes a great viewing experience for the kids.

While the food and atmosphere are middle of the road, they make excellent beer. Their **Stumbler's Stout** is one of the best oatmeal stouts around town. Winning silver in the 2012 World Beer Cup, Stumbler's is solid all around with chocolate, vanilla, and fruit flavors shining in the dry taste. **Paddler's Porter** is a seasonal brew that's definitely worth seeking out in the winter months. With dark malts, milk chocolate, and vanilla, it's definitely a very tasty dessert beer. While the bulk of their beers are sold in the pub, you can find 22-ounce bottles of a handful of their beers mostly around the Portland area. Make sure to bring growlers, as they'll gladly fill those for you.

If you visit, the food menu is your typical pub food of appetizers, salads, sandwiches, burgers, and pizza with a touch of seafood, such as fish and chips, calamari, and coconut shrimp.

Hop Heaven
Style: IPA
ABV: 7.5 percent
Availability: Year-round

Although you could probably call the entire Northwest a hop heaven, Columbia River Brewing's Hop Heaven IPA is aptly named. Once you see the hop cone on the label with a halo around the top, you should expect some great hoppiness. Taking a sip, you'll soon realize they don't let you down. Brewed with 5 malts, 5 hop additions, and 2 dry hop blends, the well-balanced malt, citrusy, pine, and grapefruit all play together in a solid IPA. It's not overly bitter, but you definitely get a bite of hops that lingers.

Portland

THE COMMONS BREWERY

1810 SE 10th Ave., Portland, OR 97214; (503) 343-5501; CommonsBrewery.com; @commonsbrewery
Founded: 2011 **Founder:** Mike Wright **Brewer:** Mike Wright **Flagship Beer:** Urban Farmhouse Ale **Year-round Beers:** Urban Farmhouse Ale, Flemish Kiss **Seasonals/Special Releases:** Pale Evening Ale, Blonde, Little Brother, Sticke, Haver Bier, Wit, Pils, Madrone, Biere de Garde, and many more **Tours:** No **Taproom:** Yes

The Commons Brewery is like the little engine that could. What started out as an idea to turn a 1.5-barrel garage brewing system into a full-fledged production brewery turned into Beetje Brewery, a small Portland-based nanobrewery. Not long afterward, in an effort to brew more beer and expand the business, owner Mike Wright moved the brewhouse out of the garage and into a true commercial system.

While the nanobrewery had grown into a 7-barrel system, it was also time for a name change. The original name, Beetje, is a Flemish word that roughly means "little." Shedding the original name, the now-larger brewer became known as The Commons Brewery. Located in the Hosford-Abernathy neighborhood of Portland, the small artisan brewery is in an area full of great beer culture.

The beer is inspired by European brewing traditions, with a strong use of Belgian yeast. Year-round they brew an **Urban Farmhouse Ale,** which won a bronze medal in the 2012 World Beer Cup; **Flemish Kiss,** a Belgian pale ale; and a rotation of **Pale Evening Ale, Madrone, Pils,** and **Blonde,** which is their pale ale. All have a strong Belgian presence with a slight Northwest twist. Because they still have a fairly small brewing system, The Commons is able to produce a lot of varieties of seasonal and special beers. Their creativity has led to some pretty impressive beers for such a small brewery.

Beer Lover's Pick

Urban Farmhouse Ale
Style: Saison
ABV: 5.3 percent
Availability: Year-round
The Urban Farmhouse Ale won the Bronze Medal in the 2012 World Cup for the same reason people love to drink it: It's a great saison. The hazy golden color shines beautifully and the almost white head sticks around for a while. Belgian yeast, bananas, and other fruits make up the smell, with more yeast, malts, and a touch of lemon giving it a terrific flavor. The subtly spicy saison is a complex session beer at only 5.3 percent ABV that fits just about every season.

To try their beer, you'll need to either find it on tap around town, seek out their bottles around town, or head over to the brewery's tasting room on Friday or Saturday night. The tasting room consists of 8 taps filled with their beers. Have a glass or fill up a growler to take home. They also generally have a few 750-milliliter bottles of their brews that have been bottle conditioned and are ready to be enjoyed either on the premises or to go.

GIGANTIC BREWING COMPANY

5224 SE 26th Ave., Portland, OR 97202; (503) 208-3416; GiganticBrewing.com; @giganticbrewing
Founded: 2012 **Founders:** Van Havig and Ben Love **Brewer:** Van Havig **Flagship Beer:** Gigantic IPA **Year-round Beers:** Gigantic IPA **Seasonals/Special Releases:** The City Never Sleeps, St. Tennenholz, Rauchweizen and the Bandit, and many more
Tours: No **Taproom:** Yes

One of the most anticipated breweries in Oregon opened its doors in 2012 to great reviews. Gigantic Brewing is the result of two brewers who are well respected in the local brewing industry coming together to create quality beer. Van Havig, long-time brewer at Portland's Rock Bottom Brewery, and Ben Love, formerly of Hopworks Urban Brewery, have created a production brewery in an industrial area of the Reed neighborhood in Portland. The two focus on doing what they do best: creating really solid beer. Gigantic doesn't offer a brewpub or food, though they do offer a tasting room and champagne bar serving drinks each day of the week. Fitting with the location, the brewery itself has a very industrial look. Like many local breweries, this one has a rollup door in front that leads into the simple taproom welcoming patrons to come in and drink beer or fill up a growler to go. There is also plenty of space to sit outside if it gets too crowded or the slight chance it's not raining. Interestingly, if you visit the taproom you also have some choices of champagne to consume if beer isn't your thing.

Gigantic is keeping things creative by only offering one beer in the year-round lineup. The **Gigantic IPA** is the flagship beer and represents the brewery's focus on quality very well. Other than the IPA they brew multiple special and seasonal beers to keep things fresh and interesting. As part of the camaraderie in the local brewing community, they have brewed multiple collaboration beers with breweries such as Breakside, Oakshire, and Upright. Aside from the taproom, you can find Gigantic beer throughout the area at beer bars and restaurants. They have 22-ounce bottles available complete with fun comic book–like labels that are distributed throughout the area.

The City Never Sleeps
Style: Saison
ABV: 7.3 percent
Availability: Rotating

A growing trend in brewing is to take a beer that's not traditionally dark and turn it black. The City Never Sleeps is one of the few black saisons you'll find, though it will most likely be your first love in the style. The color is black with a hue of brown topped with a creamy head. Huge aromas of Belgian yeast and smokiness lead the way to an incredibly smooth taste that follows the smell with a touch of sweetness. It's an obscure style, but it works beautifully for Gigantic.

HAIR OF THE DOG BREWING COMPANY

61 SE Yamhill St., Portland, OR 97214; (503) 232-6585; HairoftheDog.com; @hairofthedog
Founded: 1993 **Founder:** Alan Sprints **Brewer:** Alan Sprints **Flagship Beer:** Adam
Year-round Beers: Ruth, Adam, Fred, Blue Dot (kegs year-round, bottles seasonal
releases) **Seasonals/Special Releases:** Doggie Claws, Matt, Fred from the Wood, Cherry
Adam from the Wood, Fred Flanders **Tours:** No **Taproom:** Yes

In a city filled with breweries on just about every corner, Hair of the Dog Brewing has produced some of the most sought-after beers both locally and across the world. Founded in 1993 by Alan Sprints, the brewery focuses on unique beer styles that get better with age and contain higher alcohol content. One of their first beers produced in 1994 was **Dave,** a 29 percent ABV brew that was created by taking 300

Adam
Style: Old Ale
ABV: 10 percent
Availability: Year-round

Adam was Hair of the Dog's first beer brewed and is still one of the best they make. It's a recreation of a historic beer style originally brewed in Dortmunder, Germany. The dark ale has huge aromas of roasted and smoked malts, dark fruits, coffee, chocolate, and plenty of booze. Following the nose, the beer has so many complex flavors that you could start to lose yourself in its intricacies. It's awesome. There is also a rare version called Adam from the Wood, which is Adam aged in American oak barrels. If you find it, do yourself a favor and order it ASAP.

Portland

gallons of **Adam,** their first brewed beer, and freezing it three times to remove the water. Though Dave hasn't been created since, it helped put the brewery on the map worldwide.

Most of their beers are bottle conditioned by taking beers that are ready for bottling and adding some freshly brewed beer that's just starting to ferment. This process helps the beer start to ferment again in the bottle, producing better and more complex flavors as it ages.

Back in 1994 the very first customer of Hair of the Dog was Fred Eckhardt, one of the great beer writers and historians, who has accomplished a lot for the brewing industry. He is also the inspiration for the beer **Fred,** a golden special ale that uses

10 hop varieties from 5 different counties. With the use of aromatic and rye malts, Fred is a very full-bodied ale that has a nicely toasted and hoppy flavor yet contains a warm and spicy bite.

The taproom, located at the brewery in an industrial area of the central east side of Portland, offers a selection of beers on tap, special-edition bottle sales, and a small array of food. With high ceilings, exposed wooden beams, brightly painted walls, huge windows, and skylights, the taproom is a very cheerful place to sit and drink some incredibly delicious beer and eat some better-than-expected food. The menu includes salads, cheeses, meats, pastas, and desserts that all pair well with the beers on draft. They also offer vintage bottles of their beers that are for consumption on site only.

HARVESTER BREWING

715 SE Lincoln St., Portland, OR 97214; (503) 928-4195; HarvesterBrewing.com; @harvesterbrew

Founded: 2011 **Founder:** James Neumeister and John Dugan **Brewer:** James Neumeister **Flagship Beer:** Pale Ale **Year-round Beers:** Pale Ale, Red Ale, Dark Ale, IPA **Seasonals/Special Releases:** Experiment Ale Series **Tours:** No **Taproom:** No

Over the past few years, the rise of gluten-free products in the marketplace has started to make things easier for those with celiac and other related diseases, those with wheat allergies, or those just staying away from it for other health reasons. The options for beer drinkers have been few and far between, with most gluten-free beers tasting nothing like the regular variety. Because of this, many beer drinkers have jumped ship from their favorite beverage as soon as they cut out gluten from their diets. This is where James Neumeister and John Dugan decided to step in and build up Harvester Brewing, Oregon's only exclusively gluten-free brewery. Without the use of wheat or barley, the duo have crafted up a variety of recipes that have given gluten-free drinkers hope for better beer.

Using ingredients such as chestnuts, sorghum, certified gluten-free oats, pure cane sugar, and a variety of hops, Harvester has been able to produce ales with some amazing characteristics that can stand up next to their wheat- and barley-filled counterparts made at other breweries. As best as they can, they source ingredients locally, with both their hops and chestnuts coming from Oregon's Willamette Valley. The brewery bottles just a few beers, including a **Pale Ale, Red Ale, IPA,** and **Dark Ale** along with a rotating beer in the experimental series. With chestnuts taking the place of malts, the beers have a distinctly nutty flavor that cuts through the sweetness of the sorghum and gives their beers a lot of balance.

Pale Ale
Style: Pale Ale (gluten free)
ABV: 5.8 percent
Availability: Year-round
Those with gluten intolerances, rejoice. Harvester Brewing's gluten-free Pale Ale is packed with great flavors in a beer that is missing only the gluten. With a slightly lighter golden color than your typical American pale ale, this bad boy is incredibly clear. With a blend of nuttiness from chestnuts, herbal hops, and a sweetness from the use of sorghum instead of barley, this pale ale has a refreshing character all its own. If you're looking for a gluten-free beer that actually tastes like beer, give this a shot.

Portland

Because even a little gluten can cause people a lot of pain, they have decided to strictly bottle their beers to ensure quality control and keep even the slightest amount of gluten from coming in contact with the beer. Harvester beers are available at a number of bottle shops, gluten-free stores, specialty grocers, and restaurants in Washington and Oregon. While they don't offer a taproom, they do open up for dock sales every Thursday so you can come buy beer by the case. With a dedication to making quality beer without the gluten, Harvester is forging ahead and making brews that anyone can enjoy despite diet restrictions.

HOPWORKS URBAN BREWERY

2944 SE Powell Blvd., Portland, OR 97202; (503) 232-4677; HopworksBeer.com;
@hopworksbeer

Founded: 2007 **Founder:** Christian Ettinger **Brewer:** Christian Ettinger **Flagship Beer:** Hopworks IPA **Year-round Beers:** HUB Lager, Crosstown Pale Ale, Velvet ESB, Hopworks IPA, Survival Stout, Deluxe Organic Ale **Seasonals/Special Releases:** Rise Up Red, Abominable Winter Ale, Ace of Spades, Secession Black India Pale Ale, Noggin Floggin, Galactic Imperial Stout **Tours:** Yes **Taproom:** Yes

If any brewery captured the very essence of Portland culture, it would most likely be Hopworks Urban Brewery (HUB). Their heavy emphasis on organic, local, green, and sustainable business blended with a love of bikes and good beer helps make a brewery that is designed perfectly for its city. The brewery itself is set up with sustainability in mind. From using a biodiesel-fired brew kettle and delivery trucks to sending their organic spent grain for use by a local cattle rancher, HUB has created the city's first eco-brewpub.

They have the same philosophy for their building and equipment as they do for the beer and food they sell. Each beer is made with organic ingredients and crafted by a team of brewers with a lot of experience, resulting in some pretty tasty brews, most of which are packed with hops, just like the name implies. The year-round offerings, such as **HUB Lager, Hopworks IPA,** and **Survival Stout,** are all solid choices. However, they really excel at producing some high-quality seasonals. The **Abominable Winter Ale** is a great option for hop lovers in the winter months. It's slightly sweet with a great balance of citrus and piney hops and roasted malts.

Beer Event

BiKETOBEERFEST

Every year Hopworks Urban Brewery organizes BiKETOBEERFEST, a celebration of bikes, beer, and bands. The one-day event at the brewery has a full schedule that includes 15 of their own beers. For bikers, there are multiple competitions including the famous Huffy Huck to see who can throw a bike the farthest. Stunt teams also come out and show off some crazy biking skills. You can even join one of the organized rides that start out at the Hopworks BikeBar on N. Williams Avenue. Throughout the day multiple bands provide live entertainment, and kids are welcome.

Hopworks offers a large brewpub upstairs that is set up with sustainable foods, is very kid friendly, and has a lot of amenities for bikers, such as generous amounts of bike parking as well as a bike repair station. There is ample seating both inside and outside on the patio, depending on Portland's weather. You feel as if you might be eating in a bike shop, as there are bike frames and parts everywhere. They even have banana bike seats above the urinals in the men's room. HUB also has a second bike-themed location called the Hopworks BikeBar in northeast Portland at 3947 N. Williams Ave.

You can take a tour of the brewery every Sat at 3 p.m. You'll receive a full tour of their system with explanations of how they make their beer as well as sample tastings. Reservations aren't required but are highly encouraged.

Beer Lover's Pick

Ace of Spades
Style: Double IPA
ABV: 9.2 percent
Availability: Rotating
Named after the British heavy metal band Motörhead's 1980 hit song and album, HUB's Ace of Spades rocks just about as hard. The hopped-up brew won a gold medal at the 2009 Great American Beer Festival in the imperial IPA category. The addition of hops at every point in the brew process gives you lots of citrus, tropical fruit, and pine, with a pleasant sweet malt backbone, in both the aroma and flavor that finishes with a spicy bite. It's a big beer with lots of bitterness, yet incredibly balanced. Be careful, though—Ace of Spades isn't meant for the weak.

LAURELWOOD BREWING COMPANY

5115 NE Sandy Blvd., Portland, OR 97213; (503) 282-0622; LaurelwoodBrewpub.com; @laurelwood1

Founded: 2001 **Founders:** Mike De Kalb and Cathy Woo–De Kalb **Brewer:** Vasillios Gletsos **Flagship Beer:** Organic Free Range Red **Year-round Beers:** Organic Free Range Red, Organic Pale Ale, Space Stout, Hooligan, Mother Lode Golden Ale, Workhorse IPA, Tree Hugger Porter, Gearhead IPA **Seasonals/Special Releases:** Stingy Jack Pumpkin Ale, Vinter Varmer, Ink Heart Cascadian Dark Ale, Organic Portland Roast Espresso Stout, Portlandia Pils, Hop Monkey IPA, and many more **Tours:** No **Taproom:** Yes

While most brewpubs and breweries aren't known for being the most family-friendly establishments, Laurelwood Brewing Company has made it their mission to create a place where people of all ages can gather and have a great time.

Beer Lover's Pick

Workhorse IPA
Style: IPA
ABV: 7.5 percent
Availability: Year-round
Laurelwood's Workhorse IPA is one of the brewery's biggest sellers for good reason: It's delicious. Workhorse is a great representation of a West Coast–style IPA that isn't too bitter yet is booming with hops. They use Simcoe, Amarillo, Columbus, Cascade, and Nugget hops, which give it a great aroma of citrus, pine, and a touch of grass. The malt is subdued in taste, with great citrus and a touch of bitterness toward the end. If you visit one of their pubs, try pairing it with a Greek lamb gyro or Thai chicken wrap to help cut through the spices.

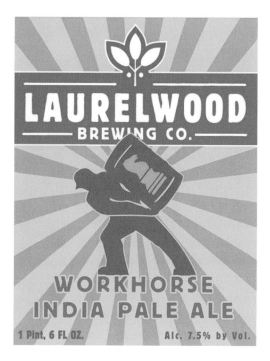

Since 2001, owners Mike De Kalb and Cathy Woo–De Kalb have created a family-friendly brewpub that does a lot to support the community. The atmosphere is really relaxed, with each of the 5 locations offering a play area for toddlers to hang out while their parents sip a cold drink and still keep an eye on them. Though the place is extremely kid friendly, it's set up in a way that makes it a great meeting place for everyone, even if you just want to catch the game on one of the TVs in the bar.

The multiple locations include the flagship brewpub on Sandy Boulevard, which is also where the brewery is located; two locations at Portland International Airport; a restaurant across the river in Battle Ground, Washington; and the newest location in the Sellwood-Moreland neighborhood.

Laurelwood's claim to fame is having brewed Oregon's first certified organic beers, and they continue to include several in their year-round offerings. The brewery produces 22-ounce bottles of a handful of their year-round brews, and releases a few seasonals, such as the **Vinter Varmer** and **Ink Heart Cascadian** dark ale. While they have a great range of both year-round and seasonal beers, their **Organic Free Range Red** continues to be the most popular and is a great addition to their home-made barbecue sauce. While the menu varies among the locations, they have a wide selection of food, with beer being an integral ingredient for many of their dishes. Make sure to try the bratwurst burger, which consists of a delicious bratwurst patty served with a fondue of **Mother Lode Golden Ale**, sauerkraut, and spicy mustard made with **Tree Hugger Porter,** all on a soft pretzel bun.

LOMPOC BREWING
3901 N. Williams Ave., Portland, OR 97212; (503)288-3996; LompocBrewing.com; @lompocbeer
Founded: 1996 **Founders:** Pete Goforth and Bob Rice **Brewer:** Dave Fleming
Flagship Beer: C-Note Imperial Pale **Year-round Beers:** C-Note Imperial Pale, Proletariat Red, LSD, Sockeye Cream Stout, Centennial IPA, Condor Pale Ale, Fool's Golden Ale, Kick Axe Dry Hopped Pale Ale **Seasonals/Special Releases:** 8 Malty Nights, Batch 69 Baltic, C-Songs Greetings, Monster Mash, Heaven's Helles, Oktoberfest, Saazall, Mai Bock, Brewdolph **Tours:** No **Taproom:** Yes

Over the years, Lompoc Brewing has taken many shapes to make it what it is today. Pete Goforth and Bob Rice first founded it as a brewery in 1996 to distribute craft beer to their network of taverns with the original name of Old Lompoc. They ended up hiring homebrewer Jerry Fechter to build and run the brewery, even though he didn't have experience in commercial brewing. In 2000 Fechter partnered with Horse Brass Pub owner Don Younger and purchased the brewery and renamed it the New Old Lompoc. Since then, Lompoc Brewing has opened a handful of other brewpubs, including the Fifth Quadrant, Sidebar, Oaks Bottom Public House, and Hedge House. In 2012 the original New Old Lompoc brewery and brewpub was torn down and all brewing operations were moved to the Fifth Quadrant location, although a new brewpub will open in a new building at the same location in summer 2013.

With a healthy dose of seasonal and special releases as well as a solid year-round lineup of Northwest-inspired house beers, Lompoc crafts some of the finest beers in the state. One of their most popular beers, **C-Note Imperial Pale Ale,** will excite any hophead. The name comes from the 7 "C" hops used in making the 100 IBU ale: Crystal, Cluster, Cascade, Chinook, Centennial, Columbus, and Challenger. Another classic is **LSD** (Lompoc Special Draft), a unique strong ale brewed with 6 hops that has a touch of smokiness. They also produce a variety of barrel-aged and specialty beers that are available only through their brewpubs. Many of their beers are available in 22-ounce bottles throughout the Portland area as well as in kegs, which are available at the brewery.

Each of the Portland locations has a full food menu you can enjoy with your beer. While the menus vary, you can expect to find typical pub food with a touch of their own creativity. Salads, soups, sandwiches, burgers, and an assortment of entrees are available. Both their barbecue pulled pork sandwich and chipotle black bean chili are created with their **Sockeye Cream Stout** and are solid options.

Batch 69
Style: Baltic Porter
ABV: 7.7 percent
Availability: Spring

Released in spring, Lompoc's Batch 69 is a Baltic porter that's brewed using lager yeast, giving it a nice and smooth finish. It pours a light black with a mocha head that looks as though you could slice it like a cake. Coffee, chocolate, smoke, and toasted malts lead the way with a slightly bitter finish. The mouthfeel is velvety smooth in this light-bodied porter, making it a little too easy to drink. There does seem to be a little variation in the flavor between bottles and years, but it's still a delicious beer.

MACTARNAHAN'S BREWING COMPANY

2730 NW 31st, Portland, OR 97210; (503) 228-5269; MacsBeer.com; @macsbeer
Founded: 1986 (originally named Portland Brewing Company) **Founders:** Fred Bowman and Art Larrance **Brewer:** Ryan Pappe **Flagship Beer:** MacTarnahan's Amber Ale **Year-round Beers:** MacTarnahan's Amber Ale **Seasonals/Special Releases:** Full Bloom Craft Lager, Summer Grifter IPA, Inkblot Baltic Porter, Hum Bug'r, Goose Bump Imperial Stout, Sling Shot Pale Ale, Spine Tingler **Tours:** No **Taproom:** Yes

In the mid-1980s the Portland beer scene was in its infancy and several new breweries were entering the market each year. During this time Portland Brewing was founded by Fred Bowman and Art Larrance, who set out to save the city from the boring beer that was leading the market. To build their business they ended up looking for investors to buy stock in the company, one of whom ended up being Mac MacTarnahan, a local businessman. After 12 years in business the brewery started to get in financial trouble and MacTarnahan stepped in and essentially bought out Portland Brewing. The company was then sold in 2004 to Pyramid Breweries and they changed the brand name to MacTarnahan's Brewing Company. The company is now owned by North American Breweries, and the name has been changed to Portland Brewing Company as of January 2013.

While many breweries tend to have a full lineup of year-round offerings, MacTarnahan's keeps it simple by offering only **Amber Ale** all the time. However, they have a handful of rotating seasonal releases that adorn Northwest store shelves with their comic book–like labels and names that stand out in a crowded marketplace,

Beer Lover's Pick

MacTarnahan's Goose Bump
Style: Imperial Stout
ABV: 9 percent
Availability: November–January
Brewed in the winter, Goose Bump is an imperial stout that packs in a lot of flavor. It's deep brown in color with very little head retention. However, it leaves some beautiful lacing on the glass to remind you how good it was. The aroma is all about the coffee beans, with bitter chocolate, licorice, and roasted malts making their presence known. Just like the smell, the taste is all coffee with a slight sweetness. This smooth and creamy stout brewed with coffee beans is complex and incredibly enjoyable and will have most coffee fans doing a happy dance.

such as **Grifter, Spine Tingler,** and **Inkblot.** Their seasonals range from a light summer lager called **Full Bloom** to a heavy imperial stout called **Goose Bump.**

The MacTarnahan's Taproom, located at the brewery in an industrial section of northwest Portland, offers over 12 beers on tap from both MacTarnahan's Brewing and Pyramid Brewing Company. While the food menu isn't extensive, they do offer a nice array of sandwiches, salads, and burgers. Their fish and chips are made with Mac's Amber Ale batter and served with garlic fries, perfect for pairing with either a pint of the amber or their Full Bloom lager if it's available. While there, take a peek at their copper brew kettles, which give the industrial building a somewhat antique feel.

NATIAN BREWERY

1321 NE Couch St., Portland, OR 97232; (971) 678-7116; NatianBrewery.com; @natianbrewery

Founded: 2009 **Founder:** Ian McGuinness **Brewer:** Ian McGuinness **Flagship Beer:** Old Grogham Imperial IPA **Year-round Beers:** Old Grogham Imperial IPA **Seasonals/ Special Releases:** Undun Blonde Ale, Lumberjane Stout, Big Block IPA, Destination Honey Red, Makeshift Organic Golden Ale, Autumn Chocolate Amber Ale, Old Grogham Winter IPA, Everyday IPA, CuDA Cascadian Dark Ale, CoDA Organic Cascadian Dark Ale, La Luz Summer Ale, and many more **Tours:** No **Taproom:** No

In Oregon there has been a trend in the marketplace over the past few years of small nanobreweries starting up around the state. Depending on whom you ask, the actual size to be considered a nanobrewery varies. Despite the size that classifies a brewery as a nano, it is safe to say that Natian Brewery started out as one, with a small 1.3-barrel system. At that size, it meant that brewer Ian McGuinness was brewing a lot to keep up with demand for his beer. After years of operating on the small scale, Natian was able to upgrade to a larger 10-barrel brew system, allowing the production-only facility to start offering more of the beers in cans. It is impressive, though, that they were able to can a few beers, such as their **Undun Blonde Ale, Old Grogham Imperial IPA,** and **CuDA Cascadian Dark Ale,** while they were still operating on the small system. Equally as impressive is that Natian has been at multiple area beer festivals including the Oregon Brewer's Fest, one of the largest in the US. With a 1.3-barrel system, they were able to brew only about 2 kegs per batch, so to enter such a large festival, they had a lot more brewing to do than the larger breweries there.

Besides finding their beer in cans, the Portland brewery offers their beers on draft at select restaurants and beer bars throughout the area. Being a small brewery, Natian tends to brew multiple special releases that can be hard to find. Undun

CuDA Cascadian Dark Ale
Style: Cascadian Dark Ale
ABV: 7.4 percent
Availability: Seasonal

While many parts of the country refer to this style as a black IPA, most of the time around Portland it's known as a Cascadian dark ale. The dark brown color with thick tan head will get your mouth watering. CuDA is an interesting beer, as it's a little heavier on roasted nutty malts and leaves the Amarillo hops as a subtle accent, with a characteristic spicy floral and citrusy orange flavor. Available in the spring in cans and on draft, this is a CDA that is worth drinking.

Blonde Ale was the first of their beers released in cans. It's a sessionable blonde ale with a smooth mix of floral hops and a balanced malt finish—great for drinking on warm summer days. In the winter they released **Old Grogham Winter IPA**, a hopped-up IPA with rum-soaked oak spires added in the final stages of fermentation. This gives it some nice vanilla and caramel notes to play with the bitterness of the beer.

OCCIDENTAL BREWING COMPANY

6635 N. Baltimore Ave., Portland, OR 97203; (503) 719-7102; OccidentalBrewing.com
Founded: 2011 **Founders:** Dan Engler and Ben Engler **Brewer:** Dan Engler **Flagship Beer:** Kölsch **Year-round Beers:** Hefeweizen, Kölsch, Altbier, Dunkel **Seasonals/ Special Releases:** Voorjaar Tripel, Lucubrator Doppelbock, Dunkelweizen, Silvesterbrau Bock **Tours:** No **Taproom:** Yes

Although the Northwest is known for crafting big, hoppy beers, Occidental Brewing Co. has decided to take a different approach. Instead of IPAs and pale ales dominating the lineup, they've chosen to specialize in creating typically German-style beers. Situated at the base of the St. Johns Bridge in Cathedral Park Place, Occidental, which means "western," opened in 2011 in one of the few neighborhoods in Portland without a brewery. Currently they're a production brewery with a taproom open 5 days a week. While their beer is the only thing served in the taproom, you can bring in your own food and drink the German-inspired beers. In the taproom check out the fairly massive can collection, which would entertain most beer-history nerds. The bar top is covered in hundreds of bottlecaps, making it great entertainment while you sip on a beer and try to see how many of the beers you've drunk in the past. You can try the year-round line as well as special and seasonal brews and even take them home in your own growler or Cornelius keg. Besides the taproom, their beers are available at multiple restaurants and beer bars around the area. However, they have yet to bottle any of them, so they are available only on draft.

Dunkel

Style: Dunkel

ABV: 5.1 percent

Availability: Year-round

The Dunkel style isn't regularly brewed in Oregon. More commonly found imported from Germany, Dunkels are lower in alcohol and make great session beers. Occidental's Dunkel is produced year-round and is almost too easy to drink. Brewed with clean-fermenting ale yeast, the dark caramel-brown beer has a thin tan head with lots of malt and bread, and a touch of hops. Its flavor starts off like a loaf of bread with sweet malt and finishes with a nice bitter bite from the noble hops.

The year-round offerings include a classic Bavarian Hefeweizen, Kölsch, alt, and a Dunkel, utilizing hops from both the Northwest and Europe. The **Hefeweizen** is crafted using German Hallertau hops and a true Weizen yeast, making it a refreshing, citrusy beer that doesn't need the added lemon to enhance the flavor. The **Altbier** is a slightly hopped-up version of a traditional German alt that has some great spicy notes. With a slightly different approach than other Northwest breweries, Occidental definitely stands out with a unique offering in a somewhat crowded beer scene.

UPRIGHT BREWING COMPANY

240 N. Broadway, Ste. 2, Portland, OR 97227; (503) 735-5337; UprightBrewing.com; @uprightbrewing

Founded: 2009 **Founder:** Alex Ganum **Brewer:** Alex Ganum **Flagship Beer:** None **Year-round Beers:** Four, Five, Six, Seven, Engelberg Pilsener (draft only) **Seasonals/ Special Releases:** Sole Composition, Flora Rustica, Fantasia, Late Harvest, Blend Love, Fatali Four, Billy the Mountain, Gose, Oyster Stout, Pure Wit **Tours:** No **Taproom:** Yes

Located adjacent to the Rose Garden Arena in the basement of the Leftbank Building, Upright Brewing provides Portland with a unique mix of old-world classic brewing and unusually creative beers. Specializing in farmhouse-inspired recipes of Belgium and France blended with local ingredients and a Northwest twist,

Upright produces incredibly flavorful and complex brews. The brewery uses many old-world styles of brewing, such as aging in old wine barrels and using open-top fermenters for some batches.

Owner and head artisan brewer Alex Ganum named the brewery as a reference to legendary jazz musician Charles Mingus, who is well known for playing the upright bass. Ganum set out to craft beers with the same creativity and uniqueness that Mingus had for his compositions. The results are a blend of year-round beers utilizing classic ingredients with seasonal and one-off beers that tend to get a little crazy. The year-round offerings include **Four, Five, Six,** and **Seven,** farmhouse ales with

Flora Rustica
Style: Saison
ABV: 5.1 percent
Availability: Summer
Flora Rustica is a unique Northwest-style saison. Brewed with yarrow and calendula flowers, both the flavor and aroma are heavily floral. Like a lot of saisons, it has a spicy bite, but with more herbal undertones and hoppy bitterness. The yellowish-orange color of the beer with its white frothy head is like a work of art. It tempts you in the glass to take a drink, and you will be glad when you finally do. The low alcohol and unique flavor make this out to be an interesting yet versatile drink.

fairly simple names, which give a nod to each beer's starting gravity. Their **Oyster Stout,** which won the 2012 World Beer Cup bronze medal, uses both oyster liquor and whole oysters, giving the beer a lightly salty flavor with a distinct mineral finish. If you're a salt lover, give the **Gose** a try if you can find it. It's a centuries-old German-style beer made with salt and coriander that produces a unique flavor.

While mainly a production brewery, Upright offers a limited taproom that is open Fri 4:30 to 9 p.m., Sat and Sun from 1 to 6 p.m., and 6 p.m. until tipoff during home Blazers games. If you've never been there, it can be a little hard to find. Just enter through the doors on the west side of the building and take the elevator down to the basement. Food is very limited, so just go for the beer and live music on Sunday. You can purchase bottles to take home as well as bring in your own Cornelius keg to be filled up with one of the year-round beers.

WIDMER BROTHERS BREWING

929 N. Russell St., Portland, OR 97227; (503) 281-2437; WidmerBrothers.com; @widmer_brothers

Founded: 1984 **Founders:** Kurt and Rob Widmer **Brewer:** Joe Casey **Flagship Beer:** Hefeweizen **Year-round Beers:** Drifter Pale Ale, Drop Top Amber Ale, Hefeweizen, Omission **Seasonals/Special Releases:** Rotator IPA Series, W' Series, Brrr, Pitch Black IPA, Nelson Imperial IPA, Oatmeal Porter, Citra Blonde Summer Brew, Okto Festival Ale, and many more **Tours:** Yes, 2 and 3 p.m. Fri, and noon, 1, and 2 p.m. Sat. **Taproom:** Yes

It was in 1984 when brothers Kurt and Rob Widmer first opened their brewery in Portland and started what would become the largest-producing brewer in the state. At the time they opened, the number of breweries in the US was in decline and only 83 breweries were operating. They first launched an alt beer, but it was nearly impossible to get the clear-beer drinkers of the time to give it a try. After brewing up a Weizen, they finally found their footing and created **Widmer Hefeweizen,** which has been leading the way for them ever since. Generally served with a lemon wedge, their Hefeweizen is responsible for turning many people on to good craft beer.

Today while other breweries of similar size tend to stick to a handful of beers meant to please the mass public, Widmer is ever innovating and is constantly releasing new seasonal and special brewed beers. Most recently they launched **Omission,** a line of gluten-free beers brewed with traditional barley. The gluten levels are then reduced through their proprietary brewing process, creating a very drinkable and delicious pale ale and lager. Aside from that they brew multiple IPAs in their **Rotator Series,** release one new beer each year in the **W' Series,** and brew multiple seasonals throughout the year.

The Gasthaus Pub is just across the street from the brewery and carries a variety of beers available only on draft and offers a wide selection of traditional pub food with a Northwest twist. Many items on the menu are cooked using their **Drop Top Amber Ale** including steamer clams, fondue pretzels, smoked bratwurst, and kielbasa. They also have a separate menu for those needing to cut the gluten out of their diet.

Each Friday and Saturday you can sign up to tour the massive brewery. You will see how their brewing process works and take a look at their four 1,750-barrel fermentation tanks, which were installed in 2012. Reservations are required.

Beer Lover's Pick

Pitch Black IPA
Style: Cascadian Dark Ale
ABV: 6.5 percent
Availability: January–April

Widmer's Pitch Black IPA was originally brewed as a one-time release in their W' series in 2010. After great feedback, they decided to turn it into one of their seasonal beers released January through April. Pitch Black is a Cascadian dark ale brewed with Alchemy and Cascade hops and 5 different malts, resulting in a toasty yet hoppy ale. The roasted malt is the headline in the taste, with pine, lemon, coffee, and chocolate playing along. For a beer that isn't overly bitter, this is a solid beer that would pair well with a lot of different meats on the grill.

Widmer Brothers Oktoberfest

You don't have to go to Germany to celebrate Oktoberfest. Each year Widmer Brothers hosts an Oktoberfest block party that attracts around 5,000 beer enthusiasts. The event offers a wide range of Widmer beers including their popular seasonal Okto Festival Ale. Along with plenty of beer, they have German-style food, accordion players, and other live music throughout the day. In 2012 the festival added an extra day, making it a two-day event allowing beer lovers more time to get their Oktoberfest on and thin out the packed crowds a little.

Brewpubs

AMNESIA BREWING COMPANY

832 N. Beech St., Portland, OR 97217; (503) 281-7708; AmnesiaBrews.com; @amnesiabrewing

Founded: 2003 **Founders:** Kevin and Kristina King **Brewer:** Kevin King **Flagship Beer:** Desolation IPA **Year-round Beers:** Desolation IPA, Dusty Trail Pale Ale, Copacetic IPA, Slow Train Porter, Alt **Seasonals/Special Releases:** Mother Plucker Fresh Hop Ale, Trail Hazer, Red Handed Red Ale, OK Ale, Mellow Yellow, Impale Imperial Pale Ale

Amnesia Brewing, situated in North Portland off Mississippi Avenue, has an incredible feel of the Portland culture. The no-frills brewpub spends the time creating great beer and not worrying about luring people in with fancy buildings or even a huge selection of food. From the outside, the converted warehouse makes you feel as if you're about to walk into an auto shop instead of a brewery. Inside you're met with a bar, old wooden floors, a few tables, and not much else, although there is a very laid-back feel to the place. The covered outdoor patio is amazing, with huge wooden tables that provide a ton of space for people and dogs alike. If it isn't raining, or at least not raining too hard, make sure to grab a drink and enjoy the patio.

Going with the no-frills theme of the building, the food menu is very basic and is all cooked outside on a barbecue. Choose between a sausage plate, a sausage and cheese plate, a burger, or a tofu brat. If none of that sounds good, just go for the beer. It's really good. Going with the Portland tradition, Amnesia loves to brew hoppy beers. One of the year-round selections is **Copacetic IPA,** a very impressive hazy IPA that isn't too bitter yet is packed with lots of piney hops. At 6.2 percent ABV, it's a great choice for grabbing a few drinks with some friends. The **Slow Train Porter** is a delicious option for the dark-beer lovers out there. It's extremely dark and packed with chocolate, toasted malt, and coffee flavors, with a subtle hoppiness that makes it refreshing anytime. They currently don't bottle their beers, but you can pick up a growler at the brewpub.

BREAKSIDE BREWERY

820 NE Dekum St., Portland, OR 97211; (503) 719-6475; BreaksideBrews.com;
@breaksidebrews

Founded: 2010 **Founders:** Scott Lawrence and Tony Petraglia **Brewer:** Ben Edmunds
Flagship Beers: IPA and Aztec Ale **Year-round Beers:** Aztec Ale, Dry Stout, Hoppy
Amber, IPA, Witbier **Seasonals/Special Releases:** Over 100 different special releases

Situated in the underserved neighborhood of Woodlawn in northeast Portland, Breakside Brewery has provided the area with great food and some amazing and unique beers. The brewpub itself is nestled in the midst of the neighborhood, making it a great spot for locals to get a meal or stop and have a beer while walking their dogs. With 2 rollup doors leading into the bar, plenty of outdoor seating at long wooden tables, and an upper eating area, the open space makes it feel larger than it really is. Although the space is very comfortable, the beer is what really makes the place shine. Instead of pumping out the same boring lineup of beers many brewpubs stick with, head brewer Ben Edmunds pushes the edge of creativity and concocts beers you won't find anywhere else. With a mix of traditional styles, barrel-aged, historical, and even cocktail-inspired recipes, there is a constantly rotating list of brews being served next to the year-round selections. In 2011 alone the small brewpub created close to 100 different beers, each with a unique yet well-crafted flair. In late 2012, Breakside opened a new production facility in Milwaukie complete with a 30-barrel brewing system, allowing the brewery to distribute outside of the pub and giving room for future growth.

The 5 year-round beers include the smooth and chocolaty **Dry Stout,** a **Witbier, Hoppy Amber, IPA,** and **Aztec Ale,** a strong ale made with cocoa and a mix of habanero and serrano chiles. The IPA is well balanced with a huge floral nose, yet a sweet and grapefruit-like flavor that isn't overpowering in bitterness. It's a perfect beer to pair with most of their pub food, which, like the beer, is well thought out and made with some of the best ingredients in the Northwest. Sandwiches, burgers, wraps, and a handful of entrees make up the menu. The Breakside Burger is highly recommended for blue cheese fans out there; the cheese is stuffed into the center of the patty and then topped with roasted wild mushrooms and caramelized onions. While the prices are a touch on the high side, you are paying for much higher quality food than at a lot of brewpubs around town.

FIRE ON THE MOUNTAIN BREWING COMPANY

3443 NE 57th Ave., Portland, OR 97213; (503) 894-8973; PortlandWings.com; @portlandwings

Founded: 2011 **Founders:** Jordan Busch and Sara Sawicki **Brewer:** Ben Nehrling **Flagship Beer:** Wonderin' Rye **Year-round Beers:** Electric Mud, Shocks of Sheba, Wonderin' Rye **Seasonals/Special Releases:** X-tinguisher Wheat, Hoosier Amber, Lefty Lager, Winter IPA, Cherry Brun

If you're a fan of chicken wings, you're probably familiar with Fire on the Mountain in Portland. For years the restaurant served the city with some of the best chicken wings around, taunting risky eaters with the El Jefe sauce. While they were known for their food, the beer selection was generally top-notch. After years of serving beers from predominantly Oregon-based breweries, they decided to add a brewery of their own to serve fresh beer along with their wings. The 7-barrel brewery, located at their Freemont location, provides a unique mix of beers to all three of the Portland-area restaurants.

In true Portland fashion, the **Shocks of Sheba IPA** is a hoppy but balanced Northwest-style IPA named after the reggae program *Shocks of Sheba* on Portland's KBOO radio station. **Electric Mud,** a chocolate oatmeal stout named after blues musician Muddy Waters's 1968 album, makes a great beer to soothe the heat from the food. The menu at all three of the restaurants is similar: wings, appetizers, sandwiches, and burgers. At the Freemont location you can also order an array of New York–style pizza. Although all of the food is pretty darn good, you must order the chicken wings if you're a carnivore. Nothing pairs with good beer as well as wings. With 12 sauces to choose from, you can have it as spicy or as mild as you want. If you opt for the spicier end of the spectrum, pair it with Shock of Sheba or **X-tinguisher Wheat.** Order some sweet potato fries on the side and you have yourself a great meal.

LUCKY LABRADOR BREWING COMPANY

915 SE Hawthorne Blvd., Portland, OR 97214; (503) 236-3555; LuckyLab.com; @luckylabpdx

Founded: 1994 **Founders:** Gary Geist and Alex Stiles **Brewer:** Alex Stiles **Flagship Beer:** Super Dog **Year-round Beers:** Black Lab Stout, Stumptown Porter, Super Dog, Crazy Ludwig's Alt, Blue Dog Pale Ale, Reggie's Red, Organic Golden Ale, Hawthorne's Best Bitter **Seasonals/Special Releases:** Black Sheep CDA, Triple Threat IPA, Scottish Holiday, Pavlov's Russian Imperial Stout, Wheat Stout, Solar Flare, Got Hops?, No Pity Pale, and many more

One of Portland's most well-known and respected brewpubs, Lucky Labrador Brewing, has been serving residents quality beers since 1994. Slowly growing over the years, they now operate four pubs throughout the city that each fit perfectly into their respective neighborhoods. The original pub is located in an old roofing and sheet metal warehouse on Hawthorne Avenue in southeast Portland. Each of the pubs offers plenty of open space to relax with a cold beer, mingle with friends, and hang out with your canine in a very comfortable atmosphere. Lucky Labrador is the epitome of a neighborhood pub. With great beers, decent food, and a feeling that you belong, it is one of the most down-to-earth pubs Portland has to offer as long as you don't expect the waitstaff to treat you like a big-name celebrity.

The beer list is constantly rotating, with multiple styles including barleywines, Russian imperial stouts, IPAs, rye beer, a porter, and many others. If you can find **Pavlov's Russian Imperial Stout,** do yourself a favor and order it. It's aged in Pinot Noir barrels and port barrels, giving it a unique and complex flavor. As far as the year-round beers go, you can't go wrong with **Crazy Ludwig's Alt,** one of the best altbiers in Portland, or **Black Lab Stout,** a very underrated foreign-style stout. Each of the four locations offers a slightly different menu, but each centers on sandwiches and some pretty tasty pizzas, which can be bought either by the slice or as a whole pie. If you're looking for a good neighborhood pub and want to bring your dog, make sure to stop by any of the Lucky Labrador locations.

THE MASH TUN BREW PUB

2204 NE Alberta St., Portland, OR 97211; (503) 548-4491; TheMashTunBrewpub.com
Founded: 2005 **Founder:** Christian Bravard **Brewer:** Christian Bravard **Flagship Beer:** Alberta Pale Ale **Year-round Beers:** Alberta Pale Ale, Summit IPA, ESB **Seasonals/Special Releases:** Blackberry Oatmeal Pale Ale, Concordia Cream Ale, Razorback Red

The Alberta Arts district in northeast Portland is known for its thriving art community that draws a diverse group of people. Like most of the city, the neighborhood has a love of beer and independently owned businesses. Inside this district on Alberta Street sits The Mash Tun. Founded in 2005, the small brewpub provides a comfortable place for both locals and visitors to gather and enjoy good beer and food. The space is friendly with inside seating and a nice relaxing bar. Step a little farther toward the back and it opens up to one of the best outdoor patios the city has to offer, especially if it's a warm summer evening. Many people bring their dogs with them, which gives it a somewhat down-home and comfortable yet exciting vibe. With the free jukebox, pool table, and darts, you have good reason to stick around.

They've recently installed a new 7-barrel brewhouse pumping out batches of Northwest-inspired beers. While the beers aren't considered the best in the city, they are well crafted. The **Summit IPA** is unique in that it is made by using only Summit hops, giving it a very sweet citrus aroma and a bitter orange rind flavor. For the lighter beer drinkers, the **Concordia Cream Ale** is brewed using flaked maize in the mash that gives the beer a smooth mouthfeel. With the addition of Willamette hops, it gets a slight herbal and woody aroma that isn't too noticeable. It's an easy-drinking beer.

Your typical pub food fills the menu with appetizers, salads, soups, burgers, and sandwiches. One of the unique offerings is the pita pizza, which you can customize. If you want to pair a beer with your meal, just ask the waitstaff, as they are typically very helpful.

MCMENAMINS

430 N. Killingsworth, Portland, OR 97217; (503) 223-0109; McMenamins.com; @captainneon

Founded: 1974 **Founders:** Mike and Brian McMenamin **Brewer:** Each of the 17 breweries in Oregon has its own head brewer **Flagship Beer:** Hammerhead **Year-round Beers:** Hammerhead, Ruby, Terminator Stout, India Pale Ale **Seasonals/Special Releases:** Irish Stout, Workingman's Red, Copper Moon, Thundercone, Black Widow Porter, Sleepy Hollow Nut Brown, Kris Kringle

When people think of beer in Oregon, the name McMenamins generally comes to their mind first. In 1974 Mike McMenamin opened up his first tavern, called the Produce Row Cafe. Over the next 6 years, Mike and his brother Brian bought and sold multiple pubs. In 1984 Oregon passed a law allowing small breweries to sell their products on site and the two quickly jumped on the idea of opening the state's first brewpub. The same year they opened, McMenamins became the first brewery to use fruit legally in the US by adding raspberries to the Ruby ale. Fast-forward to the present time and the company has grown to over 60 locations throughout Oregon and Washington state.

While beer is still central to the business, McMenamins is now so much more. From the multiple theater pubs, concert venues, hotels, and brewpubs, you can order a beer as well as their own wine, distilled spirits, and coffee. While the drinks and food are great, the locations are a big draw, as many are renovated historical properties. Some highlights include Edgefield, a former Multnomah County poor farm; Kennedy School, a former elementary school turned into a hotel, theater, and multiple restaurants; and the Crystal Ballroom, with a floating floor great for concerts.

In Oregon alone 17 locations act as breweries producing classics such as **Terminator Stout, Ruby,** and **Hammerhead,** as well as each producing its own seasonal brews. Each brewpub has a menu that varies based on location, but you can't go wrong with ordering the Cajun tater tots. Try the Captain Neon Burger if you like bacon and blue cheese, and pair it with a Rubinator, which is half Terminator Stout and half Ruby ale.

Beer Event

Lighthouse Brewfest

It seems like you can go pretty much anywhere in Oregon and find a McMenamins brewery. Throughout the year their many breweries get together for multiple festivals, including the yearly Lighthouse Brewfest in Lincoln City. Almost 20 McMenamins breweries enter an original beer that is brewed to a style chosen by a random drawing. Each of the brewers is also required to submit a tiny image to represent the particular brew. The one-day event is a great way to experience unique beers not found in any of their other pubs.

MIGRATION BREWING COMPANY

2828 NE Glisan St., Portland, OR 97232; (503) 206-5221; MigrationBrewing.com; @migrationbrewco

Founded: 2010 **Founders:** Colin Rath, McKean Banzer-Lausberg, Eric Banzer-Lausberg, and Mike Branes **Brewer:** Mike Branes **Flagship Beer:** MPA (Migration Pale Ale) **Year-round Beers:** Terry's Porter, Clems Cream, Luscious Lupulin IPA, Old Silenus **Seasonals/Special Releases:** Red Bier, Deuce Double IPA, Glisan Street Dry Hop, Bam Bam Amber, Black Hearted

"Clean industrial" is how you might classify Migration Brewing Company, located off Northeast Glisan Street. Migration opened in 2010, creating a very Portland brewpub experience for the surrounding neighborhood. Like many pubs in Portland that have converted old buildings into breweries, they have turned what was once an old muffler shop into a local watering hole serving up a variety of delicious brews. Going through the large rollup door that leads to the big open space complete with exposed ductwork and wooden beams, you almost get the feeling you've been here before. Inside you find multiple wooden tables, couches, a TV to watch the Blazers or Timbers games, and some dartboards. The space is perfect on sunny Portland days, as there is a fairly large outdoor patio area with lots of wooden tables to relax at. One minor note is that you do need to head inside to order at the bar, but that's not a big deal.

Their beer consists mainly of ales that include a full spectrum of colors, styles, and tastes, each based on a traditional recipe. The **Luscious Lupulin IPA** is a pretty solid Northwest-style IPA packed with quite a bit of hops and bitterness, but it is easy to drink. **Black Hearted Ale,** a special-release Cascadian dark ale, packs in great bready roasted malts and citrusy and spicy hop flavor in an easy-to-drink, dark-as-night brew. While the food menu is small, it all pairs well with beer. Choose between a variety of hot or cold sandwiches and a handful of appetizers. While not mind-blowing food, everything is delicious and should please both meat-eating and vegetarian beer lovers. Come by for their happy hour Mon through Fri, 3 to 6 p.m., and during all Blazers and Timbers games.

OLD MARKET PUB & BREWERY

6959 SW Multnomah Blvd., Portland, OR 97223; (503) 244-2337; DrinkBeerHere.com
Founded: 1994 **Founder:** Andy and Shelly Bigley **Brewer:** Tomas Sluiter **Flagship Beer:** British Bombay IPA **Year-round Beers:** British Bombay IPA, Multnomah Village Golden, Rat Dog ESB, Great White Wheat, Hop On!, Mr. Toad's Wild Red, Black Magic Stout, Pacific Porter, Ol' Granny Smith, Pinochle Pale Ale, Mr. Slate's Gravelberry Ale, Hot Tamale **Seasonals/Special Releases:** Maple Vanilla Stout, Berried Alive

One of Portland's oldest, yet often overlooked brewpubs has been brewing beer and serving a big selection of delicious foods since 1994. The Old Market Pub & Brewery off SW Multnomah Boulevard is located in what was once Comella's Produce Market. The restaurant and brewery provides ample room both inside and outside for visitors to come eat and to enjoy themselves. Inside, the pub is fairly large with room for quite a few people, although it does tend to get packed during the weekends. In the back there are pool tables, shuffleboard, and games that give it a relaxed atmosphere. They have a philosophy of green living that is evident by the large solar panels covering the roof that supply the bulk of their energy. By the brewhouse is a large silo for organic grains.

At any given time, they generally have at least 10 of their beers on draft. All are created with 100 percent organic ingredients. The lineup includes everything from your typical styles, such as **Pacific Porter** and **British Bombay IPA,** to more interesting beers, such as **Hot Tamale,** a golden ale made with fresh habanero and jalapeño peppers. Often they have rotating seasonal and special releases that include some unique barrel-aged beers that will interest any beer geek. Along with their beer, Old Market Pub is known for having some amazing food. The pizza, pasta, and calzones are tasty and excellent for eating alongside a few beers. Finish off your meal with an adult root beer float, consisting of vanilla ice cream and your choice of stout or porter mixed in.

OLD TOWN BREWING CO. (OLD TOWN PIZZA)
5201 NE MLK Blvd., Portland, OR 97211; (503) 200-5988; OldTownPizza.com; @oldtownpizzapdx
Founded: 2012 (restaurant in 1974) **Founder:** Adam Milne **Brewer:** None **Flagship Beer:** None **Year-round Beers:** Pilsner, Wheat, Pale Ale, IPA, Irish Red, Stout, Porter **Seasonals/Special Releases:** S.T.E.A.M., Winter Ale, Saison

Old Town Pizza has been a Portland restaurant icon since 1974. In the 1970s actor Willem Dafoe was a regular and could often be found on a couch in the mezzanine of the original restaurant. Portland Trail Blazer center Bill Walton was also known to ride his bike to Old Town Pizza and order a large vegetarian pizza and a pitcher of Henry's. The historic original building is said to be haunted by a ghost named Nina, a woman who was killed when the building was a hotel years ago while she was working as a prostitute. With such rich history, the restaurant is now known for more than just its past. Today the owners operate two locations and brew their own beer at the newest location on NE MLK Boulevard, where they started brewing in 2012. Known for their pizza, they are making a name for themselves in two other areas Portland is known for: biking and beer.

Old Town Brewing Co. is the first brewery in Portland to offer beer delivery via bikes. If you're within a 2-mile radius of either location, you can call to have pizza and beer delivered by bicycle. You can even order a full keg and have it delivered straight to your party, business, house, or even a hotel room. They offer a fairly standard lineup of beers that includes **Pale Ale, IPA, Stout, Irish Red, Porter, Pilsner, Wheat,** and a few seasonal beers that rotate. All of the beer is brewed to pair well with the pizzas, which are always delicious. The thin-crust pizzas are among the best in the city. For those who need gluten-free crusts, they have you covered. Both locations offer a great experience for both dining and drinking beer, but how cool is it that you can get your beer delivered straight to you on a bike?

PHILADELPHIA'S STEAKS & HOAGIES

6410 SE Milwaukie Ave., Portland, OR 97202; (503) 239-8544; PhillyPDX.com
Founded: 1987 (brewery founded in 1994) **Founders:** Steve and Amelia Moore
Brewer: David Vohden **Flagship Beer:** Betsy Ross Golden **Year-round Beers:** Betsy Ross Golden, Two Street Stout, Ginger Hefeweizen, Independence IPA, Blackberry Porter, Coffee Stout, Philly's Pils, Rocky Red, American Wheat, Habanero Ale **Seasonals/Special Releases:** Cherry Wheat, Oak Barrel Fermented Pale, Dry Hopped Pilsner, Liberty Fell Fresh Hop Pale Ale, and many more

With so many breweries located around Oregon, it is inevitable that a few of the smaller ones will fall through the cracks and be neglected by the local beer scene. Walking into Philadelphia's Steaks & Hoagies, you can understand a bit why they don't show up on the local beer scene often. With a name that doesn't mention brewpub, brewery, or beer, it's easy to pass them over as just a neighborhood sandwich shop. The Portland location is in the Sellwood-Moreland neighborhood and has been brewing beer fairly quietly since 1994. Walking by, you'll notice a neon sign that says "brew pub" hanging in the window, but once you enter it's not well displayed that they brew their own beer using what was once Oregon's smallest brewery setup. The interior pays homage to the city of Philadelphia with Phillies paraphernalia and that of other city icons lining the walls. Along with the Portland restaurant, the owners also offer a second location in West Linn.

Philadelphia's is a sandwich shop first, brewery second. The cheesesteaks are pretty tasty and rank among the best in the city. You can choose from a menu of your typical Philadelphia-inspired steak, chicken, and Italian sandwiches. The beer is unique yet unrefined. With 11 taps, they generally have their own beers available along with a couple from local breweries. One notable beer to try is the barrel-aged **Betsy Ross Golden Ale.** It's a golden ale aged in a Syrah wine barrel, giving the beer a nice oak and fruity flavor. Other beers include ingredients such as habaneros, jalapeños, cranberries, strawberries, and apricots, making them tempting to try. Go for the delicious food; stay for the beer.

PINTS BREWING COMPANY

412 NW 5th Ave., Portland, OR 97209; (503) 564-BREW; PintsBrewing.com; @pintsbrewing
Founded: 2012 **Founder:** Chad Rennaker **Brewer:** New brewer to be announced
Flagship Beers: Rip Saw Red, Steel Bridge Stout, Seismic IPA **Year-round Beers:** Red Brick Rye, Rip Saw Red, Seismic IPA, Steel Bridge Stout, Tavern Ale **Seasonals/Special Releases:** Legalize Wit, Next Generation Strong Ale

The Northwest is known for two specialties: great beer and great coffee. Pints, located at the edge of the Pearl District in Oldtown/Chinatown, combines both of these drinks in a unique way not seen by other local brewpubs. On weekday mornings the location is known as Pints Everyday Coffee and acts as your typical urban coffee shop with locally brewed coffee. After the morning coffee rush, they turn into Pints Urban Taproom, a brewpub featuring their own lineup of beers as well as a few guest taps from other local breweries and a selection of regional wines. The building itself is a touch of modern design with a mix of old brick walls fitting in nicely in the urban Portland setting. On nice days you can sit outside on the sidewalk with your drink of choice or head inside and relax at the bar or even on a couch. Throughout the week you can stop by for live music, but make sure to check the events page on the website first.

The brewery, located in the basement, has been brewing since 2012. With the brewery's philosophy of creating quality simple beer, you won't find many crazy recipes. The year-round offerings include an IPA, Stout, Red Ale, NW Pale, and an ESB, all brewed to style. You can find a handful of seasonal and special brews throughout the year on tap as well, although they focus on crafting great beers that are meant to please the masses. **Tavern Ale,** described as a Northwest ESB, is a surprisingly delicious and sessionable beer that's brewed with UK malts and Northwest hops. The **Seismic IPA** is all you'd expect in a solid IPA, with an incredible nose and a sweet citrusy hop flavor that goes down way too easy. The food is a bit hit or miss, as they do grill burgers and brats occasionally, but don't come expecting a full meal.

ROCK BOTTOM BREWERY
206 SW Morrison St., Portland, OR 97204; (503) 796-BREW; RockBottom.com/Portland; @rockbottompdx
Founded: 1994 (Portland location) **Founder:** Frank Day **Brewer:** Charlie Hutchins
Flagship Beer: None **Year-round Beers:** Kölsch, White Ale, Red Ale, IPA Special Dark
Seasonals/Special Releases: Swan Island Lager, Volksweizen Wheat, Velvet Pale Ale, Sunny Day IPA, Oregonic Amber, Morrison Street Stout, and many more

In a city known for supporting local businesses, there is always that one business that doesn't quite fit the Portland mold but still is successful. Located in the heart of downtown Portland, Rock Bottom Brewery is one of the few chain breweries located in the state. However, to completely call it a chain restaurant is a bit unfair to how it operates. Yes, it is owned by a large corporation and has a lot of similarities from location to location across the country, but the brewery has a lot of freedom to try new recipes and create some amazing and clean beers. Each Rock

Bottom Brewery has its own brewmaster who gets to use creativity to produce a wide variety of seasonal and special beers available only at that location and sometimes at a few select locations around town. One of the specialties brewed in Portland is the **Morrison Street Stout** series, which changes based on the season. In the spring a dry **Irish Stout** is offered, followed by **Cream Stout** in the summer. During the fall you can find **Oatmeal Stout** and in the winter months warm up with a big **Imperial Stout** that is incredibly dark, smooth, and chocolaty. They have about 5 year-round beers that are similar to those at other locations, and generally at least 5 seasonal options to choose from.

Although there is some nice outdoor seating on the sidewalk at the restaurant, the real fun is inside. As it fills up with foodies and beer drinkers alike, the energy increases and it can get a bit loud. Head on upstairs to play some pool and have a drink with friends or just belly up to the bar if you're not hungry. If you're in the mood for food, they have a huge menu of burgers, pizza, sandwiches, salads, soups, steak, and an abundance of other options. Rock Bottom is definitely a great spot to go with picky eaters, as everyone will be able to find something they like on the menu.

SASQUATCH BREWING COMPANY

6440 SW Capitol Hwy., Portland, OR 97239; (503) 402-1999; sasquatchbrewery.com; @sasquatchbrew

Founded: 2011 **Founder:** Tom Sims **Brewer:** Tom Sims **Flagship Beers:** Woodboy Dry-hopped IPA and Red Electric **Year-round Beers:** Healy Heights Pale Ale, Woodboy Dry-hopped IPA, Bertha Brown Ale, Red Electric, Untimely Summer Ale **Seasonals/ Special Releases:** Swamp Ale, Drop It Like It's Hop'd, and many more

Southwest Portland, especially in the Hillsdale area, had been a fairly under-served part of the city when it came to breweries—until Sasquatch Brewing opened up shop in 2011. Located in a residential area in a building that can be easy to miss unless you're looking for it, Sasquatch brings the neighborhood a mix of great food and beer. The space itself gives the feeling that you're sitting in a mountain lodge waiting for the weather to clear. A few outdoor tables line the sidewalk, which are highly sought after on warm days, making it a great spot to watch cars drive by while you sip on a cold beer. Sasquatch is very family friendly and they cater to families with young kids. As the evening gets later, though, the kids tend to head home, creating a great hangout for those without children. The brewery offers a small selection of house-made beers and local guest taps along with hard cider and wine.

Why So Much Hops?

It isn't a secret that beers in the Northwest tend to be a bit hoppier than those in the rest of the country. In Oregon there is a constant battle going between brewers to make beers with more hops than ever before. We're seeing beers that aren't normally known to have a strong hop presence, such as reds and browns, being blasted with double and triple the amount of hops. As the beers get hoppier, happy Northwesterners continue seeking out the next big hop bomb to try.

So why does the Northwest have such a love of hops?

One of the biggest reasons is that the majority of hops are grown in Washington, Oregon, and Idaho. Through much of the first half of the 20th century, Oregon was the nation's leading hop-producing state. Today the state is the second-largest hop producer in the country, behind its neighboring state of Washington. Along with Idaho, the three states produce the majority of the hops grown in the US, which is second only to Germany in hop production worldwide. Oregon's Willamette Valley is similar in both appearance and climate to Germany, and both are located on the 45th parallel. For years hop-growing has been a big part of the state's agriculture, and many of the hop farms that exist today are third-, fourth-, and even fifth-generation family hop farms.

Not only are hops grown right in the state, much of the scientific research has been done at Oregon State University's Crop Science Department. Many hop varieties, such as Cascade, Willamette, Sterling, Ultra, Mt. Hood, Liberty, and Crystal, were crossed, culled, and cultivated at OSU. While the Oregon hop industry has had its ups and downs, the state continues to be one of the premier regions in the world for both hop-growing and research.

The hop harvest generally takes place around August and September, giving many Oregon-based breweries access for a wide variety of fresh hop beers. With such an abundance of the great flower that goes into making beer, it's easy to see why it's so loved in Oregon.

Healy Heights Pale Ale is a classic American-style pale ale that pairs well with pretty much all of the food. At 5.6 percent ABV, it's nicely hopped and smooth, making it a great choice to knock back a couple. They also offer a well-balanced **Woodboy Dry-hopped IPA,** which has just enough bitterness to notice, but not enough to make you squish up your face and run. The food menu offers a great mix of vegetarian options and meat dishes utilizing local beef and seafood. Start off with the deep-fried kimchee pickles, one of the best options on the appetizer list. The fish and chips are made with catfish, a fish not found in many Portland-area restaurants. Both vegetarians and meat lovers will enjoy the veggie burger with avocado relish. It's one of the best in town.

TUGBOAT BREWING COMPANY
711 SW Ankeny St., Portland, OR 97205; (503) 226-2508; d2m.com/Tugwebsite
Founded: 1992 **Founder:** Terry Nelson **Brewer:** Terry Nelson **Flagship Beer:** Chernobyl Stout **Year-round Beers:** Chernobyl Stout **Seasonals/Special Releases:** Hop Gold, Thunderbolt Pale Ale, Tugboat IPA, Amber Lamps, ESB, Ankeny IPA, Munich Style IPA

As one of Oregon's oldest and smallest brewpubs still running today, Tugboat Brewing Co. is often overlooked in a city with so many beer options. Established in 1992 by owner/brewer Terry Nelson, the nautical-themed brewpub fits snugly in downtown Portland, where it provides patrons a relaxing place to hang out and drink a wide variety of beer. The pub itself is like a time capsule that takes you back to the early 1990s while giving you an authentic Portlandia experience. Old wooden tables and booths fill the space while hundreds of old books and board games line the walls. It has the feeling you'd get stepping into your aunt's old beach house. In the corner is a small stage where on many nights you can catch some live jazz music while sipping on a beer and snacking on some food.

The beers are a little different than other Portland breweries, as they specialize in British-style strong ales. With slightly higher alcohol content in most of their offerings, you are sure to have a great time. Because they have a smaller brewhouse, the year-round beers aren't always available. However, they do have multiple guest taps featuring both international and local beers. Tugboat Brewing is most known for **Chernobyl Stout,** one of Portland's most potent and delicious Russian Imperial stouts. At 13.5 percent ABV, it has nice roasted malts with flavors of dark chocolate, dried fruits, licorice, and espresso. Be careful, though, as the alcohol is hardly noticeable, which is why they serve it in an 8-ounce glass. Aside from the beer, they offer a small selection of food, such as mac and cheese, nachos, fruit and cheese, and a pulled pork sandwich, although it's probably not the best place to catch a full meal.

Beer Bars

APEX

1216 SE Division St., Portland, OR 97202; (503) 273-9227; ApexBar.com; @apexbar
Draft Beers: 50 **Bottled/Canned Beers:** Over 100

Apex is a beer bar off SE Division Street in Portland that isn't for everyone, and they are more than all right with that. While many businesses cater to every need of the customer, Apex has created a unique identity for itself and won't stray from what it wants to be. While they don't accept credit or debit cards (cash only), allow kids or dogs, allow any mainstream sports shown on the TVs (even if it's the Blazers in the playoffs), offer table service, or have any food on the menu or parking for cars, they do offer some of the best and rarest beers in the city.

Inside you are met with a barrage of beer and cycling decor, with multiple bikes hanging around. If you're up for some fun, they offer a pinball room complete with small tables between each machine for your beer. The music gets loud with a mix of rock and dubstep blasting from the speakers, so head outside if you're not into the music. Outside it gets even better with tons of outdoor seating and a relaxed, friendly atmosphere. You do need to get up and go to the bar to order your drinks, but it's not a big deal. At the bar is a 50-inch TV showing all 50 beers on draft, which helps make your selection a bit easier. With beers like Dogfish Head 120 Minute IPA, Russian River Pliny the Younger, and Pliny the Elder, as well as many other rare beers making appearances, it's easy to see why Apex was rated as one of the 100 best bars in America in 2012.

Although they don't offer food, there are multiple excellent restaurants within walking distance, and Apex allows you to bring in food. They do offer a live beer menu on the website, so you can check out what's flowing through the draft lines before you head on in for a drink.

BAILEY'S TAPROOM

213 SW Broadway, Portland, OR 97205; (503) 295-1004; BaileysTaproom.com;
@baileystaproom
Draft Beers: 20 **Bottled/Canned Beers:** 75+

Situated on the corner of SW Broadway and SW Ankeny in downtown Portland, Bailey's Taproom does one thing really well: serve good beer. Walking in, you feel as if you're in a coffee shop, except there's a bar with 20 tap handles waiting for you to choose your drink. Inside you're met with unfinished brick walls, high ceilings, windows all around, concrete floors, and exposed ductwork, which all play into the bar's somewhat industrial yet rustic feel. One of the first things you'll notice is the big-screen display behind the bar listing the current beers on tap along with its ABV, price, and even how much is left in the keg. They offer beer in 20- and 10-ounce sizes, which is great if you want to try multiple beers (and with their selection, you will). If you want to bring some beer home, you can buy bottles to go or fill up a growler with what's on draft.

The setting is relaxing enough that you can kick back and chat with friends or make some new ones. Although they don't serve food, they encourage you to bring it in from other locations. If you like Mexican food, stop by Santeria, which is next door on your way to Bailey's.

With the constantly rotating taps emphasizing Oregon breweries, everyone should find a beer he or she will enjoy at every visit. Each month Bailey's has multiple events that do tend to draw a crowd, so show up early. In January they offer CellarFest, where you'll find many aged beers ready for tasting. The anniversary barrel-aged event takes place each August, followed by BelgianFest in November.

BAZI BIERBRASSERIE
1522 SE 32nd Ave., Portland, OR 97214; (503) 234-8888; BaziPDX.com; @bazipdx
Draft Beers: 17 **Bottled/Canned Beers:** About 15

In Portland you don't need to head all the way to Belgium to get a taste of a true Belgian beer bar. Just head to the Hawthorne District and look for the pumpkin-orange building on 32nd Avenue. Walk past the outdoor seating unless the sun is shining and step into the beautifully decorated bar. Rich colors fill the walls, in contrast with the rugged red floor of the small space, giving it a European flair and making you feel immediately welcome. In front are multiple tables to eat at, while on the left are a couple of comfortable couches to kick back and watch local sports on the 114-inch big screen. Fans of the Blazers, Timbers, and Ducks will be able to catch most games on the big screen, while soccer fans often can find both MLS and European games. Head a little farther to the back and you'll see the wood bar featuring 17 beers being poured from an authentic European-style tap system. Speaking of beer, lovers of Belgian-style beers will love the rotating tap list. A handful of the 17 beers on draft are Belgian-influenced beers from US and local breweries, such as The Commons and Upright, while the great majority are imported from Europe. The bar also has a fantastic selection of both traditional-style cocktails and cocktails made with beer.

Following the European-style ambience and beer list, you'll find a selection of locally sourced and organic Belgian-inspired food that pairs perfectly with the drinks. Start off with some truffle frites (fries tossed in truffle oil), pork belly skewers, or a charcuterie plate before enjoying one of the specialty entrees. For those seeking a good deal, make sure to come during one of the two daily happy hours.

See Hilda Stevens's recipe for **Moules de Blonde** on p. 220 and for **Jeanneke Beer Cocktail** on p. 225.

THE BEERMONGERS
1125 SE Division St., Portland, OR 97202; (503) 234-6012; TheBeerMongers.com; @thebeermongers
Draft Beers: 8 **Bottled/Canned Beers:** 525

On the corner of 12th and Division sits the somewhat nondescript-looking bottle shop and bar known as The BeerMongers. With a glass front door and a small rollup door as the entrance, it feels as if you're walking into a small warehouse. However, a few feet in and you can spot the bar and multiple beer fridges packed with delicious brews from all over the world. The shop is small, yet not intimidating in any way. If you like great beer without all the frills, The BeerMongers has you covered. The bar serves 8 rotating beers on tap that are focused on seasonal and rare beers, along with many from small local Oregon breweries that can be consumed on site or poured into a growler. Along with the tap selection, they serve over 500 bottles that can be bought and taken home, or consumed in the bar with no corkage fee. With an amazing selection of beers from all over the world, there are plenty of options for you to choose from. The staff is very knowledgeable and available to help in your selections when needed. For the price-conscious beer drinker, they offer some of the best prices in town.

While they don't offer food, you can bring in food from any of the nearby restaurants to eat while enjoying good beer. The bar does have a flat-screen TV, making The BeerMongers a decent destination to watch a game in a friendly and laid-back atmosphere. Throughout the year they also offer events such as meet the brewer, cellar sales, tastings, and holiday parties. If you're looking to buy a keg to go, they have you covered. They'll even help you order in something if they don't have it in stock.

BELMONT STATION
4500 SE Stark St., Portland, OR 97215; (503) 232-8538; Belmont-Station.com; @belmontstation
Draft Beers: 16 and 1 on cask **Bottled/Canned Beers:** Over 1000

Belmont Station is Oregon's oldest and one of the most well-respected bottle shops and beer bars around. Started as a bottle shop in 1997, Belmont Station

1000
BEERS

BELMONT STATION

added the Biercafe 10 years later, allowing customers to drink one of the 1,000-plus bottled beers, one of the 16 rotating beers on tap, or a beer on cask at the time of purchase. With a beer selection unlike that of any other shop in Portland, it's pretty much impossible to not find something you'll enjoy drinking. While a big majority of their beers are from West Coast breweries, you can find bottles from all over the US as well as from breweries internationally. Aside from just beer, they also carry an extensive collection of meads and cider and a handful of wine and sake.

"Meet the brewer" nights are a common occurrence at the Biercafe and often-times you can try rare, aged, or one-off beers you won't find elsewhere at their events. Each July they also put on an event called Puckerfest that celebrates sour, wild, and funky beers. Adventurous beer lovers can come out and try unique and fun beers from multiple breweries.

The shop and adjacent Biercafe pack a lot into a not-so-big space. Inside the Biercafe you are met with walls plastered with beer signs and tap handles, a few tables, and a bar, perfect for grabbing a drink after a tough day of shopping in the bottle shop. The food menu includes a handful of options such as snacks, sand-wiches, soups, salads, and sweet treats. Beer is the main attraction here, so come expecting to get some great beer and you won't be disappointed.

Puckerfest

Every July during Oregon's Craft Beer Month, Belmont Station hosts Puckerfest, a weeklong celebration of sour and wild beers. Each day a different brewery or two take over the tap with 10 to 14 funky beers along with multiple "meet the brewer" nights where brewers come to talk about the beers they brought. For sour-beer fans it is one of the most anticipated events during the month. Belmont Station's Biercafe extends its hours for the event, which tends to get packed during the evening.

CONCORDIA ALE HOUSE

3276 NE Killingsworth St., Portland, OR 97211; (503) 287-3929; Concordia-Ale.com;
@concordiaale
Draft Beers: 22 **Bottled/Canned Beers:** Over 150

Finding a good neighborhood watering hole in Portland that serves up a great selection of beer and food isn't too difficult. This is especially true if you're in northeast Portland in the area of Concordia Ale House. With an impressive beer selection, extensive food menu, relaxed neighborhood atmosphere, and plenty of entertainment, it's a great spot to kick back and enjoy yourself. While the building itself is fairly plain and not that special, the warm atmosphere upon entering draws you in. The interior is separated into 3 areas: a bar area, an eating area, and a game room complete with a free pool table, pinball machines, video games, and even video poker.

While it's a very entertaining place to go, the beer menu helps the place shine. The rotating tap list of 22 draft beers and over 150 bottles is carefully selected to offer a range of styles and breweries to fit many tastes. The draft beers are heavily West Coast focused with an occasional import. The bottles, however, are from all over the world with a big focus on Belgian beers. Each year Concordia Ale House puts on a weeklong Beer Brawl event that compares breweries from Washington, Oregon, and California to find out which state has earned the best-beer title. Twelve beers are selected and patrons get in on the action by doing a blind taste test and choosing the winner.

Aside from beer, Concordia serves a menu of your typical pub appetizers, salads, burgers, sandwiches, tacos, pastas, and entrees. On the weekend you can order breakfast and even pair it with a good stout or wheat beer. For the non–beer drinkers, the full bar includes cocktails and wine.

COUNTY CORK PUBLIC HOUSE

1329 NE Fremont, Portland, OR 97212; (503) 284-4805; CountyCorkPublicHouse.com
Draft Beers: 20 **Bottled/Canned Beers:** 10

While the County Cork Public House appears to be your typical Irish pub serving up pints of Guinness and dishing out shepherd's pie to the masses, when you spend some time there you'll quickly realize it's so much more. The interior is somewhat quaint, with Irish signage, tall ceilings, a couple of dartboard stables, and pictures of the pope, Ted Kennedy, and JFK lining the walls. While Irish beers are on tap, they have a great mix of both imports and West Coast beers. Fans of Russian

Portland

River Brewing will love that Pliny the Elder and a handful of their other beers are regularly on tap as well as the occasional appearance of Pliny the Younger. You'll also usually find Full Sail, Deschutes, Murphy's Irish Stout, and a rotating cask beer, among others, all served in both imperial pints and 10-ounce glasses. Stop by for happy hour Mon through Fri, 4 to 6 p.m. for a discount on beer and food.

On Tuesday and Friday you usually can catch live folk music from local musicians. It can fill up quickly on Friday night, but that's all part of the fun. When the weather is right, you can go sit on the patio, drink some cold beer, and enjoy the Portland air. County Cork is a very family-friendly pub, so feel free to bring the kids. They even offer a kids' menu.

While the food menu is filled with traditional Irish pub grub, such as fish and chips, red beet salad, bangers and mash, Murphy's stew, and shepherd's pie, it's all well crafted, delicious, and consistent. No matter if you bring your friends or your family, County Cork Public House is a great place to go have a great time.

GREEN DRAGON

928 SE 9th Ave., Portland, OR 97214; (503) 517-0660; PDXGreenDragon.com;
@pdxgreendragon
Draft Beers: 62 **Bottled/Canned Beers:** 40

If you're a fan of bars with a ton of rotating craft beer options on tap, you'll easily fall in love with the Green Dragon. Located in southeast Portland on 9th and Yamhill, the Green Dragon has been named by *Imbibe Magazine* as one of the 100 best places to drink beer in America, and it's easy to see why. With 62 beers on draft, there is never a shortage of great beers from across the country. The restaurant was bought in 2008 by Rogue; however, the tap list has stayed open to multiple breweries, making it a great place to get local and sometimes hard-to-find beers.

Inside the restaurant is Buckman Botanical Brewery, another Rogue-owned brewery that is run as a separate entity. Along with Buckman is the Oregon Brew Crew's 1-barrel nanobrewery as well as a distiller. It's the only place in the country you can get a drink and watch 2 active brewers and a distiller working at the same time. Walking into the Green Dragon, you get the feeling you're almost in a warehouse. The place is clean and open, and has a simple decor. With concrete floors, wooden tables, skylights, and 2 bars with multiple taps, it is a very relaxed environment to hang out with a group of friends. There is a lot of room inside, though it can get crowded in the evening, but a fun and exciting vibe emanates from the mass amount of good-beer drinkers. Make sure to attend one of the "meet the brewer" nights, where they bring in a brewer along with his or her beer for great discussions and even better drinks.

Along with the generous amounts of taps offered here, there is also a decent food menu filled with soups, salads, sandwiches, and burgers. For dessert try a beer float. Choose any of the beers on draft served over fresh vanilla ice cream. That's right, beer makes any dessert better.

Portland

Firkin Fest

Rogue's Green Dragon is host to the annual Firkin Fest. The one-day event features 30 Oregon breweries serving unique firkin beers. Firkin beers are unfiltered, unpasteurized, and naturally carbonated beers poured from a cask at cellar temperature. Each year the beers are served along with gourmet cheese, meat, and chocolate for a unique experience.

HENRY'S TAVERN

10 NW 12th Ave., Portland, OR 97209; (503) 227-5320; HenrysTavern.com;
@henrystavern
Draft Beers: 100 **Bottled/Canned Beers:** About 5

Located in the iconic Weinhard Brewery complex in Portland's Pearl District, Henry's Tavern has become a perfect gathering spot for both beer lovers and their non–beer loving friends. Built in 1908, the building has a long history with beer, as it housed one of Portland's first breweries, Henry Weinhard's, up until it was sold to Miller Brewing Company in 1999 and brewing operations were moved out of town. After a remodel of the complex, the building now contains offices and shops, and houses Henry's Tavern in the brewhouse building where the original Weinhard Brewery smokestack still stands.

Walking into Henry's, you are met with a warm and comforting atmosphere with wooden floors, old brick walls, 24-foot ceilings, dim lights, and a feeling you are in for a good time. The 2-story building is split into 3 areas according to your mood. In the bar you can choose from the 100 beers on tap, with the majority of them local brands. While they generally aren't difficult-to-find beers, Henry's has great options for everyone's tastes. Henry's has 2 happy hours every day, providing some great food selections, such as the signature Gorgonzola fries or tempura prawns.

If you sit at the bar, make sure to check out the ice rail that surrounds it to keep your beer cold. Upstairs in what was once the hops storage room is a more relaxed bar where you can kick back and play some pool with friends while drinking your choice of beer. Down below in the dining room it's slightly quieter and much more of a restaurant atmosphere. The menu is packed with options, all of which are created to pair well with the beers; just ask your waiter for help selecting the perfect food and beer combo.

HORSE BRASS PUB
4534 SE Belmont St., Portland, OR 97215; (503) 232-2202; HorseBrass.com; @horsebrasspub
Draft Beers: 59 **Bottled/Canned Beers:** 25+

One of the great Portland institutions known throughout the world, the Horse Brass Pub brings together great beer, English and American food, and the old standard game of darts into a traditional English-style pub atmosphere. The dimly lit southeast Portland establishment is covered in dark woodwork and British signs, making you feel as if you're actually sitting in England, drinking a 20-ounce imperial pint. Aside from the decor and the food, the beer isn't dominated by England, although they do offer a handful of imports on tap, including Bass Pale Ale, Young's Double Chocolate Stout, Morland Old Speckled Hen, and Newcastle Brown Ale. While some standard brews are on tap, the multiple rotating taps are where the Horse Brass Pub has made a name for itself. With a heavily dominated West Coast rotation mixed with a handful of imports and East Coast brews, any beer geek will feel the joy of Christmas morning every time he or she looks at the tap list. Not only is the selection filled with rare and local brews, generally there are multiple beers on cask that you just don't see every day.

The food is a mix of potpies, sandwiches, salads, banger sausage, and other English-style menu items. However, if you've never visited before, you have to try their legendary fish and chips, crafted with halibut and house-made beer batter. Pair that with the house beer made by Rogue, Younger's Special Bitter, and you'll have a great experience.

Former Horse Brass Pub publican Don Younger, who passed away in 2011, did so much for the craft beer scene in Portland. He took his pub and led the way for great beer to be easily accessible in the city. While it's been in the Portland scene since 1976, the Horse Brass Pub is still as relevant today and makes for a great and fun-filled experience.

Portland

PROST!
4237 N. Mississippi Ave., Portland, OR 97217; (503) 954-2674; ProstPortland.com;
@prostportland
Draft Beers: 12 **Bottled/Canned Beers:** 15

In the heart of the historic Mississippi District and surrounded by a sea of food carts, Prost! serves as an escape to the typical Portland beer culture. Instead of featuring taps filled with hoppy Northwest-style IPAs and stouts as dark as the backside of the moon, the owners have decided to give patrons a taste of the German bier hall. A selection of Pilsners, lagers, Weissbiers, Oktoberfests, Dunkels, and other German-style beers populates the tap lines and bottle selection. Each beer, including the rotating taps, is imported from Germany from breweries such as Spaten, Ayinger, and Paulaner, with each served in authentic and appropriate glasses. Whether you're looking to drink huge amounts of beer in *das boot* (2 liters) or want to try multiple styles in a half-liter glass, they are ready to serve you.

Besides authentic German beer, the atmosphere is what makes the Prost! experience so memorable and exciting. The building, which was built in 1894 and housed a drugstore and a church, was renovated in 2009 and turned into the friendly bier hall that it is today. From the wooden communal tables, bar stools, and exposed beams, you get the feeling you've entered Bavaria. While the inside is cozy and tends to get packed just about every night, the outside beer garden in the back is a perfect escape to a good time on those nice Portland evenings.

To complete the German experience, Prost! offers a small menu consisting of semi-traditional German fare: bratwursts, pretzels, sauerkraut, pickles, and rye bread. If you're not in a bratwurst type of mood, they do allow you to bring in food from one of the nearby food carts as long as you order a drink. For those who don't feel like having beer, they do offer a full cocktail bar and a decent wine selection.

ROSCOE'S
8105 SE Stark St., Portland, OR 97215; (503) 255-0049; RoscoesPDX.com; @roscoespdx
Draft Beers: 18 **Bottled/Canned Beers:** Around 20

Looks can be deceiving—a statement that rings true for Roscoe's, a southeast Portland craft-beer bar in the Montavilla neighborhood, on SE 81st and Stark. You'd probably drive on by if you didn't know what's on the inside. From the outside of the building, it looks like it could be your typical dive bar located in a not-so-great part of town. Once you step inside, you're in a whole new world filled with great beer, food, and entertainment. The interior is covered in aged wood and is in a U-shape, separating the bar and eating area from the game room. Inside, the game room contains a couple of pool tables, pinball machines, and video poker, perfect for having a good time, drinking excellent beer, and listening to a great selection of music on the jukebox.

On tap you'll find 16 rotating beers and 2 on nitro. The beers tend to heavily favor the West Coast, but Roscoe's does like to switch it up, and you can often get rare or hard-to-find beers. Monthly they put on themed beer summits and turn the taps over to a specific style of beer. It could be all stouts from different breweries, or IPAs; every event is different. Along with beer summits, they often do blind tastes where tasters try to identify each beer.

The menu contains a handful of pub food mixed with some southern cuisine, such as po' boys, jambalaya, gumbo, and red beans and rice. While the food is great on its own, you can also place orders from Miyamoto Sushi next door and have it delivered into Roscoe's. Great food and beer along with lots of entertainment in a fun atmosphere make Roscoe's an outstanding destination for those looking to unwind and have a good time.

SARAVEZA BOTTLE SHOP & PASTY TAVERN

1004 N. Killingsworth St., Portland, OR 97217; (503) 206-4252; Saraveza.com; @saraveza
Draft Beers: 9 **Bottled/Canned Beers:** Over 250

Saraveza Bottle Shop & Pasty Tavern is not your typical bottle shop. Like many bottle shops, they have fridges filled with over 250 cold beers lining the walls, each stocked with beers from all over the world. However, going to Saraveza without sitting down and enjoying a draft beer and some Midwestern-inspired food just doesn't give you the full experience. Walking in, you feel the Wisconsin influence with Green Bay Packers signs and stickers interspersed with those from the local Portland Trail Blazers and Oregon beer companies. The decorations are sure to make any beer lover happy, with tables made with bottle caps, old beer bottles lining the wall, and even a leg lamp reminiscent of that from the movie *A Christmas Story*. With an always-great selection of beer on draft that is constantly rotating, Saraveza has an option for everyone. If you don't like what's on tap, just browse the huge selection of beer in the fridge, and you can consume it on site. Throughout the year they hold multiple events, with free bacon night occurring the second Monday of every month.

The food follows the Midwestern flair, with pasties, which are pastries stuffed with meats and vegetables, being the main attraction. They are served alongside a

Beer Event

Saraveza's IIPA Fest

For hopheads there isn't anything much better than Saraveza's IIPA fest. The two-day event packs more than 20 rotating taps of huge imperial IPAs from all over the country. While most of the beers are from the hop-loving West Coast, you can find beers from multiple breweries across the country, such as Dogfish Head, Boulevard, Oskar Blues, and Victory. Both days you can listen to live music and find some great food. They also offer mason jars to go, just in case you don't get enough hop-infused beer at the festival.

mixture of pickled vegetables and accompanied by a selection of sauces. Other tasty options include brats, smoked trout board, and an appetizer of cream cheese–stuffed jalapeños that pair well with many of the beers they have on tap.

Saraveza's very relaxed environment serves as both a great local hangout spot as well as a destination to stock up on some hard-to-find beers. The staff is generally very friendly and loves to talk about beer and help with any questions you have when it comes to selecting your next drink.

SPIRIT OF 77
500 NE MLK Jr. Blvd., Portland, OR 97232; (503) 232-9977; Spiritof77Bar.com; @spiritof77bar
Draft Beers: 8 **Bottled/Canned Beers:** 15

For the sports fanatic, nothing goes better with beer than watching your favorite team with a group of like-minded people. While Portland isn't known for dominating professional sports, the city has a fond love for the ups and downs of the Trail Blazers. Back in 1977 the Blazers, led by Bill Walton, won the only championship the city has seen in professional sports. Portlanders who were around at the time still talk about that team as if it were yesterday, reminiscing how exciting it was. With that same excitement, Spirit of 77 has captured the city's love for its team and turned it into a well-crafted sports bar. Located down the street from the Rose Garden Arena, the bar has multiple screens and a huge 9-foot-by-16-foot big screen to show the main attraction. There isn't a reason to miss a game unless you want to watch an out-of-town team. You can even relax during commercial breaks and halftime and play some free Pop-A-Shot, foosball, or darts.

While the beer selection isn't as large as at other beer bars in town, this is the place to go to grab a quality beer and watch sports in a fun atmosphere. The 8 taps rotate frequently, with Portland breweries making appearances on most of them. To make things fun, they put together a Pop-A-Shot tournament with brewers from local breweries. The winner gets a permanent tap at Spirit of 77 for their brewery for an entire year. Throughout the year the place also holds multiple beer-related events to draw beer lovers in the door.

Spirit of 77 isn't your typical sports bar. It feels more like a loud Portland hangout that features sports. With high rafters, worn wood, and tables looking somewhat like cafeteria seating so everyone can see the game, there is always excitement in the air. The food menu is small, extending only to salads, sandwiches, and a handful of appetizers. Make sure to come early if it's a big game; the place can get packed.

THE VICTORY BAR
3652 SE Division St., Portland, OR 97202; (503)236-8755; TheVictoryBar.com; @victorybar
Draft Beers: 6 **Bottled/Canned Beers:** 60

The Victory Bar, located in southeast Portland's Richmond neighborhood, is part Northwest, part Europe, and all about the drinks. It's like dive bar meets classy Belgian restaurant, creating a cozy yet almost communal atmosphere. The welcoming interior is dimly lit with a somewhat Belgian flair, making it a great spot to grab drinks with friends or take a date for a semi-romantic evening. Victory is made to please drinkers of any preference with a full selection of wine, rare and unique liquors, and, of course, beer, both on tap and in bottles and cans. Although there are only 6 beers on tap, each is unique and well thought out, which makes each one stand out. With this mix of local and global beers that can be tough to find even in a beer mecca such as Portland, beer lovers won't be disappointed. Along with the draft beers, they have a fairly large selection of bottles that are mostly imports and heavily Belgian focused. With a well-thought-out beer list and a great atmosphere, it's easy to see why *Imbibe Magazine* named The Victory Bar as one of the 100 best places to drink beer in America.

Besides great beer, wine, and spirits, Victory has a small food menu consisting of mostly European-focused appetizers that is known throughout the city. The baked spaetzle with gruyère cheese is a must-try and pairs well with many of the Belgian beers. If you eat meat, the venison burger is the best in the city. Split it with a friend and order the poutine fries, smothered in cheese curds and bacon gravy. Victory is open only after 5 p.m., so stop by after work or make a date of it.

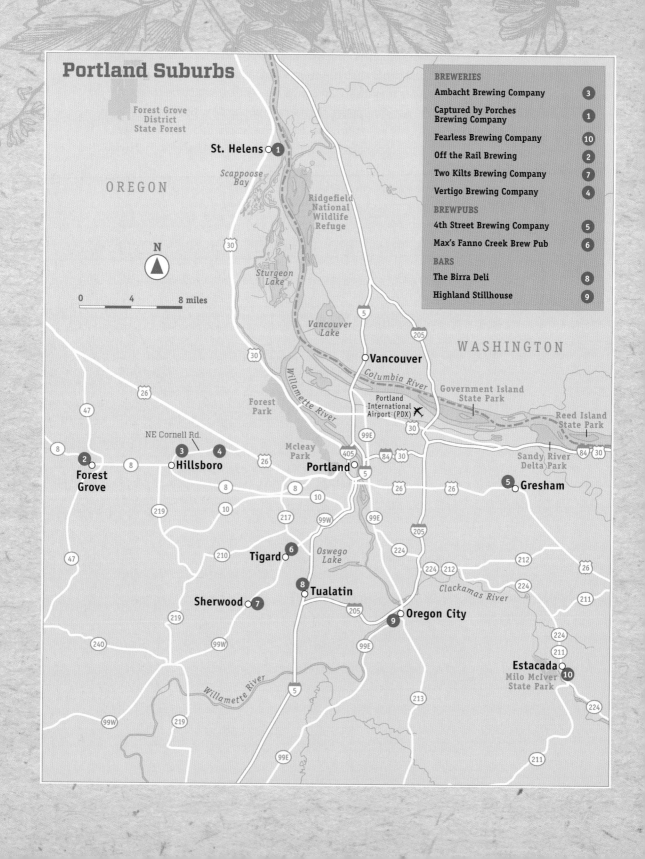

Portland Suburbs

Forest Grove
District
State Forest

St. Helens ○ **1**

Scappoose
Bay

OREGON

Ridgefield
National
Wildlife
Refuge

30

Sturgeon
Lake

N

0   4   8 miles

Vancouver
Lake

Vancouver ○

Columbia River

WASHINGTON

30

Government Island
State Park

Forest
Park

Willamette River

Portland
International
Airport (PDX) ✈

Reed Island
State Park

84   30

26

47

NE Cornell Rd.

McLeay
Park

99E

405

84   30

Sandy River
Delta Park

8   **2**   8   **3**   **4**

Hillsboro

26

Portland ○

5

5 Gresham

Forest
Grove

219

8   8

10

26   26

205

10

217

99W   99E

224

212   26

210   **6**

Oswego
Lake

224   212

224

211

47   Tigard

8   Tualatin

Clackamas River

Sherwood   **7**

205

9 Oregon City

224

219

99W

240   99W

Willamette River

5

99E

213

211

Estacada ○ **10**
Milo McIver
State Park

224

99E

211

BREWERIES

Ambacht Brewing Company	**3**
Captured by Porches Brewing Company	**1**
Fearless Brewing Company	**10**
Off the Rail Brewing	**2**
Two Kilts Brewing Company	**7**
Vertigo Brewing Company	**4**

BREWPUBS

4th Street Brewing Company	**5**
Max's Fanno Creek Brew Pub	**6**

BARS

The Birra Deli	**8**
Highland Stillhouse	**9**

Portland Suburbs

For years the suburbs of Portland haven't had an identity of their own in the beer world. Sure, you can find great beers that are produced in Portland, but it wasn't quite as easy as if you were in the city. Luckily, over the past few years the beer culture of Portland is starting to spread outward and take root in the surrounding cities. What makes the suburbs even better is that they haven't taken on a "me too" attitude to beer. Instead most of the breweries are making a name for themselves by producing delicious and unique beer.

In Hillsboro both Ambacht Brewing and Vertigo Brewing have been brewing some unique beers that have the beer community taking notice. Two Kilts Brewing in Sherwood is brewing up a variety of solid beers, while down in Estacada Fearless Brewing is growing their distribution by crafting a handful of great-tasting brews. As more and more breweries keep popping up in the suburbs, we are seeing them carving out their own identities in areas needing great locally produced beers.

Breweries

AMBACHT BREWING COMPANY

1055 NE 25th Ave., Ste. N, Hillsboro, OR 97124; (503) 828-1400; Ambacht.us; @ambachtale
Founded: 2007 **Founder:** Tom Kramer **Brewers:** Tom Kramer and Brandy Grobart
Flagship Beer: Honey Triple **Year-round Beers:** Golden Farmhouse Ale, Dark Farmhouse Ale, Golden Rose Farmhouse Ale **Seasonals/Special Releases:** Golden Rye Farmhouse Ale, G++ Ale, Pie Cherry Pale Farmhouse Ale, Matzobraü, Honey Tripel **Tours:** No **Taproom:** Yes

In a state known for producing hoppy IPAs, Ambacht Brewing Company has decided to take a different approach. As one of the few Oregon breweries that doesn't brew your typical American-style beers, Ambacht instead specializes in Belgian-inspired ales. Founder Tom Kramer was a brewer of Tuck's Brewery, a now-closed Portland brewery. Once Tuck's closed, the brewing equipment and space was sold to Congregation Kesser Israel, a Jewish synagogue. Kramer purchased the brew system and moved it to its new home in Hillsboro to start Ambacht, whose name is Dutch for "handmade," which is how all their beers are made.

The brewing philosophy is to simply brew quality Belgian-inspired ales with organic and local ingredients. Each beer is bottle conditioned with natural Oregon blackberry honey, providing sweetness and a unique flavor. One of the most interesting beers Ambacht produces is **Matzobraü.** After Passover many families have leftovers, so to make use of the extra matzo, Ambacht asks for donations to be used in Matzobraü. The end result is a very drinkable, yet unique Belgian pale ale with 6.5 percent ABV that comes around once a year, just after Passover. Other beers include a range of farmhouse ales brewed with ingredients such as pie cherries, rose hips, rye, and plenty of malt, hops, and yeast. Time is an important factor in how the beers turn out, with an average of 3 months from brew day to when they are ready to hit the store shelves.

Ambacht's beer is generally found around the Portland area in 22-ounce bottles at bottle shops and farmers markets, as well as on draft at select locations. Twice a week they open up the brewery on Thursday and Sunday so you can purchase the beer fresh and direct.

Golden Farmhouse Ale
Style: Saison
ABV: 6.5 percent
Availability: Year-round

Ambacht's Golden Farmhouse Ale is an easy-drinking saison-style ale that has been bottle conditioned with local blackberry honey. It pours a hazy golden orange and has enough honey, citrus, and a slight spicy yeast in the nose to get your mouth watering. The yeast is a bit subdued in the flavor, with lots of honey and fruit being the dominant players. The balance of ingredients makes it incredibly drinkable and quite delicious. Golden Farmhouse Ale is a somewhat light and crisp beer that is versatile for pairing with all kinds of foods.

CAPTURED BY PORCHES BREWING COMPANY

40 Cowlitz St., St. Helens, OR 97051; (971) 207-3742; CapturedByPorches.com; @capturedbyporch

Founded: 2007 **Founders:** Dylan Goldsmith and Suzanne Moddhe **Brewer:** Dylan Goldsmith **Flagship Beers:** Invasive Species IPA **Year-round Beers:** Invasive Species IPA **Seasonals/Special Releases:** Miskatonic Dark Rye, Emma, Punctured by Corpses Undead Porter, Red Rye Ale, Friday Rye, Vagablonde Ale, Apricot Blonde, Cuddly Panda Porter, Two Cats Kölsch, Hefeweizen, CbP Lager **Tours:** No **Taproom:** Has beer buses

What started off as a homebrew club has morphed into one of the more interesting breweries in the state. After years of determination to get their brewery set up, founders Dylan Goldsmith and Suzanne Moddhe decided to open up shop in St. Helens, Oregon, and Captured by Porches was born. While the small brewery is located in St. Helens, they offer their beer in Portland, not in tasting rooms or pubs, but on buses. With 3 beer buses located throughout the city, beer drinkers can get a true Portland food cart experience while sipping on their brews.

Each of Captured by Porches' beers is unfiltered, carbonated naturally, and brewed with local and organic ingredients when possible. Besides the buses, they distribute kegs of their beers around the area along with offering a small selection of 750-milliliter bottles. When buying their beer in bottles, note that they bottle them in reusable bottles and charge you a $1 deposit per beer that you can get back upon returning it to the brewery. **Invasive Species IPA** is their single year-round beer. It's

Beer Lover's Pick

Two Cats Kölsch
Style: Kölsch
ABV: 5.2 percent
Availability: Spring and summer
If you look at the majority of the labels on Captured by Porches beers, you'll notice most have a bird of some sort. Two Cats Kölsch takes a different approach with two mean-looking cats in the middle of a fight. The beer gets its name from an Irish limerick about fighting cats. Although Two Cats has a little bite, it's a mellow golden yellow summertime beer that's more geared toward relaxing. A light citrus and grass flavor powers through a somewhat tart and dry body, creating a very sessionable summer brew.

a hazy IPA with a large malt body and slightly citrusy hops brewed in the traditional British style. A beer that's worth trying if you come across it is the **Red Rye Ale.** While not something that is going to please every palate, it's a very interesting ale that's brewed with unmalted rye, Tettnanger hops, and Bavarian wheat yeast. It's like barnyard meets hop field with some spicy yeast thrown in.

Currently the brewery in St. Helens is production only, so you can't get their beer there. If you're over on Sauvie Island, one of the buses is located on Kruger's Farm. The other two are at 3221 SE Division St. and at North Lombard and Burr in Portland. You can experience the old-school bus turned into a lounge and bar, making it one of the most unique beer experiences in Oregon. Where else can you sit on a school bus with a beer in your hand and not get in trouble?

FEARLESS BREWING COMPANY

326 S. Broadway St., Estacada, OR 97023; (503) 630-2337; Fearless1.com; @fearlessbrewing.com

Founded: 2003 **Founders:** Ken and Bennett Johnson **Brewer:** Ken Johnson **Flagship Beer:** Scottish Ale **Year-round Beers:** Clackamas Cream Ale, Scottish Ale, Loki Red Ale, Porter, India Pale Ale, Peaches & Cream Ale, Mjolnir **Seasonals/Special Releases:** Strong Scotch Ale, Maibock, Niord NWPA **Tours:** No **Taproom:** Yes

Fearless Brewing Company, a Viking-themed brewery and brewpub in Estacada, Oregon, has been brewing beer with the waters of the Clackamas River since 2003. The name Fearless actually comes from a nickname given to owner Ken Johnson from his dad in his younger days. Started as a brewpub in the small town known for its history of logging, the brewery for years served the locals an array of well-crafted beers. Over time they have expanded to include distribution around the state on draft as well as a handful of beers available in 16-ounce tallboy cans.

One of the beers available on store shelves is **Mjolnir Imperial IPA.** Mjolnir is the hammer of Thor in Norse mythology, which can be seen on the bottom of the green can. The power that name suggests comes in the form of alcohol content in the imperial IPA. Both the 7.7 percent ABV and 98 IBUs are surprisingly hidden, which could come back and whack you in the face like a hammer if you drink too many at once. If you prefer darker beers, check out the **Porter.** It's a very standard porter that's well crafted with nice flavors of roasted malts, coffee, chocolate, and a touch of bitter hops.

The brewpub has a very small-town feel, fitting perfectly in the downtown area of Estacada. With a comfy couch and chairs, plenty of tables, old family pictures, and memorabilia on the walls, you get the feeling you're part of the local family. They

Scottish Ale
Style: Scottish Ale
ABV: 5.3 percent
Availability: Year-round

With so many hoppy beers in the Northwest, it's nice to take a break and drink something a little more malt forward. Scottish ales are typically low in hops and high in malts, and Fearless Brewing's Scottish Ale is no exception. Brewed to style, the beer has an aroma filled with sweet caramel malt with a slight toastiness and a touch of pine. The flavor follows with a smoky sweet maltiness, pine, and a nutty finish. It's a little lighter than other Scottish ales, with fairly low carbonation, resulting in a truly sessionable beer.

even list on the menu who is in the pictures, all relatives of husband-and-wife owners Ken and Bennett Johnson. They offer a range of pub food that includes wraps, sandwiches, burgers, salads, soups, and a handful of appetizers.

Owner and brewer Ken Johnson got his start as a homebrewer and opens up Fearless each year to host the annual Slurp and Burp Open, put on by the Strange Brew Homebrew Club. Homebrewers from around Oregon and Washington can enter their brews for a chance to win a number of awards, including a chance to be brewer for a day with Ken.

OFF THE RAIL BREWING

2040 A St., Forest Grove, OR 97116; (503) 866-5924; OffTheRailBrewing.Posterous.com; @offtherailbrew

Founded: 2001 **Founders:** Dan and Antionette Bragdon **Brewer:** Dan Bragdon
Flagship Beer: Over the Mountain **Year-round Beers:** War Pigs Wheat, Paranoid, Hysteria, Coal Porter, Mad Man IPA, Sweet Leaf Amber **Seasonals/Special Releases:** Bon Scott, Over the Mountain, Misty Mountain Hop, Poker Stout, Blizzard of Oz, Sin After Sin, Rhoad's Red, and many more **Tours:** No **Taproom:** No

Although Off the Rail Brewing has been brewing since 2001 west of Portland in Forest Grove, they don't have the name recognition of many of the other newer breweries in the area. But don't let that stop you from seeking them out; they know how to make some really solid beers. Owners Dan and Antionette have their hands in all aspects of the business, from brewing to distribution. The two have built up a business that would make Ozzy Osbourne and Randy Rhoads proud. One of the first things you'll notice about the brewery is the influence the two rockers have on their marketing. Their name of Off the Rails comes from the lyrics of Ozzy Osbourne's song "Crazy Train." If you come across posters from the brewery around town, you'll notice the resemblance in the artwork to many heavy-metal album covers.

Along with the name, most of the beers are named after songs by the two, with just a few exceptions. **Sweet Leaf Amber** gets its name from a song by Osbourne's

Beer Lover's Pick

Over the Mountain
Style: American Stout
ABV: 5.5 percent
Availability: Seasonal

Over the Mountain is one of the most underrated stouts in Oregon, mainly because it's not one of the easiest beers to find. Sitting in the glass, it's a dark, almost black yet brown color with a thin, dark tan head. Huge aromas of chocolate come billowing out to lure you in. Dark chocolate, roasted coffee, caramel, and herbal flavors all play together in balance, giving it some very drinkable complexities. If you enjoy a good stout, seek out this creamy brew named after yet another Osbourne song. You'll have to find it on draft, as it's not bottled.

band Black Sabbath on the album *Master of Reality.* One of the most popular is **Mad Man IPA.** Named after Osbourne's second solo album, *Diary of a Madman,* the IPA isn't your typical Northwest hop bomb. It's a malt-forward IPA with a subtle sweetness and just a touch of bitterness that would make a great intro beer for those who don't like bitter beers. The beers don't just have interesting names, they are well brewed using mostly local ingredients.

Since Off the Rails is self-distributed, you won't find their beers outside of the Portland metro area very often. Off the Rail also doesn't have a taproom or bottle their beers, though you can head into Forest Grove or Portland and find at least a few of their beers on draft.

TWO KILTS BREWING COMPANY

14841 SW Tualatin Sherwood Rd., Ste. 5, Sherwood, OR 97140; (503) 625-1700; TwoKiltsBrewing.com; @twokiltsbrewing
Founded: 2011 **Founders:** Chris Dillon and Alex McGaw **Brewers:** Chris Dillon and Alex McGaw **Flagship Beer:** Scotch Ale **Year-round Beers:** IPA, Pale Ale, Scotch Ale, Porter **Seasonals/Special Releases:** Russian Imperial Stout, Belgian Strong Dark, Belgian Blonde, Heather Ale, Black Lager, Belgian Red, Calluna Vulgaris, Oatmeal Stout, Hefeweizen, and many more **Tours:** No **Taproom:** Yes

Over the years craft breweries have been popping up all over the suburbs of Portland in areas from which people have previously had to drive into the city if they wanted fresh beer from the source. In Sherwood, Oregon, the first to open up

Beer Lover's Pick

Scotch Ale
Style: Scotch Ale
ABV: 6.5 percent
Availability: Year-round
Scotch ales, as opposed to Scottish ales, tend to have a little higher alcohol content. Two Kilts Scotch Ale is on the lower end for its style, at 6.5 percent, but that is still a hefty amount. It has a nice light amber-brown color with a small head that quickly leaves. Stick your nose in the glass and you can smell the sweet and roasted malt that shows up in the flavor along with a slight bitterness. It's a tasty beer that's perfect for drinking on its own, or with a plate of cheese and salami.

was Two Kilts Brewing Company. Located in a business park that doesn't have much of a brewery look on the outside, the small 8-barrel brewhouse is growing rapidly by providing brews to an eager local crowd. Started by two homebrewing friends, Two Kilts produces a variety of beer styles with inspirations from multiple countries. When coming up with a name for the brewery, they wanted to find something in common. Co-owner Chris Dillon was proud of his Irish heritage and Alex McGaw was proud of his Scottish lineage, so they came up with the name Two Kilts Brewing.

The brewery likes to mix things up with the beers, and each time you visit there are different beers on the draft lines. From the **Belgian Blonde, Belgian Red,** and **Belgian Strong Dark Ale** to the **IPA, Pale Ale, Scotch Ale,** and **Porter,** Two Kilts covers a wide variety of styles.

The taproom is the best place to find their beers. While they don't serve food, it's a small place to relax and watch a game on TV or just mingle with other beer lovers. If it's quiet, ask if you can get a glimpse of the plaid forklift that looks like it's wearing a kilt. While they are growing, you'll be able to start finding their beer more places around the area. A bottling line is in the works and should soon be sending their beer into stores in 22-ounce bombers.

VERTIGO BREWING
21420 NW Nicholas Ct., Hillsboro, OR 97124; (503) 645-6644; VertigoBrew.com; @vertigobrew
Founded: 2008 **Founders:** Mike Haines and Mike Kinion **Brewers:** Mike Haines and Mike Kinion **Flagship Beer:** Friar Mike's IPA **Year-round Beers:** Apricot Cream Ale, Arctic Blast, Friar Mike's IPA, Razz Wheat, Schwindel Alt, Smokestack Red Ale, TBD Blonde **Seasonals/Special Releases:** High-Altitude Amber, High Dive Rye, Spring Harvest Hefe **Tours:** No **Taproom:** Yes

Vertigo Brewing is the result of a couple of homebrewing friends who decided to venture out on their own and start a brewery. When cofounders Mike Haines and Mike Kinion first started out, they were brewing on a small 1-barrel system. Even when they were smaller, they were brewing beer for the Oregon Brewers Festival, which required them to brew a lot. Since then more people have tried their beer and realized how good it was, so they've been able to expand to a slightly larger 7-barrel system as well as open up a taproom next to the brewery in Hillsboro. They pride their beer on how it stands out from the saturated market of the Northwest.

Two of their most popular beers are made with fruit. The **Razz Wheat** is packed with raspberries, and the **Apricot Cream Ale** with apricots. The Apricot Cream Ale has a nice hint of apricot that goes down easy during the summer months. With competition from other big breweries, Vertigo received a tap at Henry's in Portland

Razz Wheat
Style: American Wheat Ale
ABV: 5.3 percent
Availability: Year-round

Some hot days you just need a nice light, refreshing beer. No matter if you're out camping, boating, or just enjoying the Oregon summer, Vertigo's Razz Wheat is a crisp wheat beer that is meant to satisfy. They use 15 pounds of raspberries in every barrel and it's very apparent. It results in a hazy amber beer with a pinkish hue and some nice raspberry aromas and flavors. It's not an incredibly complex beer that will have beer geeks debating all of its intricacies, but Razz Wheat is perfect when you just need some light, crisp, easy-drinking summertime relief.

during the summer for the fruit-packed ale. They had so much great feedback on the beer that Henry's asked them to create a house beer that was exclusive to their restaurant. Between the two, they came up with **Smokestack Red,** a red ale packed with caramel and a touch of bitter hops. Their most popular beer is **Friar Mike's IPA.** Although both owners are named Mike, the beer is actually named after one of their former coworkers. It's an easy-drinking English-style IPA that's fairly mild, yet well balanced and full of flavor.

Next to their brewery in Hillsboro is the taproom that features many of Vertigo's beers on draft. Although they don't offer food, you can get a growler filled at a pretty reasonable price. Outside of the taproom, they have bottles and draft versions of their beers around the Portland area and are quickly growing more accounts around the state.

Portland Suburbs

Brewpubs

4TH STREET BREWING COMPANY

77 NE 4th St., Gresham, OR 97030; (503) 669-0569; 4thStreetBrewing.com;
@4thStBrewing

Founded: 2004 **Founder:** Adam Roberts **Brewer:** Adam Roberts **Flagship Beer:**
Eager Beaver IPA **Year-round Beers:** Gresham Light, Demented Duck Amber, Black
Roots Blonde, Powell Porter, Eager Beaver IPA **Seasonals/Special Releases:** Kolsch,
Double Red, Get Jiggy Wit It, Nut Brown Ale, Mai Bock, Czech Pilsner, American Pale Ale,
and more

What happens when you name a brewery after the street you're on and then change locations? For the Main Street Ale House, a move from the original location on Main Street in Gresham to a new building on 4th Street meant a name change was in order. Rebranded in 2008 as 4th Street Brewing, the huge brewpub provides locals a great place to drink fresh beer, eat meals, and generally have a great time. The larger location features 9 TVs playing sports in the sports bar, a family-style restaurant, and a second floor with 2 meeting rooms that can hold a couple hundred people. Inside it's comfortable while maintaining a somewhat corporate look.

Their beers are all served in imperial pints. With 5 year-round beers and 7 seasonals on tap, there is always a lot to choose from. The year-round beers are quite common, with a light lager, amber, blonde, porter, and IPA, while the seasonals are a touch more exciting, but nothing too out of the norm. **Get Jiggy Wit It** is a seasonal Belgian white ale brewed with paradise seed, orange peel, and coriander. With only 4.3 percent ABV, it's an easy-to-drink summer ale. **Demented Duck Amber** is a light-bodied amber with very little nose. The flavor is all about the sweet malts and Saaz hops from the Czech Republic, making it one of their better house beers.

If you're looking for food, they have a lot of options. Burgers, sandwiches, pasta, pizza, salads, fish, and other comfort foods fill out the menu. The food isn't life-changing, but you should be able to find something on the menu to please everyone.

MAX'S FANNO CREEK BREW PUB

12562 SW Main St., Tigard, OR 97223; (503) 624-9400; FannoCreekBrewPub.com;
@FannoCreekBrew

Founded: 2007 **Founders:** Connie and Marvin Owen **Brewer:** Tim Barr **Flagship
Beer:** None **Year-round Beers:** Pagan Pale Ale, St. Fanno, X IPA, Ivan the Imperial IPA,
Raspberry Stout, Vanilla Cream Porter, Reverend's Daughter, IPA, Golden Ale, Dry Hopped
Pacific Red **Seasonals/Special Releases:** Oktoberfest, Political Pilsner, Imperial
Majesty, and many more

Located on Main Street in Old Town Tigard near Fanno Creek, Max's Fanno Creek Brew Pub is a comfortable family-style restaurant. Interestingly enough, the pub was named after the original brewer, Max, who has since left, leaving his name on the sign as well as multiple beer recipes. In the front there are multiple picnic tables where you can get a view through the window of the 10-barrel brewhouse while sipping on some brews. Inside there is plenty of seating, with a down-home atmosphere. The bar is one of the main centerpieces of the pub, as it's built with old-growth crow's foot hemlock that's approximately 600 years old. Sitting at the bottom of the Columbia River for nearly 200 years, the wood was salvaged and crafted into the bar it is today.

The pub itself generally has 10 house beers on draft at any given time, with a wide range of styles. While IPA lovers will appreciate their citrusy and well-balanced Northwest-style **IPA,** they brew a range of styles that makes it easy for most people to find something they'll enjoy. Their **Vanilla Cream Porter** is worth ordering. The beautiful dark brown beer has big roasted chocolate malt flavors with hints of vanilla and a smooth, creamy finish.

Choosing food from the menu can be a little tough because they have so many tasty options. A suggestion: Choose one of the many starters to munch on along with a beer to tide you over while you browse through the salads, chowder, burgers, sandwiches, pizzas, fish, seafood, pasta, steak, tacos, and even a chicken burrito. Also make sure to check out the Nano Beer Fest they hold once a year in the summer where you can try multiple beers from many local small breweries.

Nano Beer Fest

The summer is packed with beer festivals, one of which is the Nano Beer Fest held every year at Max's Fanno Creek Brew Pub. Held in the parking lot, the event is open to multiple smaller breweries from around the state that each bring select seasonal brews. The three-day event offers live music each day along with plenty of food and lots of beer. You can check out nanobeerfest.com for details of the next event.

Beer Bars

BIRRA DELI
18749 SW Martinazzi Ave., Tualatin, OR 97062; (503) 783-1037; BirraDeli.com; @birradeli
Draft Beers: 7 **Bottled/Canned Beers:** Over 600

While the Portland beer scene is pretty amazing, the suburbs tend to get a little overlooked. Hidden inside a strip mall in the city of Tualatin is Birra Deli, a shining beacon of good beer in the 'burbs. The name comes from the Italian word for beer, *birra,* mixed with "deli." When you enter, you quickly realize that those are the two best and well-chosen words for what they offer. While the space is small, it is laid out in a way that works. It has a feeling of both a bar and a deli mixed with a bottle shop. Throw in some video poker in the back along with a couple TVs and you have a great little suburban hangout spot. The neon glow of beer signs and fridges helps light the place around the edges and deli-style tables fill the middle, inviting you to sit down and have a drink.

A selection of hot and cold sandwiches and wraps help soak up the suds. While they are your typical deli-style sandwiches, they have a condiment station featuring house-made mustards and pickled vegetables to make your sandwich unique. Though the deli is good, the beer is where they really excel. With 7 rotating taps and a huge selection of bottles, there is no reason to leave thirsty. The beers come from all over the country with a pretty decent selection of imports. You can drink the beer inside or take it home. They will even give you a discount when you buy a 6-pack. Multiple times throughout the month they host beer club tastings where you can sample beers from specific breweries. For $5 you get beer tasting and sandwiches, a deal you can't beat. They also offer a fairly extensive list of kegs for your next gathering. Just be sure to give them a call in advance.

THE HIGHLAND STILLHOUSE
201 S. 2nd St., Oregon City, OR 97045; (503) 723-6789; HighlandStillhouse.com; @StillhousePub
Draft Beers: 13 **Bottled/Canned Beers:** 50+

Finding a traditional Scottish pub in the Portland area can be a challenge. While a few claim they are a taste of Scotland, most don't make the cut. If the Scottish experience is what you're looking for, go no further than the Highland Stillhouse in Oregon City. As one of the most underrated pubs in the state, the Highland Stillhouse offers an experience you can't find elsewhere. Inside you feel like you might be in

Scotland, with old wood everywhere, rounded doors, a beautifully crafted wooden bar, and, of course, Scottish flags hanging from the ceiling. There is also a covered porch with space for a lot of people to sip some beverages and take in the views of the river and old mills. While the place is pretty cozy and comfortable, the selection of drinks is by far the best part. They have a great liquor selection, but the beer and whiskey is what they are best known for. Whiskey lovers will enjoy a selection of almost 500 varieties; it takes quite a while to read through the whole menu. Beer lovers aren't left out, as the beer lineup is carefully selected.

With 13 beers on draft, 4 beers on nitro, and a few on cask, beer lovers are well taken care of. The selection varies with a mix of locals, domestics, and imports. The bottle selection numbers around 50, with a heavy selection from Europe. Choosing what to drink is the most difficult part of visiting. To go with your beverage, they have a whole menu of Scottish- and American-inspired pub food. Fish and chips, bangers and mash, cottage pie, scotch eggs, pasties, and even haggis balls are on the menu. While everything on the menu is a pretty good choice, the fish and chips are excellent and pair well with a nice ESB.

The Coast & Western Oregon

WASHINGTON

PACIFIC OCEAN

Inset A

Columbia River

8th St.

7th St.

Astoria

Shively Park

Astoria Reservoir

Youngs River

0   4000 ft.

See inset A
1-4

Clatsop State Forest

Forest Grove District State Forest

Cannon Beach

Tillamook State Forest

Vancouver

Portland

OREGON

Pacific City

Newport

SE Bay Blvd.

Yaquina Bay

Yaquina Bay State Recreation Site

SE OSU Dr.

0   4000 ft.

Inset B

Lincoln City

See inset B
8-11

Toledo

Siuslaw National Forest

Florence

N

0   15   30 miles

BREWERIES

Astoria Brewing Company	2
Astoria Brewery Company– Wet Dog Cafe	1
Fort George Brewing + Public House	3
Pelican Pub & Brewery	6
Rogue Ales	10
Wakonda Brewing Company	13

BREWPUBS

Bills' Tavern & Brewinghouse	5
Rogue Ales–House of Spirits	11
Rogue Ales Public House–Astoria	4
Rogue Ales Public House–Newport	9
Rusty Truck Brewing Company	7
Twisted Snout Brewing and Public House	12

BARS

| Bier One | 8 |

The Coast & Western Oregon

Although the Oregon Coast doesn't have many great beer bars or the number of breweries offered in many other areas of the state, it's still not too difficult to find award-winning beer. Many people will think of Rogue out in Newport and all of their unique and original beers. Along the coast other breweries are joining in the craft-beer scene and producing some truly remarkable beers. In Astoria both Fort George and Astoria Brewing have created a lineup of beers that rank right up there with some of the best in the state. In Pacific City the Pelican Pub & Brewery is pushing the limits on beer and food pairing as well as winning a ton of awards for beer. For those looking for an exciting vacation, try driving the Oregon coast and stop at the many great breweries and brewpubs on your way. You won't miss out on quality beer just because you're in predominantly tourist areas.

Breweries

ASTORIA BREWING COMPANY

144 11th St., Astoria, OR 97103; (503) 325-6975; WetDogCafe.com
Founded: 1997 **Founders:** Steve and Karen Allen **Brewer:** John Dalgren **Flagship Beer:** Bitter Bitch Imperial IPA **Year-round Beers:** Da Bomb Blonde, Volksweissen, Old Red Beard Amber, Solar Dog IPA, Stone Cold Strong Ale, Poop Deck Porter, Bitter Bitch Imperial IPA, Bad Ass Imperial Stout, Lincoln Lager, West Coast Lager, Strawberry Blonde, Astoria ESB **Seasonals/Special Releases:** Kirby Kolsch, Fresh Hop, BrewBerry, and many more **Tours:** No **Taproom:** Yes

In 1995 a new restaurant opened in the coastal town of Astoria called the Wet Dog Cafe. Two years later a brewery was added under the name Pacific Rim Brewery. By 2005 the name of the brewery had changed to Astoria Brewing Company to commemorate the first brewing company in Astoria that was established in 1872 and had long since closed down. The small brewpub operated at its beautiful location overlooking the Columbia River but was busting at the seams with demand for its beer. To expand, the owners purchased the building that had housed the Chartroom bar and Andrew & Steve's restaurant for 95 years. Having turned it into a brewery and taproom, they now brew at both locations. With the expansion, they were able to buy a canning line so their beers could start being distributed around the area.

The beers produced at the small brewery have been impressive, leading to a handful of regional awards, and even first place in the 2004 Great American Beer Festival for **Stone Cold Strong.** With a beautiful amber color, caramel and toffee aroma, and sweet malt, dark fruit, and caramel flavor, it's a well-rounded strong ale. **Poop Deck Porter** is another year-round beer that's more than just a funny name. It's packed with so much coffee flavor that you can get away with replacing your morning cup of joe with it.

With a focus on being sustainable, Astoria Brewing has solar panels on the roof of the Wet Dog Cafe that generate the power to heat the brewery's hot water tanks. If you're in Astoria, you can find the beer at both locations, so bring a growler to fill. If you enjoy really hoppy beers, make sure to fill it up with their award-winning **Bitter Bitch Imperial IPA.**

Bitter Bitch Imperial IPA
Style: Imperial IPA
ABV: 8.2 percent
Availability: Year-round
Astoria Brewing Company
is known for Bitter Bitch
Imperial IPA. With a female
dog on the label looking
like she's about to bite you,
you feel compelled to give
the beer a try. Just like the
name implies, it's got a bitter bite with layers of floral, citrus, and piney hops
leading to a sweet but bit-

ter taste. The caramel malt fights its way in, but the hops end up winning the fight.
It's a fairly dry beer that has some impressive drinkability for what it delivers.

FORT GEORGE BREWERY

1483 Duane St., Astoria, OR 97103; (503) 325-7468; FortGeorgeBrewery.com;
@FortGeorgeBeer
Founded: 2007 **Founders:** Jack Harris and Chris Nemlowill **Brewer:** Jack Harris
Flagship Beer: None **Year-round Beers:** 1811 Lager, Quick Wit, Divinity, Sunrise
Oatmeal Pale Ale, Nut Red Ale, Vortex IPA, Working Girl Porter, Cavatica Stout
Seasonals/Special Releases: Co-hoperative, Coffee Girl, Drunkin Pumpkin, Spruce
Budd Ale, The North Series, Bad JuJu, Badda Boom Stout, Bourbon Barrel Cavatica Stout,
Hellcat, Kentucky Girl, Magnifera Indica Belgae, Murky Pearl, and many more **Tours:** Yes,
Sat and Sun at 1 and 4 p.m. **Taproom:** Yes

Fort George has quickly become one of Oregon's most beloved breweries. The
brewery and public house is located on the original settlement site of Fort
Astoria, which was founded in 1811. The fort was the Pacific Fur Company's primary
trading post in the Northwest and was the first American settlement on the Pacific

coast. For a brief time the British took control of it and renamed it Fort George, after King George III. Years later, in 1924, the Fort George building was built to house an automotive station and repair facility that ran through the late 1990s. After the building was abandoned for a short time, founders Jack Harris and Chris Nemlowill restored it into a beautiful brewery and have expanded brewing operations to pretty much take over the entire city block.

As Fort George has expanded, distribution across the Northwest has grown. In both kegs and 16-ounce cans, their beers are showing up in new places all the time. **Cavatica Stout** is one of their most popular beers available in cans. Named after the brewer's affinity for spiders, with a name made popular by Charlotte A. Cavatica in the book *Charlotte's Web,* this is one dark and bold stout. There are so many flavors in it that you can spend quite some time dissecting all of the artful nuances. At times you can find the bourbon barrel–aged version of Cavatica, which sits in Maker's Mark bourbon barrels for 2 months before it's released.

If you're in Astoria, you need to make a trip down to visit the public house or taproom. Better yet, make a day of it and visit both. Each offers a full food menu and live music, although most music happens in the public house. Bring a growler or two to fill up, and stop by on the weekend for a tour of the brewery.

Vortex IPA
Style: IPA
ABV: 7.7 percent
Availability: Year-round

If you're looking for a fairly intense IPA that will have your taste buds zinging, crack open a can of Fort George Vortex IPA. While it looks cloudy, the glowing orange color is almost angelic. The huge light beige head can last awhile, so be careful while you pour. As soon as the beer is poured, make sure to breathe in the powerful citrus, pine, and caramel malt aromas. While the malt is in the taste, this IPA is all about the hops. It's sweet, bitter, and full of pine and citrus. The name comes from a close encounter with a tornado in Nebraska when they were hauling new brewing equipment across the country from Virginia to Astoria.

PELICAN PUB & BREWERY

33180 Cape Kiwanda Dr., Pacific City, OR 97135; (503) 965-7007; YourLittleBeachTown
.com/Pelican; @thepelicanpub
Founded: 1996 **Founders:** Jeff Schons and Mary Jones **Brewer:** Darron Welch
Flagship Beer: Doryman's Dark Ale **Year-round Beers:** Kiwanda Cream Ale,
MacPelican's Scottish Style Ale, India Pelican Ale, Doryman's Dark Ale, Tsunami Stout,
Silverspot IPA **Seasonals/Special Releases:** Riptide Red, Nestucca ESB, Ankle-Buster
Ale, Surfer's Summer Ale, Winema Wit, Elemental Ale, Full House, Bad Santa, Angler's
Amber Ale, Saison du Pelican, Bridal Ale, Mother of All Storms, and many more **Tours:** No
Taproom: Yes

While beer is great on its own, it's usually better when food is involved. It's even better when you add beer to the food itself, which is often the case at

Mother of All Storms
Style: Barleywine
ABV: 13.5 percent
Availability: November

Released once a year around November, Mother of All Storms is an English-style barleywine that's been aged in Kentucky bourbon barrels. This gigantic beer pours a dark brown color with a thin off-white head that dissipates quickly. Billowing bourbon, dark fruits, caramel malts, oak, and toffee aromas will have you smelling this powerhouse for quite some time. The taste follows the nose with vanilla and candied fruits added to the mix. The strong boozy flavor doesn't hide the 13.5 percent ABV, giving it a warm finish that is perfect for weathering just about any storm.

Pelican Pub & Brewery. Starting the brewery in the mid '90s on the beautiful Oregon coast, Jeff Schons and Mary Jones didn't know much about brewing. While attending a craft brewers conference in Portland to learn more about the process, they found their brewmaster, Darron Welch. Though he didn't have a lot of industry experience when he started, he has turned the pub into an award-winning brewery that is producing some very exciting beers. Listing all of their awards over the years might take an entire book of its own. From the Great American Beer Festival and the North American Beer Awards to the World Beer Cup and a host of other honors, they have a well-decorated wall, to say the least.

Pelican Pub & Brewery offers 6 house beers year-round both on draft and in bottles. Along with those they brew 2 or 3 beers for each season and have a handful of special releases on draft and in bottles. Their year-round **Tsunami Stout** is one of the best stouts in the state. The pitch-black stout is packed with chocolate, caramel, coffee, and fruit flavors that all come together in a creamy body. **Doryman's Dark Ale** is another year-round brew that originated as an award-winning homebrewing recipe their brewmaster had created prior to brewing professionally. The great balance of malts and hops in the brown ale has been a favorite ever since.

When creating both their beer and food for the pub, pairing is extremely important. Not only do they pair food with beer, but a lot of their food items also use it as an ingredient to enhance the flavor. **Kiwanda Cream Ale** is used in many of their dishes, including the tower of onion rings, steamed clams and mussels, fish and chips, and a wide range of other entrees. If you're nearby, Pelican Pub & Brewery is a place where any beer lover must stop for both an amazing meal and award-winning beer.

See Ged Aydelott's recipe for **India Ale Gazpacho** on p. 218 and for **Doryman's Dark Ale Apple and Raisin Bread Pudding** on p. 223.

ROGUE ALES

2320 SE Osu Dr., Newport, OR 97365; (541) 867-3660; Rogue.com; @RogueAles
Founded: 1988 **Founders:** Jack Joyce, Bob Woodell, and Rob Strasser **Brewer:** John Maier **Flagship Beer:** Dead Guy Ale **Year-round Beers:** Dead Guy Ale, Double Chocolate Stout, American Amber Ale, Brutal IPA, German Maibock Hazelnut Brown Nectar, Mocha Porter, Portland State IPA, Shakespeare Oatmeal Stout, Younger's Special Bitter **Seasonals/Special Releases:** Double Dead Guy, Festivale, Juniper Pale Ale, Kells Irish Style Lager, Santa's Private Reserve Ale, Voodoo Doughnut Maple Bacon Ale, Yellow Snow IPA, and many more **Tours:** Yes, weekdays at 1, 3, and 5 p.m. **Taproom:** Yes

While most people think of Newport when they think of Rogue, the brewery actually got its start in Albany, Oregon, where the brewing was done in the basement of a small pub. About a year into it, CEO Jack Joyce started looking for a location for another Rogue pub and landed in Newport. Stuck in the beach town due to an unusual snowstorm, he ran into Mohave Niemi, founder of the famous Mo's Clam Chowder chain. She had space for the next Rogue pub and gave it to him at a generous price under the conditions that he put a picture of her naked in a bathtub on the wall (the photo is still there today) and that he "feed the fisherman," meaning to give back to the local community. Not long after, the beer was brewing and the Rogue empire started to grow. Today the company runs the main brewery in Newport along with public houses in Newport, Portland, Astoria, and San Francisco. They also run their own hop and barley farms, as well as Chatoe Rogue Farmstead

Double Chocolate Stout
Style: Imperial Stout
ABV: 9 percent
Availability: Rotating

Rogue's Double Chocolate Stout stands out from so many beers, and not just because of its all-red bottle. This imperial stout is both a chocolate lover's and a beer lover's dream. The pitch-black color gives it a mysterious look that requires plenty of time to investigate. Dark and milk chocolate will blast you in the aroma, but keep smelling and you'll notice hidden complexities of baked cookies, vanilla, caramel, and roasted malts, among others. The flavor is dominated by rich chocolate and vanilla, with toasty malts and a touch of hops making

their presence known at the end. Take your time with this beer to fully enjoy its sweetness.

Nano Brewery, Oregon's first on-site hopyard brewery. In Eugene they own and operate Eugene City Brewery and in Issaquah, Washington, they run Issaquah Brewhouse, each with its own line of beers.

Rogue produces a wide range of beers that span the spectrum from the traditional to the strange. One of the oddest beers they've produced is **New Crustacean**, a beer with a yeast strain that actually came from head brewmaster John Maier's beard. As a joke they sent in some of his beard hair to test it for yeast, and found they could use it in a beer. On a more traditional note, **Dead Guy Ale** is one of the beers that helped put Rogue on the map. The **German Maibock** has been a staple on store shelves all over the region for years.

WAKONDA BREWING COMPANY

1725 Kingwood St. #4, Florence, OR 97439; (541) 991-0694; WakondaBrewery.com; @WakondaBrewing
Founded: 2004 **Founder:** Juanita Kirkham Ron Shearer, Sean Fitzsimmons, Tim McGinnis **Brewer:** Richard Rossi **Flagship Beer:** Black Elk Stout **Year-round Beers:** Timberbeast IPA, Black Elk Stout, Beachcomber Creme Ale **Seasonals/Special Releases:** Sneaker Wave Imperial Pilsner, 7 Devils IIPA **Tours:** No **Taproom:** Yes

Florence, Oregon, is known more for its tourism and retiree culture than for being a beer city. Unless you spend much time there, you might not even know that one of Oregon's smallest breweries, Wakonda Brewing Company, has been producing quality beer since 2004. Starting out as just a production brewery, Wakonda offered its beer locally on draft at only a handful of establishments. While it has been on tap at locations in Eugene and occasionally Portland, you'll most likely need to travel to Florence to find it. Today the small brewery, which is producing fewer than 2 barrels a month, offers most of their beer in the tasting room.

Wakonda Beachcomber Creme Ale
Style: Cream Ale
ABV: 6.5 percent
Availability: Year-round
When the weather is warm at the beach, a nice refreshing cream ale pairs nicely with the bright sun beams. The Wakonda Beachcomber Creme Ale is one of the best you'll find along the Oregon coast. Clean and golden with a small head, this is one creamy and smooth beer. A slight orange and lemon flavor is balanced with a solid malt and hop profile that finishes a bit dry. If you're outside of Florence, it can be hard to find as it's served strictly on tap.

While they aren't out to become a huge brewery, they are brewing up some solid beers. The **Timberbeast IPA** is well balanced with a solid malt bill that balances out the citrusy hops. Ask the locals about the **Sneaker Wave Imperial Pilsner** and they will most likely smile and tell you it will sneak up on you. With 11.5 percent ABV that isn't very noticeable, it's way too easy to drink for the amount of alcohol in it. Drink it with caution.

If you're visiting Florence, make sure to check that the tasting room is open. It can be a bit tough to find but is worth the trip. The small room is like a college friend's basement, where music is featured more than the beer. Live music shows are a regular occurrence, making it a place you go to hang out, meet people, and have a great time while drinking beer. It's not a place where you'll have in-depth conversations about the intricacies of the yeast used. They don't offer food, so make sure to bring your own or eat before you visit.

Brewpubs

BILL'S TAVERN & BREWHOUSE

188 N. Hemlock St., Cannon Beach, OR 97110; (503) 436-2202; BillsTavernAndBrewhouse
.com
Founded: 1923 (remodeled in 1997) **Founder:** Ken Campbell and Jim Oyala **Brewer:**
Ken Campbell and Jim Oyala **Flagship Beer:** Duckdive Pale Ale **Year-round Beers:**
Duck Dive Pale Ale, Blackberry Beauty, Foggy Notion Weissbier, Rudy's Red, 2x4 Stout,
Asa's Premium Blonde, Ragsdale Porter, Evil Twin IPA **Seasonals/Special Releases:**
Asa's Premium Blonde, Curiously Strong, Auld Nutcracker, and many more

Right in the middle of the main drag of Hemlock Street in Cannon Beach sits Bill's
Tavern & Brewhouse. The old wooden Oregon coast–style building fits perfectly
in the small beach town, although it could be easy to walk by without realizing that
they produce some really good beers. The outdoor seating faces the main sidewalk,
creating a comfortable place to sit on nice days and do a little people-watching.
Walking inside, you'll notice a U-shaped pub with a restaurant on one side and more
of the bar area on the other, with the feel of a wood-filled beach lodge. When it's
stormy outside there is a comforting feeling of hunkering down with a nice beer and
relaxing in the security of the building. The brewery can be viewed through windows
above the bar, which is where all of the magic happens.

Bill's brews all of their beers on the second-floor brewery, and produces some
outstanding beers for a beach town. **Blackberry Beauty** is one of their most interesting offerings. It has a subdued sweetness, yet is very tart and full of wheat—
perfect for those sunny days at the coast. Another of their easy-drinking beers is
Duck Dive Pale Ale. With nice citrus and malt up front, you then get hit with a
touch of slightly bitter hops at the end.

If you're hungry, there's a selection of typical coastal fare: burgers, fish, soups,
and salads. Because you're at the beach, you can't go wrong with either the cod or
halibut fish and chips or the clam chowder, both of which are among the best the
small town has to offer. On the family side of the restaurant, kids are welcome, and
there tend to be quite a few.

RUSTY TRUCK BREWING COMPANY

4649 SW US 101, Lincoln City, OR 97367; (541) 994-7729; RustyTruckBrewing.com
Founded: 2011 **Founder:** Brian Whitehead **Brewer:** Paul Thomas **Flagship Beer:**
None **Year-round Beers:** Back Seat Wheat, Beach Blonde Ale, Fender Bender Amber

Ale, Low Rider Lager, Moonlight Ride Blackberry Ale, Procrastinator Stout, Road Wrecker IPA, Slant 6 Pale Ale, Stupiphany Imperial Red Ale, Taft Draft Toffee Porter **Seasonals/Special Releases:** Cherry Chocoholic Porter, Rauch 'n' Roll, Rostig Bier Oktoberfest Lager, Pedal to the Metal, Belsnickle's Strong Ale, and many more

Driving along US 101 through Lincoln City, you might notice an old red 1958 Chevy flatbed truck that looks to be rusting away on the side of the road. Instead of driving past it, turn into the parking lot and have a Rusty Truck Brewing beer or two at Roadhouse 101. The old truck, which is owner Brian Whitehead's, serves as a landmark to steer you in to the restaurant and brewery. Roadhouse 101 has been a blues- and rockabilly-themed restaurant serving the beach town for a few years, complete with bowls of peanuts that can be thrown on the floor, dollar bills pinned to the ceiling, and bright neon signs. In 2011 the restaurant opened its own brewery on the premises with the name Rusty Truck Brewing Company.

The 10-barrel system brews beer that is consumed mainly within the restaurant, but is situated in a building with plenty of room to grow in the future. The beers range in styles typical of Northwest brewpubs; however, they all have their own unique twist. **Road Wrecker IPA** is one of the top sellers. It's a fruity-tasting IPA with mild hop presence that hides its 6.8 percent ABV pretty well. Another local favorite is the **Stupiphany Imperial Red Ale** that is nice and chewy with a warm 8 percent ABV that will help ease the pain of those times when you come to the realization you did something stupid.

If you love huge portions of American food and live music, Roadhouse 101 is right up your alley. Burgers, seafood, ribs, steak, pizza, sandwiches, and salads are served, so there is no reason to walk away hungry.

TWISTED SNOUT BREWERY AND PUBLIC HOUSE

318 S. Main St., Toledo, OR 97391; (541) 336-1833; TwistedSnout.com; @TwistedSnoutPub
Founded: 2011 **Founders:** Doug and Dayle Rider and Stu and Becky Miller **Brewers:** Doug Rider and Stu Miller **Flagship Beer:** None **Year-round Beers:** Gateway Golden Ale, Oops!, Wilbur's White Wheat, Twisted Snout IPA, Red Headed Step Hog, Honey Oatmeal Porker **Seasonals/Special Releases:** Dayle Earnhog, Raspberry Squeal, Savory Sow IPA, Spruce Hog Ale, Spruce Boar Ale, WPA

For meat and beer lovers, nothing is better than really good barbecue and delicious craft beer. In Toledo, Oregon, you can find an almost perfect pairing of the two. For the past few years a local joint called Pig Feathers has been serving some of the best barbecue in the state. Owner Stu Miller had also been a homebrewer and when the space next to his restaurant became available, he swooped in with his partners to open up Twisted Snout Brewery and Public House. While the businesses operate as different establishments, you can walk between the two and order beer and food at each. The brewery side of the business isn't that large, but they have made great use of the space with plenty of tables and places to sit and enjoy their beer.

They offer a selection of mainly American-style ales that include 6 year-round beers and a rotation of seasonal beers. The **Honey Oatmeal Porker** is a chocolaty porter brewed with oats and wildflower honey from Queen Bee Apiaries in Corvallis. It has a delicious and smooth porter taste with just enough of the sweet honey flavor to make it unique. Another beer worth a drink is named **Oops!** Such a name piques your curiosity, tempting you to try it. Luckily the name comes from an error while making a golden ale—adding more hops than planned, resulting in a very hoppy golden ale.

In the pub you can order a handful of food items special to the pub, such as the Cajun steamed oysters when they are in season. You can also order from the full Pig Feathers menu, including the amazing baby back ribs with your choice of 4 sauces. If you're passing through Toledo, make sure to come hungry. You won't be disappointed.

Beer Bars

BIER ONE

424 SW Coast Hwy., Newport, OR 97365; (541) 265-4630; Bier-One.com;
@bierone_newport
Draft Beers: 15 **Bottled/Canned Beers:** 200

Most of the Oregon coast is a desert when it comes to good craft beer. The towns along US 101 generally aren't the best places to go if you're looking for decent beer from other parts of the state or country. If you mention Newport, you'll probably think of Rogue, which dominates much of the taps alongside a sea of macro beers in local restaurants and bars. However, more than Rogue can be found in the beach town, which is great for craft beer lovers. Bier One, a small beer shop and bar right on US 101 in Newport, is the place to go. More than just a bar with 15 rotating taps, Bier One also offers a full bottle shop of craft beer, a good selection of homebrewing equipment, as well as winemaking supplies. Along with beer, they also have a selection of meads and wine, both by the bottle and by the glass.

The tap list rotates frequently with beers from not just the Northwest, but nationally and internationally as well. Located in the same city as Rogue, they rarely carry their beers on draft, because you can find them at other area bars. They focus on a lot of Northwest breweries that you can't find at many other establishments, making it a unique place to visit. The store itself has a local feel to it and is set up to entertain. Periodically they offer foosball tournaments as well as live music and parties. There's also a pool table and TV, so if you're in Newport, this is a great place to relax and have really good beer. If you're hungry, they generally have a small and rotating food menu.

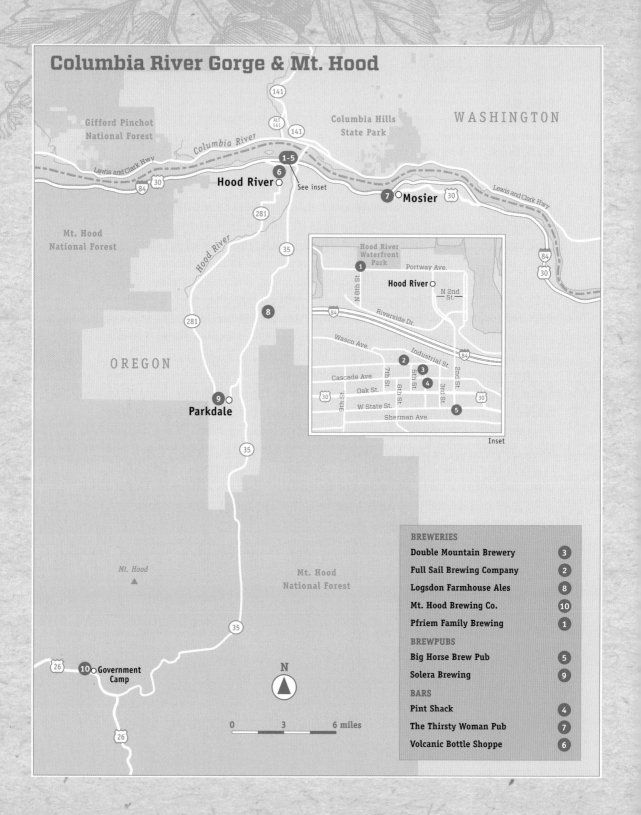

Columbia River Gorge & Mt. Hood

WASHINGTON

Gifford Pinchot
National Forest

Columbia Hills
State Park

Columbia River

Lewis and Clark Hwy

141

ALT 141

141

1-5

6

Hood River

See inset

7 Mosier

Lewis and Clark Hwy

84

30

84

30

281

35

Mt. Hood
National Forest

Hood River

281

8

OREGON

9 Parkdale

35

Mt. Hood

Mt. Hood
National Forest

35

26

10 Government
Camp

26

N

0   3   6 miles

Inset

Hood River
Waterfront
Park

1

Portway Ave.

N 8th St

Hood River

N 2nd St.

84

Riverside Dr.

84

Wasco Ave.

Industrial St.

2nd St.

Cascade Ave.

2

7th St.

5th St.

3

30

Oak St.

6th St.

4

3rd St.

30

9th St.

W State St.

5

Sherman Ave.

Inset

BREWERIES

Double Mountain Brewery	3
Full Sail Brewing Company	2
Logsdon Farmhouse Ales	8
Mt. Hood Brewing Co.	10
Pfriem Family Brewing	1

BREWPUBS

Big Horse Brew Pub	5
Solera Brewing	9

BARS

Pint Shack	4
The Thirsty Woman Pub	7
Volcanic Bottle Shoppe	6

Columbia River Gorge & Mt. Hood

Over the past few years the Columbia River Gorge, specifically the Hood River area, has become a hot spot for great craft beer. With Full Sail Brewing being the center of the beer scene for so long, multiple smaller brewers have decided to set up shop in the area. Right across the street from Full Sail is Double Mountain Brewery, one of the state's fastest-growing breweries. The area is also home to multiple boutique-style breweries, such as Logsdon Farmhouse Ales, Pfriem Family Brewers, and Solera Brewery, each of which are brewing up some remarkable and unique beers. Although the population isn't as large as in other areas in the state, the ratio of breweries per capita is the highest in the state.

Aside from some great breweries, step into most restaurants in the area and you'll be treated to a great beer selection. The Columbia River Gorge and Mt. Hood area is also arguably the most scenic in the state for beer drinking.

Breweries

DOUBLE MOUNTAIN BREWERY

8 4th St., Hood River, OR 97031; (541) 387-0042; DoubleMountainBrewery.com;
@DoubleMountain
Founded: 2007 **Founders:** Matt Swihart and Charlie Devereux **Brewer:** Matt Swihart
Flagship Beer: IRA **Year-round Beers:** Kölsch, The Vaporizer, India Red Ale, Hop Lava
Seasonals/Special Releases: Black Irish, Spicy Brown Ale, Two X Four, "Little G" ESB,
Tripel Nipel, Red Light District, Molten Lava, Devil's Kriek, Dapper Dan Nitro Brown Ale,
Rainier Kriek, and many more **Tours:** No **Taproom:** Yes

Located just down the road from Full Sail Brewing in Hood River, Double Mountain Brewery is the creation of Matt Swihart and Charlie Devereux, both former employees at Full Sail. Founded in 2007, Double Mountain has become one of Oregon's fastest-growing breweries, mainly because they produce some incredible beers. The name "Double Mountain" refers to a view in Hood River where you can see both Mt. Adams and Mt. Hood from one location. It's also a name now seen on many tap handles throughout the Northwest in all sorts of restaurants and bars. Their beers have been available mainly on draft in multiple locations as well as their taproom. A recent expansion into the building next door to their original brewery has opened up a lot of room for future growth, including a new line that is bottling half liters.

Double Mountain offers 4 year-round beers, which are brewed with one of their 2 house yeasts. The unfiltered 5.2 percent **Kölsch** is light-bodied, yet is a slightly hoppier version than other beers in the style. **The Vaporizer** is a dry and clean pale ale dry-hopped with Challenger hops, refreshing for both hot summer days and cold winter nights. The **India Red Ale,** or IRA, is a beautiful red ale with hop flavors of an IPA. It's a truly delicious beer that is complex, yet easy to enjoy. **Hop Lava** is a Northwest-style IPA that's hoppy yet has a strong enough malt backbone with little lingering bitterness. Along with the year-round lineup, they offer multiple seasonals and specialties that are generally available only in the taproom. From your usual beer styles to more obscure sour beers, they aren't afraid to brew up small-batch new ideas.

While you can find their beer around the state, if you can make it to the taproom, you should. The pizza is just about as legendary as the beer. Go pretty much anytime and you'll notice just about everyone else eating pizza with their beer. While they have delicious sandwiches and salads on the menu, do yourself a favor and order the pizza along with a few pints of brew.

Rainier Kriek

Style: American Wild Ale

ABV: 9 percent

Availability: Once a year

As sour beers gain popularity, more breweries are starting to experiment with different and local fruits. Double Mountain's Rainier Kriek is a sour ale that utilizes Rainier cherries harvested from brewmaster/owner Matt Swihart's own orchard. The hazy light golden ale has a lot of tart cherry in the aroma along with a touch of funk. It's a sour beer that will make you pucker for sure. While this isn't a style that pleases everyone, those who enjoy sour beers need to seek out this Kriek. It's unique.

FULL SAIL BREWING COMPANY

506 Columbia St., Hood River, OR 97031; (541) 386-2247; FullSailBrewing.com; @fullsailbrewing

Founded: 1987 **Founder:** Irene Firmat **Brewer:** Jamie Emmerson **Flagship Beer:** Full Sail Amber Ale **Year-round Beers:** Full Sail Amber Ale, Full Sail India Pale Ale, Full Sale Pale Ale, Session Premium Lager, Session Black Lager **Seasonals/Special Releases:** LTD 03, LTD 04, LTD 05, Wassail, Old Boardhead Barleywine, Full Sail Imperial Stout, Lupulin Fresh Hop Ale, Wreck the Halls, and many more **Tours:** Yes, daily on top of every hour from 1 to 4 p.m. **Taproom:** Yes

In the 1980s, a few big breweries dominated the beer industry. Although craft breweries were on the rise, it was a difficult time to start a brewery. It was also a time when beer was viewed more as a man's drink, so the idea of a woman starting a brewery was a bit of a foreign concept to many people. It didn't stop Irene Firmat from launching Full Sail Brewing in 1987, which has become one of the biggest brewery success stories in the country. Irene left her job as a fashion buyer to start the brewery in what was an old fruit packaging plant that had been abandoned for 15 years. Using her drive, love of beer, and commitment to her employees, Full Sail has grown into the powerhouse it is today. In 1999 the company became one of the few breweries to be completely employee owned.

Under the Full Sail label, the company produces its core beers of an **Amber Ale,** **IPA,** and **Pale Ale** that are available all over the country. They also offer a handful of seasonals including 3 in their **LTD** series and **Wassail,** their holiday brewed winter warmer. Along with those they have special releases in the **Brewer's Share, Brewer's Share Experimental,** and **Brewmaster Reserve** series, which are brewed in the Full Sail brewhouse in Portland. Aside from the Full Sail label they have a series of lagers branded under the name Session that come in short, stubby, 11-ounce bottles. The company also produces multiple beers under contract for SABMiller, which includes a full lineup of Henry Weinhard's beers.

If you're in Hood River, make sure to stop by the tasting room and pub to sample the beer and order some delicious pub food. They offer a free tour every day on the hour from 1 to 4 p.m., covering their brewing process, ingredients, sustainability, and company history. Kids 12 and over are welcome as long as they are with an adult.

Old Boardhead Barleywine
Style: Barleywine
ABV: 9 percent
Availability: Year-round

Part of Full Sail's Brewmaster Reserve series, Old Boardhead Barleywine is brewed each year and is offered in 22-ounce bottles and on draft. This is one complex yet smooth beer that is a little on the lighter body side for barleywines. Deep copper in color, the beer has very little head. Aromas of caramel malts, citrus, and brown sugar rise out of the glass, tempting you to drink. A slightly citrus hop flavor is present, with fruit, caramel, and a malty backbone playing along. While not the strongest barleywine around, Old Boardhead is a great beer to sip on and it gets even better with age.

LOGSDON FARMHOUSE ALES

4785 Booth Hill Rd., Hood River, OR 97031; (541) 490-9161; FarmhouseBeer.com;
@farmhouseales
Founded: 2011 **Founder:** David Logsdon **Brewer:** David Logsdon **Flagship Beer:** Seizoen Bretta **Year-round Beers:** Seizoen, Seizoen Bretta, Kili Wit, Peche 'n' Brett, Cerasus, Far West Vlaming **Seasonals/Special Releases:** Fresh Hop Seizoen **Tours:** No
Taproom: No

Farmhouse ales have been a growing trend in the US craft beer world; however, most aren't actually brewed in a farmhouse. However, for Logsdon Farmhouse

Ales, they brew their artisan beers on an actual farm in the outskirts of Hood River. Founded in 2011, the small brewery is producing some unique beers and quickly making a name in the Oregon beer scene. Founder and brewer David Logsdon is no newcomer to the industry. He was the first head brewer for Full Sail Brewing in the late 1980s, and started Wyeast Labratories, one of the world's largest companies producing yeast and fermentation products. The 1940s barn, which once housed the laboratory for Wyeast, now houses the brewery.

On the farm is a nursery of Schaerbeekse cherry trees brought over from East Flanders in Belgium that will be used to produce future beers. All of the Logsdon

Beer Lover's Pick

Seizoen Bretta
Style: Saison
ABV: 8 percent
Availability: Year-round
Sold in 750-milliliter bottles with a beeswax seal, Seizoen Bretta is one unique saison that is worth seeking out. You won't be disappointed. It's brewed with Brettanomyces yeast and bottle conditioned with pear juice, giving it a ton of carbonation and sweet aromas and flavor. It's packed with lots of fruity aromas and brings more funk than James Brown. Citrus, Brett, floral, and spicy flavors give this amazing beer a lot of depth. The 8 percent ABV is masked well, making this a beer that goes down smooth. If you can find it on draft, order it.

Farmhouse ales are brewed using organic ingredients, and they also choose to use organic whole-leaf hops instead of pellets. With such great care for their ingredients, along with a handful of unique yeast strains, they are producing some amazing Belgian-inspired beers. The **Seizoen** is bottle conditioned and carbonated with pear juice, producing a complex and easy-drinking saison. They also produce a similar beer called **Seizoen Bretta** that uses Brettanomyces yeast along with a version called **Peche 'n' Brett,** which is the same beer oak aged and loaded with peaches. Peche 'n' Brett won a gold medal at the 2012 World Beer Cup in the American-style Brett ale category. Their **Kili Wit** is a traditionally brewed Witbier that has added African spice. Logsdon Farms donates a portion of sales from it to K2 Adventures Foundation, an organization providing community service, medical, and educational enrichment to African children.

The brewery doesn't offer a taproom, but you can find their beers throughout Oregon and in parts of Washington. Each is bottled in a 750-milliliter bottle with a beeswax seal.

MT. HOOD BREWING COMPANY

87304 E. Government Camp Loop, Government Camp, OR 97028; (503) 272-0102; IceAxeGrill.com

Founded: 1991 **Founders:** Multiple founders **Brewers:** Tom Rydzewski and Jeff McAllester **Flagship Beer:** Ice Axe India Pale Ale **Year-round Beers:** Ice Axe India Pale Ale, Cloud Cap Amber Ale, Highland Meadow Blonde Ale, Multorporter Ale, Cascadian Pale Ale, Hogsback Oatmeal Stout **Seasonals/Special Releases:** Pittock Wee Heavy Scotch Ale, Old Battleaxe Barleywine, Rookie Rye **Tours:** No **Taproom:** Yes

Government Camp, Oregon, is a gathering spot for skiers, winter sports enthusiasts, hikers, and those just passing on through the mountain. One of the few buildings you can spot while driving by on Mt. Hood Highway is the Ice Axe Grill and Mt. Hood Brewing. Located on the first floor is the brewery, which for years has supplied fresh beer to both those visiting the mountain and the locals. What was once a ski rental and gift shop was transformed into what it is today. Operations began in 1991 with a focus on serving their beer mainly in the pub. Although most of the beer is produced for on-site consumption, the brewery distributes kegs to multiple locations throughout the state as well as selling limited supplies of 22-ounce bottles at Zupan's Markets and Made in Oregon stores.

Mt. Hood Brewing offers 6 year-round beers and a rotation of seasonal selections. The flagship beer, **Ice Axe India Pale Ale,** is a 5.9 percent ABV IPA that's on the lighter side for its style. It's also the first beer they have bottled. In the winter

Hogsback Oatmeal Stout
Style: Oatmeal Stout
ABV: 4.5 percent
Availability: Year-round

Hogsback is a beer that could easily fool you if you just looked at the color. It's about as dark as you can get, yet the flavor is actually quite light. The aroma is a pleasant mix of coffee, toasted caramel, chocolate, and a touch of oatmeal. The flavor follows with an added bitterness and a hint of vanilla. With an incredibly

creamy mouthfeel, it has smooth drinkability. If you're not at the brewery, you might be able to find it on cask at the Horse Brass Pub in Portland for an even better experience.

they release **Pittock Wee Heavy Scotch Ale,** brewed with a combination of 9 malts, 3 hops, and hybrid fermentation (ale yeast, lager temperatures) to give it a nice and complex flavor. With smoky notes, a lingering sweetness, and 8.5 percent ABV, it's a fantastic beer to sip on around a warm fire.

Although their beer is available in multiple locations, visiting the brewery is a great experience. The inside of the pub is lined with Cascadian stone and timber, giving a true ski lodge feel. Not only are most of their beers available only on site, but they also offer at least one beer on cask and one on nitro. If you're feeling hungry after a long day on the slopes, they offer a selection of pizzas, sandwiches, soups, burgers, and seafood.

PFRIEM FAMILY BREWERS

707 Portway Ave., Ste. 101, Hood River, OR 97301; (541)321-0490; PfriemBeer.com
Founded: 2012 **Founders:** Josh Pfriem, Ken Whiteman, and Rudy Kellner **Brewer:**
Josh Pfriem **Flagship Beer:** None **Year-round Beers:** Wit, Blonde IPA, Belgian Strong
Blonde, IPA, Belgian Strong Dark **Seasonals/Special Releases:** Multiple seasonals
Tours: No **Taproom:** Yes

As the Hood River beer scene grows and the small tourist and sport enthusiast
town becomes known just as much for its breweries as the wind surfing, new
brewers are moving in and setting up shop. Hood River's newest brewery, Pfriem
Family Brewers (pronounced "Freem"), has moved into the city and is quickly making a name for itself by creating artisanal Belgian-style beers with Northwest soul.
Head brewer and co-owner Josh Pfriem, however, isn't new to brewing, with previous
experience at Chuckanut Brewery, Full Sail, and Squatters/Wasatch, all of which
have given him the know-how to craft some very solid and well-planned beers.

Belgian Strong Blonde
Style: Belgian Strong Ale
ABV: 7.5 percent
Availability: Year-round

If you come across Pfriem's Belgian Strong Blonde, be careful. The beautiful clear, golden-colored ale with a thick white head looks tempting yet light. With the appearance of a session beer, you could easily be fooled into thinking the 7.5 percent ABV isn't there, even upon tasting it. The house yeast gives off flavors of cloves, apples, banana, pears, and citrus, producing one complex yet light and easily consumed beer. A beautiful balance of ingredients makes drinking this ale a refreshing experience.

Situated right across the street from the Columbia River waterfront, the brewery allows you to look out and watch kite boarders and sailboarders enjoying the river while you stand in front of the 15-barrel brewery. With a beautiful tasting room covered in wood and built around the brewery, the place offers quite a family atmosphere upon entering. To match the beer styles, the taproom features a small mix of Belgian-inspired foods that pairs well with each of the beers and are made with local ingredients. While the taproom is a great place to visit, you don't have to head to Hood River to experience Pfriem beers. Between draft and 750-milliliter bottles, they are growing distribution throughout both Oregon and Washington.

One thing you'll notice from most of the beers is their incredible cleanness, which comes from the filtering process. The filtration of yeast gives their beers a very nice appearance, while keeping them in the Belgian styles in which they were created. The brewery is still very young, so the beer lineup is still changing. At the launch they offered 5 styles of beer, which included a **Wit, Blonde IPA, IPA, Belgian Strong Blonde,** and a **Belgian Strong Dark.** Each beer has its own unique characteristics, but each is fairly dry yet very drinkable. As the brewery grows, they will use their new barrel room to house wild fermented beers, allowing them to bring many unique beers to the market for years to come.

Columbia River Gorge & Mt. Hood

Brewpubs

BIG HORSE BREW PUB

115 W. State St., Hood River, OR 97031; (541)386-4411; BigHorseBrewPub.com
Founded: 2003 **Founder:** Randy Orzeck **Brewer:** Darrek Smith **Flagship Beer:** Pale Rider IPA **Year-round Beers:** Easy Blonde, Pale Rider IPA, MacStallion's Scotch Ale, Nightmare Oatmeal Stout **Seasonals/Special Releases:** Morning After Pils, Paragon, Wind Ripper, Dwed Piwate Wobberts, Vernon the Rabbit Slayer, Horsethief English Bitter, and many more

Most of the breweries in Hood River have great scenic views, yet Big Horse Brew Pub has one of the best. Situated on a hillside at the back of downtown, the pub overlooks the Columbia River Gorge as well as the town. Standing on the sidewalk out front, you'll notice a huge staircase that seems to climb forever as it extends to Winans Park. Luckily you'll need to climb only a quarter of them to get

to the pub, though more stairs wait for you on the inside. The 3-story building is set up with the brewery on the bottom floor, a pool room and restrooms on the second, and the brewpub on the third, complete with a small balcony to enjoy the beautiful scenery while you eat. Inside, the pub is very low-key, giving it a feeling of comfort for visiting tourists. With all the stairs, however, the pub isn't set up for wheelchair access.

The beers tend to be toward the hoppier side and are generally kept to popular styles that people are familiar with. One year-round favorite is the **Pale Rider IPA,** a 6.7 percent ABV beer with a great bite of bitterness, yet carrying a solid malt backbone. For those who really enjoy big, hoppy beers, **Vernon the Rabbit Slayer** is a huge 11.1 percent double IPA that makes an appearance every once in a while. Although the alcohol content is high, the balance between the citrus and piney hops along with the sweet malt flavor makes Vernon the star.

Big Horse offers a range of pub food consisting of soups, sandwiches, seafood, burgers, and appetizers. Many of the options are a little on the pricey side and sometimes service can be a little slow. But the place has a great small-town atmosphere with a beautiful view and solid beer that's worth a visit.

SOLERA BREWERY

4945 Baseline Dr., Parkdale, OR 97041; (541) 353-5500; SoleraBrewery.com; @SoleraBrewery
Founded: 2012 **Founders:** Jason Kahler and John Hitt **Brewer:** Jason Kahler
Flagship Beer: Hedonist IPA **Year-round Beers:** Berliner Weisse, Hedonist IPA
Seasonals/Special Releases: French Tickler, Goat Boxer, Shortstop ISA, Farmhouse Blonde, Parkdale Red, and many more

All over Oregon you can find many breathtaking views. Where there is a good view, you'll often find a brewery nearby. If you enjoy mixing great beer with some amazing scenery, Solera Brewery in Parkdale should be at the top of your list, as the view of Mt. Hood is pretty tough to beat. Just 17 miles south of Hood River and 8 miles from Mt. Hood, the brewpub is a perfect stop. As travelers to the mountain pass through the small town of a few hundred people, they'll drive by a 75-year-old theater that has since been converted into a brewery. Before the old building was Solera, it housed the Elliot Glacier Public House. After the doors closed, it sat empty for a couple years before it was bought out complete with the brew system, remodeled, and turned into Solera.

The term "solera" is used in aging liquids such as wine, beer, liquor, and vinegar, and blending them each year. Each year the blender takes the previous year's casks and mixes them with younger liquid and repeats this process over many years to produce a complex beer (or other liquid). A solera is the name of the containers used in the process. While beers produced using this method will be a part of their offerings in the future, they now create beers using a little more traditional brewing. **Hedonist IPA** and **Berliner Weisse** are served year-round in the pub. Interestingly enough, the Berliner Weisse is a style you don't find too often featured in a small-town brewpub, yet the locals have taken to it and it has become one of the most requested beers. At only 3.5 percent ABV, it's a true session beer that can be consumed all day.

If you're driving through or looking to make a trip out to Solera, stop in for beer, dinner, and some entertainment. They offer a small selection of sandwiches, burgers, and salads along with a rotation of live music periodically.

Beer Bars

PINT SHACK
105 4th St., Hood River, OR 97031; (541) 387-7600; PintShack.com
Draft Beers: 12 **Bottled/Canned Beers:** About 20

One of Hood River's newer tap houses, Pint Shack, offers a range of beverage and food options to please multiple tastes. Located on 4th Street between Oak and Cascade, the pub has a unique feel that is slightly Baja, slightly Northwestern, and all about good drinks. Inside, the colorfully painted walls and decor are interspersed with wine barrels and beer. With multiple tables to sit at, you can feel free to bring a large group, or if you prefer, grab a seat at the wooden bar. There's also a large rollup door that doesn't quite reach the floor, giving the space some extra light.

For the non-beer drinking friends you bring, they offer a wide selection of wines, ciders, sipping vinegars, and sake. If you love hops and malt, they have you covered. Their 12 rotating taps come from breweries all over the West Coast. Hipsters will appreciate that Pabst Blue Ribbon shows up on the tap list frequently. The rest of us can enjoy a selection of IPAs, stouts, porters, ambers, browns, and a whole list of great craft beer. Along with their taps there is a large fridge filled with bottles and cans of a variety of beers.

Multiple times throughout the month they have live music featuring a variety of styles. Music just sounds better with a good beverage in your hand. The food menu is more like an appetizer and dessert menu with such items as a salami and cheese board, hummus bowl, nachos, and a few other plate options. You can always get a stout or porter float for dessert depending on what beers are on tap. The location is great if you're looking to grab a couple of drinks and snacks after a long day of kite boarding or windsurfing.

THE THIRSTY WOMAN PUB
904 2nd Ave., Mosier, OR 97040; (541) 490-2022; ThirstyWoman.com; @thirstywoman
Draft Beers: 16+ **Bottled/Canned Beers:** 3 bottled, 21 draft

There isn't a whole lot to do in the small town of Mosier in the Columbia River Gorge. The area is known for its scenery and outdoor activities and not a whole lot else. While the population is around 500 residents, it's in a great spot near Hood River right off I-84. It's also home to the Thirsty Woman Pub, one of the most interesting beer bars the state has to offer. What started in a tiny old wood building that had more taps than seats has grown into a second building. Both buildings, known as Little Woman and Big Woman, are fully operational and cater to different needs. The Little Woman was the first of the two and is located in a building built in 1928. It's open 7 days a week and offers a variety of craft beer on tap. The Big Woman, which is the newer of the two, is built with big wooden posts and beams. Large communal-type tables are situated on the inside so patrons can eat some good pub food with their beer. There is also a back patio that has some beautiful views of the gorge.

The beer on draft rotates frequently from multiple West Coast brewers, such as Hair of the Dog, Terminal Gravity, Walking Man, Amnesia, and a whole lot more. If you're looking for food, you can choose from sandwiches, appetizers, salads, a few entrees, and burgers. They claim they have the biggest burger in town, which is most likely true because there isn't a whole lot of competition. Whatever you get, make sure to try the basket of fries served with Sriracha ranch, garlic aioli, and habanero ketchup.

VOLCANIC BOTTLE SHOPPE
1410 12th St., Hood River, OR 97031; (541) 436-1226; VolcanicBottleShoppe.com
Draft Beers: 12 **Bottled/Canned Beers:** Over 200

One thing is true if you visit Hood River: You'll never have trouble finding good beer. If you find yourself in the Heights, you'll want to make sure to stop by

the Volcanic Bottle Shoppe for a drink. Like many bottle shops around the state, it's part bottle shop and part bar. The space itself isn't huge, but is a cozy place to grab a drink. Inside it feels a bit like a coffee shop with comfortable couches and chairs around the room inviting you to kick back and enjoy yourself. Brightly painted walls help give it a fun energy, as do the tap lines and beer fridges. At this bottle shop there are just over 200 beers from all over the world. While the selection isn't massive, there definitely isn't a shortage of drinks. On tap you can find 12 rotating beers, most of which are from the West Coast. For the non–beer drinkers, they have a rather large rack of over 50 wines along with hard cider and meads.

While the inside is comfortable, the beer garden out back is perfect for enjoying those nice Hood River days. The space is fairly small, but big enough for multiple people to hang out in the fresh air. You can stop by some of their events, such as beer release parties, "meet the brewer" nights, and lots of live music shows periodically. On regular nights they do close around 9 p.m., so make sure to not get there too late. If you're looking for a place to get some work done, they also have free Wi-Fi. Who says you can't drink beer while you work.

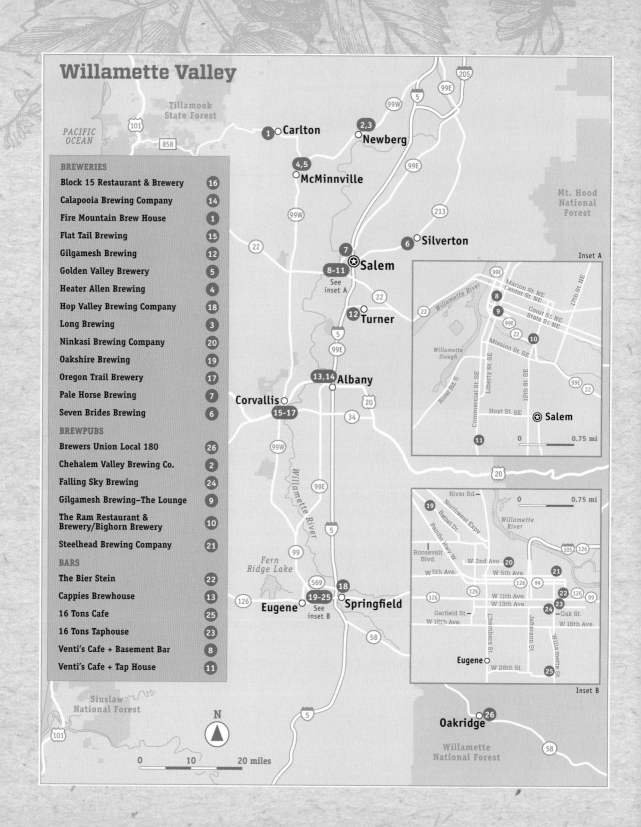

Willamette Valley

BREWERIES

Block 15 Restaurant & Brewery	16
Calapooia Brewing Company	14
Fire Mountain Brew House	1
Flat Tail Brewing	15
Gilgamesh Brewing	12
Golden Valley Brewery	5
Heater Allen Brewing	4
Hop Valley Brewing Company	18
Long Brewing	3
Ninkasi Brewing Company	20
Oakshire Brewing	19
Oregon Trail Brewery	17
Pale Horse Brewing	7
Seven Brides Brewing	6

BREWPUBS

Brewers Union Local 180	26
Chehalem Valley Brewing Co.	2
Falling Sky Brewing	24
Gilgamesh Brewing–The Lounge	9
The Ram Restaurant & Brewery/Bighorn Brewery	10
Steelhead Brewing Company	21

BARS

The Bier Stein	22
Cappies Brewhouse	13
16 Tons Cafe	25
16 Tons Taphouse	23
Venti's Cafe + Basement Bar	8
Venti's Cafe + Tap House	11

Inset A

Inset B

Willamette Valley

The Willamette Valley is the most populated area in Oregon and is home to an excellent beer culture. While Portland and its suburbs are technically considered to be part of the Willamette Valley, they have been placed in chapters all to themselves due to mass amounts of breweries. However, this leaves a large area ranging from Newberg in the north all the way down to Eugene filled with great beer culture. Both Eugene and Corvallis have had blossoming beer scenes in recent years, making way for multiple great breweries and beer bars. In Eugene Ninkasi and Oakshire have helped put the city on the map and have helped foster a city that loves its beer. Corvallis is another great beer-loving city that is home to Block 15 and Flat Tail Brewing, both of which aren't afraid to push style limits in their brewing.

All throughout the Willamette Valley, you can find a wide variety of beers brewed using a range of techniques, styles, and ingredients. The rise of craft beer popularity has helped beer drinkers more easily find great beer in restaurants, stores, and brewpubs throughout the region.

Breweries

BLOCK 15 RESTAURANT & BREWERY

300 SW Jefferson Ave., Corvallis, OR 97333; (541) 758-2077; Block15.com;
@block15brewing
Founded: 2008 **Founder:** Nick Arzner **Brewer:** Steve Van Rossem **Flagship Beer:**
None **Year-round Beers:** Glo Golden Ale, Ridgeback Red, Alpha IPA, Aboriginale,
Nebula Oatmeal Stout, Fruit Ale, Wandelpad, Print Master's Pale Ale **Seasonals/Special
Releases:** Hipster Barbie, Pappy's Dark, Figgy Pudding, Summer Knights, Hatter's Riddle,
Violet's Blueberry Berliner Weisse, Illusions, Mysticgold, Ferme de La Ville 15, Super
Nebula, and more

Prior to 2008, the college town of Corvallis had few selections when it came to brewpubs. The city was ready to get behind a local pub, so when Block 15 was opened it had quick success and a growing fan base. It didn't take long for those outside of Corvallis to take notice that the beer being brewed wasn't your standard lineup of traditional beers served at many pubs. Their beers range from traditional styles to more experimental and unique concoctions, with many being wild ales aged in barrels in the cellar.

The pub itself sits in an old building built in 1926 for the *Gazette-Times* newspaper. Inside is a traditional brewpub setting packed with wood everywhere, a restaurant and bar area, and even a game room. Down in the basement is the brewery, which has a unique feel. With rooms and hallways going all over the place, it feels like it covers the entire city block. The brewing system itself is only a 7-barrel system, but from what they offer, you'd never know it. They generally have a minimum of 12 beers on draft in the pub, with more being bottled and distributed locally. About half of the draft list is their regular lineup and the other half is seasonal and special releases. Year-round beers you can't miss include their **Alpha IPA, Nebula Oatmeal Stout,** and **Aboriginale,** although you can't go wrong with any of the offerings. Every year they age **Super Nebula,** an imperial version of their Nebula Oatmeal Stout, in bourbon casks and blend it with origin-specific cocoa nibs. The result is a unique, complex beer that is never duplicated and is released yearly.

The newest addition to Block 15 is the new European-inspired *Bier Taverne* called Les Caves just next door. It has a little more of an upscale feel to it, yet serves a couple of beers brewed by Block 15 made just for that location. While Block 15's beers can be tough to find outside of Corvallis, they are worth either seeking out or making a trip to fill up a couple of growlers.

Wandelpad

Style: Belgian Pale Ale

ABV: 6.4 percent

Availability: Year-round

Wandelpad is a delicious Belgian pale ale inspired by Westvleteren Blond and created with a Northwest love of hops. Brewed with Belgian pale and Pilsner malts, clear candi sugar, and noble hops, and fermented with Belgian Trappist yeast, Wandelpad is a very approachable beer. It pours a hazy golden color with off-white head. Light peppery spice, fruit, grass, and Belgian yeast make up the very smooth aroma. The flavor is a mix of yeasty fruit, grain, pepper, and strong hop bitterness that makes you want to sit in the Belgian countryside sipping away along with a loaf of bread and a plate of cheeses.

CALAPOOIA BREWING COMPANY

140 NE Hill St., Albany, OR 97321; (541) 928-1931; CalapooiaBrewing.com

Founded: 1993 (named Calapooia in 2006) **Founders:** Laura Bryngelson and Mark Martin **Brewer:** Mark Martin **Flagship Beers:** RIPArian IPA, Chili Beer **Year-round Beers:** Boxcar Brown, Caber Toss Scotch Ale, Luckiamute Lite, 'Pooya Porter, Devil's Hole Stout, Chili Beer, White Water Wheat, SantiAmber Ale, Riverdog ESB, Big Aft Pale, RIPArian IPA **Seasonals/Special Releases:** Yeti Blackberry Wheat, Fresh Hop Rye, Ol' Lickspigot Barley Wine, Kringle Krack Strong Ale, and more **Tours:** No **Taproom:** Yes

Originally a brewpub by the name of Oregon Trader Brewing Company, the Albany brewery was taken over by new owners Laura Bryngelson and Mark Martin and renamed Calapooia Brewing Company. Named after the Calapooia River, which converges with the Willamette River near Albany, Calapooia Brewing Company is in a bit of an odd location for a brewpub. Set as it is in an old warehouse in an industrial area, you'd never guess that many great beers were being produced inside. With a focus on brewing mainly traditional styles of beer, they have perfected it to an art and offer a lineup that is surprisingly well brewed.

Bottling beer is fairly new for the company, yet their presence is growing outside of Albany as more and more Calapooia bottles are popping up around the state. Their first bottled beer was the famous **Chili Beer.** While not a beer most people will

Chili Beer
Style: Chile Beer
ABV: 5.5 percent
Availability: Year-round
Chile beers aren't for everyone, and Calapooia's version is no exception. If you can handle the heat, then it's a must-try, well-crafted beer. Created with Anaheim, Serrano, and jalapeño peppers, this chile beer has a heck of a bite. The hazy, dark orange brew has an off-white head that doesn't last long. Make sure to give it a good smell if you love peppers, as they dominate the aroma. The flavor is all about the peppers as well, starting off with a green chile taste and moving more toward jalapeños with some heat. This would be a great beer to use in cooking.

chug, it's a unique experience that is worth a taster. Their best-selling beer is the **RIPArian IPA,** a West Coast–style IPA hopped up with Cascade, Chinook, Willamette, and Centennial hops. With a lot of sweetness and malt to balance out the bitterness, it's a solid all-around IPA. **Devil's Hole Stout** has quite a bit of fruit flavors, coffee, licorice, vanilla, and a touch of smokiness that all come together in a creamy, medium-bodied stout.

If you're near Albany, the brewpub is a must-visit. Though from the outside it's not the most impressive place, you will be pleasantly surprised. They pour about 15 taps, including their regulars and a handful of seasonal beers, so you won't go thirsty. Typical brewpub food of burgers, sandwiches, salads, and appetizers fills the menu. For a starter you will definitely want to try the Chili Beer Chili made with their own Chili Beer. Pair it with RIPArian IPA to help cut the head. Bring a growler to be filled, or even a 5-gallon Cornelius keg if you want to have some beer on tap at home.

See Calapooia Brewing Company's recipe for **Chili Beer Chili** on p. 216 and for **Chocolate Undertow Cupcakes** on p. 221.

FIRE MOUNTAIN BREW HOUSE

10800 NW Rex Brown Rd., Carlton, OR 97111; (503) 852-7378; FireMountainBrewery.com; @firemtbrewery
Founded: 2009 **Founder:** Henry Gorgas **Brewer:** Henry Gorgas **Flagship Beer:** Oregon Pale Ale **Year-round Beers:** Bogart Northwest, Bad Henry, Oregon Pale Ale, Steam Fired Stout **Seasonals/Special Releases:** Hangman Winter Fest Ale, Tan Line
Tours: By appointment **Taproom:** Yes, open Sun 11 a.m.–6 p.m.

While Carlton, Oregon, is an interesting place to find a brewery, finding one 7 miles outside of town is even more interesting. Housed in what used to be a shop where brewer/owner Henry Gorgas worked on airplanes, Fire Mountain Brew House is brewing some tasty beers using a little different style than that of many other Northwest breweries. Many of the ingredients they use are grown in Europe, giving the beer a unique flavor compared to other Northwest brews, although they brew those as well. Their malts come from the UK, France, Germany, and the US, and the hops come from the Northwest, Germany, and the Czech Republic. The 15-barrel brewery is run completely manually, so you won't find any computers running the system. Both their brew kettle and hot liquor tank are heated by steam, which is also the inspiration for the name of their **Steam Fired Stout.**

Named after the brewery's owner, **Bad Henry IPA** is not your typical Northwest IPA. English malt dominates it with flavors of spicy hops, caramel, and citrus. While not overly hoppy, Bad Henry might be a good option for those not yet accustomed to drinking the great big hop bombs of the Northwest. The rest of the brews include

Steam Fired Stout

Style: American Stout

ABV: 7.6 percent

Availability: Year-round

Chocolate fans should enjoy Steam Fired Stout, which is an almost too easy to drink stout. It pours a dark black with a nice and creamy-looking tan head. Roasted malt, dark chocolate, and coffee are dominant in the aroma with a touch of ash. With a smooth and light body, the beer goes down without a problem. Big flavors of dark chocolate, smoky roasted malts, a touch of coffee, and slight hop bitterness play together to give this beer a lot of dimension. If you see the 22-ounce bottle with a simple label that reads "Steam Fired Stout" and depicts a mountain, give it a try.

a pale ale, a couple of IPAs, a stout, and a strong ale during the winter. You probably won't find sours, light beers, or obscure styles at Fire Mountain, just well-brewed beers meant to please the majority of craft beer drinkers.

If you're making a trek out to Carlton to visit the tasting room, keep your eyes open for some happy cows munching away on Fire Mountain's spent grains. Along with sending off the spent grains to feed farm animals, the hops and spent yeast are also used as compost in an effort to keep the brewery as green as possible. Although the tasting room is just open 1 day a week, you can find the beers across the state in 22-ounce bottles. The labels are fairly easy to spot on store shelves, as they all look pretty much the same, with the exception of different-colored mountains.

FLAT TAIL BREWING

202 SW 1st St., Corvallis, OR 97330; (541) 758-2229; FlatTailCorvallis.com;
@FlatTailBrewing

Founded: 2010 **Founder:** Tonya and Iain Duncan, Dave Marliave, Jason Duranceau
Brewer: Dave Marliave **Flagship Beer:** Tailgater Kölsch **Year-round Beers:** Tailgater
Kölsch, Pale Ale, Eight Man Amber, Wheat, Rough Cut IPA **Seasonals/Special Releases:**
Tamil Black, White Heat Wit, Licentious Goat Herbed Double IPA, Mustache Rye'd Red
Ale, Jarabe Caliente Chocolate Chili Stout, MC Abbey, Smokin' Wheat, Feathertop Pumpkin
Stout, Big Fin Baltic Porter, Roggenbier, Lovin' Hoppin' Squeezin' Fusion Pale Ale, and
many more **Tours:** No **Taproom:** Yes

The American beaver is the state animal of Oregon, as well as mascot to Oregon
State University, which is located in Corvallis. Beavers are known for their flat

Beer Lover's Pick

**Lovin' Hoppin' Squeezin' Fusion Pale
Ale**
Style: American Pale Ale
ABV: 5 percent
Availability: Seasonal
Beer and rock music go hand in hand.
Brewed as a tribute to the band Journey, Lovin' Hoppin' Squeezin' Fusion
Pale Ale somehow tastes even better
when you have the band's music playing in the background. Kolsch yeast is
added along with cold fermentation,
giving this pale ale its uniqueness. In
the glass the beer is golden orange
with white frothy head and a fairly
soft aroma of citrus, rye, and spicy
hops. A well-balanced flavor of bready
malts, citrus, black pepper, and caramel mixed with a medium body makes
this an extremely pleasant beer to
drink.

tails, which was the inspiration for the name Flat Tail Brewing. Based in a perfect location near the university and the Willamette River, it's not your traditional brewery. The atmosphere screams sports bar. You'll probably rile things up if you show up wearing Oregon Ducks gear, but the beer is worth the trek, even if you're not a Beavers fan (just pretend you are). The brewing philosophy is to simply brew great beer without style limitations. While you'll find your standards, such as IPAs, pale ales, and ambers, you'll also find an array of wild ales, saisons, and fruit beers.

In the pub you can find at least 15 beers on draft, with the majority being seasonals. You can also find their 22-ounce bottles around the area in bottle shops. Their **Tailgater Kölsch** is a great crossover for those just getting into the world of craft beer as well as us seasoned beer geeks. With a bready aroma and a crisp malt flavor with a subtle spiciness, it's incredibly drinkable. For the more adventurous, look for the **Jarabe Caliente Chocolate Chili Stout.** It's brewed with Portland-grown chocolate habaneros, Bulgarian carrot peppers, and artisan cacao nibs. It's like drinking a chocolate salsa with a roasty malt backbone. Don't worry, it's better than it sounds.

The brewery itself is still fairly small, so bottles are hard to come by. However, it's worth it to make a trip out to Corvallis to fill up a couple of growlers, watch a game, and enjoy a meal. The food menu is fairly extensive with everything from burgers and sandwiches to jambalaya and meat loaf. Although it's a sports pub and brewery, the kids are still welcome and invited.

GILGAMESH BREWING
2953 Ridgeway Dr. SE, Turner, OR 97392; (503) 779-9686; GilgameshBrewing.com; @GilgameshBrew
Founded: 2009 **Founders:** Mike, Nick, Matt, and Lee Radtke **Brewer:** Mike Radtke
Flagship Beers: Mamba Year-round Beers: Mamba, Hopscotch Ale, Ridgeway IPA, Filbert Lager **Seasonals/Special Releases:** DJ Jazzy Hef, Vader Coffee CDA, El Niño Pale Ale, ABandon Brew, Chocolate Mint Stout, Harvester Fresh Hop Oktoberfest, Mega Mamba, and many more **Tours:** No **Taproom:** Yes

At first glance, Gilgamesh Brewing might sound like an odd name for a brewery. Gilgamesh was the main character in the *Epic of Gilgamesh,* the greatest surviving work of Mesopotamian literature. He was king of Uruk and a demigod (part human, part god). In the *Epic of Gilgamesh* the importance of beer was made known. It basically said that men who don't drink beer are primitive and those who do drink it are cultured. With such a strong name, Gilgamesh Brewing was launched in 2009. Three local brothers and their father founded the family-run business in Turner, Oregon. Like many new breweries, they started out brewing in their garage

ABandon Brew

Style: Saison

ABV: 13 percent

Availability: Special release

What happens when you take a 13 percent ABV saison, add cranberries from Bandon, Oregon, and then age it in Pinot Noir barrels for eleven months? You get one complex and fruity beer that has wine-like characteristics. It glows a beautiful red color with no head, looking almost like cranberry juice. A fruity cranberry, citrus, and boozy aroma floats out of the glass and hits you again once you take a drink. A slight spiciness from the yeast gives it lots of character. If you can find a bottle of it, gather some friends and share it.

before they realized they had a great product to start a business on. Their beers are available mainly on draft in various restaurants and pubs from Eugene to Seattle. Special-release beers have been bottled but can be tricky to find unless you go straight to the source.

Gilgamesh beers aren't your typical pub-style brews. While they have a few of those, they tend to brew unique beers that put them on the map. Their **Mamba** is what a lot of people know them for. It's brewed without hops by using black tea and tangerine zest instead, resulting in a somewhat sweet yet spicy beer. **Filbert Lager** is a light Pilsner with a nutty body that comes from over 8 pounds of Oregon filberts added to every barrel. A favorite seasonal is the **Chocolate Mint Stout,** brewed with Amano Chocolate cocoa nibs and mint that give it a chocolaty herbal flavor.

While the brewery is located in Turner, it's currently a production facility. In downtown Salem they run a pub called The Lounge that offers their beers on draft along with food and plenty of live music. A new property in south Salem will be opening shortly to house their brewery along with a full brewpub and will be known as The Campus.

GOLDEN VALLEY BREWERY

980 NE 4th St., McMinnville, OR 97128; (503) 472-2739; GoldenValleyBrewery.com
Founded: 1993 **Founders:** Peter and Celia Kircher **Brewer:** Mark Vickery **Flagship Beer:** Red Thistle Ale **Year-round Beers:** Third Street Wheat, PerryDale Pale, American Pale, Dundee Porter, Muddy Valley Oatmeal Stout, Chehalem Mountain IPA, Red Thistle Ale, Bald Peak IPA **Seasonals/Special Releases:** Fresh Hops Ale, Oktoberfest, Tannenbomb, Black Panther Imperial Stout, Geist Bock, French Prarie Blanche, Red Hills Pilsner **Tours:** No **Taproom:** Yes

Since 1993 Golden Valley Brewery and Pub has been supplying beer to the predominantly wine country of McMinnville. Over time the brewpub has grown by adding a second location in Beaverton and releasing a handful of their beer in 12-ounce and 22-ounce bottles in local area stores. Although beer is a big part of their business, their food plays just as big of a role. Owners Peter and Celia Kircher supply most of the pub's beef from their 76-acre all-natural Black Angus ranch. Along with their beef, they also supply quite a lot of vegetables that they grow themselves to be added to their pub food.

Golden Valley brews mostly traditional-style ales that fit in with a typical brewpub. Although they brew a wide range of beers, they really excel with their darker brews. **Muddy Valley Oatmeal Stout** is generally served on nitro in their pubs, giving the chocolaty stout a creamy body that's very smooth. Notes of roasted malt, nuts, toffee, and subtle oatmeal add to the chocolate taste and lead to a somewhat dry and satisfying finish. During the winter you can find **Tannenbomb** both on draft and in 6-packs in stores. It's a classic strong ale packed with over 125 pounds of malt per barrel, producing a hearty and warm beer with a lot of complexities. Their flagship beer is **Red Thistle Ale,** an amber-looking ale they classify as an ESB. It's all sweet caramel malts up front with very little hop flavor.

Black Panther Imperial Stout

Style: Imperial Stout

ABV: 8.7 percent

Availability: Special release

If you happen to come across the elusive Black Panther Imperial Stout, make sure to give it a try. Aged in French oak barrels from Panther Creek Cellars for two months, the big dark stout has many complexities in the aroma and flavor. Take a sip and the fairly light body allows you to navigate the dark chocolate, oak, coffee, and dark fruits, and a touch of smokiness. While it's a lot lighter than many thick imperial stouts, it's a bit too easy to drink considering the alcohol content.

If you visit either the McMinnville or Beaverton locations, they offer a taster that usually contains 10 beers and spans the length of your table. If people give you a dirty look when they see you drinking a tableful of beer, don't worry, they're just jealous. Order a taster and one of their steaks and you will leave very happy. On the way out you can buy their bottled beers to go.

HEATER ALLEN BREWING

907 NE 10th Ave., McMinnville, OR 97128; (503) 472-4898; HeaterAllen.com; @heaterallenbeer

Founded: 2007 **Founder:** Rick Allen **Brewer:** Rick Allen **Flagship Beer:** Pils

Year-round Beers: Pils, Coastal, Schwarz, Dunkel **Seasonals/Special Releases:** Bobtoberfest, Hugo (Bock), Mediator (Dopplebock), Smoky Bob, IsarWeizen, Abzug

Tours: No **Taproom:** No

McMinnville is the capital of the Oregon wine industry, yet that didn't deter owner and brewer Rick Allen from opening up a small artisan brewery in the city. Differentiating itself from the multitude of breweries in the state that tend to focus more on ales, the small production brewery focuses on brewing an array of lagers. The beers have a distinct German influence, yet Allen adds his own touch, resulting in some truly delicious beers. Starting out in 2007, Heater Allen could have easily claimed the prize for being Oregon's smallest brewer, with a small 20

Pils

Style: Czech Pilsner

ABV: 5.0 percent

Availability: Year-round

Pilsners tend to get overlooked, mainly because of the bad reputation they get from the yellow water-like beers the macro breweries brew. A well-brewed Czech Pilsner can pack a lot of flavor and complexities. Heater Allen Pils is a shining example of the style and should be considered one of the, it not the, best Pilsner brewed in the US. It pours a glowing golden yellow color with a touch of grass and malt in the nose. Delicious bread, spices, and hops create a complex flavor that makes this light-bodied and clean beer incredibly sessionable.

gallons brewed in each batch. At that size it's tough to get much exposure around the state. Luckily for thirsty Oregonians and visitors, the brewery has grown to a larger system that has allowed more distribution throughout the area, although they are still fairly small.

While many ales take only a couple weeks from the time they are brewed to when they can be consumed, lagers generally take more time and are fermented at lower temperatures. Rushing the process does affect the quality of the beer, although many brewers take shortcuts to get their beer onto the market faster. Heater Allen takes the slow approach and doesn't rush the brewing process, which results in smooth and well-crafted beers. Year-round they produce 4 beers, including **Pils, Coastal** (they call it a Northwest amber lager), **Schwarz,** and a **Dunkel.** The Schwarz, which is a Schwarzbier, is a black lager packed with 9 malts that create a complex chocolate, caramel, and espresso experience with a subtle touch of smokiness. It's not a style often found around the Northwest.

Throughout the year a few seasonal beers are thrown into the mix. One of the favorites worth seeking out is **Bobtoberfest.** Named after Rick Allen's late brother, Bob, Bobtoberfest is a take on an Oktoberfest-style beer. Smooth malts take the show with a touch of sweetness and earth hops in the finish.

While Heater Allen is a production-only facility, you may be able to give them a call if you're in the area and are looking to try some of their beers or get a quick tour.

HOP VALLEY BREWING COMPANY

980 Kruse Way, Springfield, OR 97477; (541) 744-3330; HopValleyBrewing.com; @HopValley
Founded: 2009 **Founders:** Trevor Howard, Ron Howard, Jonas Kungys, and Chuck Hare **Brewer:** Trevor Howard **Flagship Beers:** Alphadelic IPA, Double D Blonde Ale **Year-round Beers**: 541 Lager, Natty Red, Stepchild Red, Double D Blonde Ale, Alphadelic IPA, Impeller Pale Ale, VIP Vanilla Infused Porter, The Heff **Seasonals/Special Releases:** Alpha Centauri Binary IPA, Cascadian Noir, Elias Briggs Cream Ale, Pollination Honey Ale, Festeroo, Golden Road, Scruggs Pale Ale, Czech Your Head, and many more **Tours:** No **Taproom:** Yes

Located in Springfield right off I-5, Hop Valley Brewing Company serves as a brewpub for the traveler, local, and beer geek while also distributing its beers throughout the state in both bottles and cans. The building is surrounded by multiple hotels, a Denny's, and an IHOP, making it an unlikely place for a brewpub. Walking inside the brick building seems familiar, as it has the typical Northwest brewpub feel, yet the well-crafted beer separates this one from typical breweries. The 15-barrel brewhouse pumps out quite a lot of beer for the size, with a lot of it being distributed outside the pub.

As the name implies, "hoppy" is a great way to describe many of these hop-packed beers. The **Alpha Centauri Binary IPA** will give the hop addict a bitter but delicious double IPA. The **Alphadelic IPA** is a true Northwest IPA with lots of hoppy bitterness, grapefruit, malts, and floral notes that help the brewery live up to its name. **Natty Red** is an imperial red ale that has the nice malty backbone in a typical red ale, but is hopped up with Nugget, Cascade, Mt. Hood, and Columbus hops. If hops aren't your

Alpha Centauri Binary IPA
Style: Double IPA
ABV: 8.5 percent
Availability: Seasonal

Originally brewed to commemorate Hop Valley's 100th batch, Alpha Centauri Binary IPA was such a hit that they continue to bring it into the rotation. It's a big beer for those who seek out the bitter over-the-top hop bombs that can send you into a hops coma. This hazy orange double IPA is bursting with grapefruit, pineapple, mango, pine, and floral hops in the aroma. The enormous malt body is there, but the citrus, pine, grass, and spicy hops take over, giving it a hoppy yet sweet and fruity flavor. It you like DIPAs, you need to try this beast.

thing, make sure to try the **VIP Vanilla Infused Porter** that's brewed with bourbon vanilla beans. It's a beautiful porter with lots of vanilla, chocolate, and roasty notes that's perfect for making a float by adding a scoop of vanilla ice cream.

The pub itself offers a food menu consisting of burgers, sandwiches, salads, appetizers, and a handful of entrees typical of many Northwest brewpubs. You can pick up cans and 22-ounce bottles of the beer at the pub, or look for them around Oregon in multiple stores and restaurants. The brewery fills growlers on site as well as offering a mug club if you're a regular.

LONG BREWING

29380 NE Owls Ln., Newberg, OR 97132; (503) 349-8341; LongBrewing.com
Founded: 2009 **Founder:** Paul Long **Brewer:** Paul Long **Flagship Beer:** India Pale Ale **Year-round Beers:** Linda's Lager, Kolsch Style Lager, India Pale Ale, Paul's Porter **Seasonals/Special Releases:** Blonde Ale, Vienna Style Lager, Wee Heavy **Tours:** By appointment **Taproom:** No

Long Brewing isn't a name you hear too often in Oregon. The small Newberg-based brewery has been flying under the radar, while at the same time making really solid beers. Founded by brewer Paul Long, the production brewery currently produces 7 beers that are made available in 22-ounce bottles and distributed around

Beer Lover's Pick

Paul's Porter
Style: Robust Porter
ABV: 6.2 percent
Availability: Year-round
Paul's Porter isn't your typical roasted flavor porter. It's borderline stout-like, yet maintains the porter style. Pouring it in a glass, you'll notice it's one of the darkest beers you've ever seen, with a beautiful tan head. The nose has a touch of roast that's taken over by coffee, chocolate, and caramel. Take a sip and the chocolate, coffee, and caramel remain, with the addition of layered malts, resulting in a smooth and complex brew. It's a complex brew that could be enjoyed on its own, or alongside a juicy grilled steak.

Newberg, Salem, Portland, and surrounding areas. Although the beer is a bit on the pricey side, it's for a good reason. As a small brewery, the owner can be incredibly picky when it comes to choosing ingredients. The brewery uses only whole hops, personally hand selected by Paul from growers in the Willamette Valley and Yakima areas. Being small allows a very hands-on approach to brewing and produces some great tasting and balanced beers.

Year-round Long Brewing offers **Linda's Lager, Kolsch, India Pale Ale**, and **Paul's Porter.** In the summer **Blonde Ale** is released and then in the winter a **Vienna Style Lager** and **Wee Heavy Scotch Ale.** One of the most popular beers is the India Pale Ale. It's a very coppery-looking beer packed with well-balanced citrus, floral, pine, fruit, and spicy aromas and flavors with a solid malt backing. At 6.2 percent ABV and medium bitterness, it's a beer perfect for sipping anytime of the year.

While it can be tough to find outside of Newberg unless you're specifically looking for it, Long Brewing is worth a drink. Check out the website to see where you can pick up a bomber near you.

NINKASI BREWING COMPANY

272 Van Buren St., Eugene, OR 97402; (541) 344-2739; NinkasiBrewing.com; @Ninkasi
Founded: 2006 **Founders:** Jamie Floyd and Nikos Ridge **Brewer:** Jamie Floyd
Flagship Beer: Total Domination IPA **Year-round Beers:** Total Domination IPA, Believer Double Red Ale, Tricerahops Double IPA, Oatis Oatmeal Stout **Seasonals/ Special Releases:** Renewale, Spring Reign, Radiant, Sleigh'R, Maiden the Shade, Mason's Irish-Style Red Ale, Imperiale Stout, Quantam Pale Ale, Unconventionale, and many more
Tours: Yes, 2 and 6 p.m. Tues–Fri and 5 p.m. Sat **Taproom:** Yes

Currently located in Eugene's Whiteaker neighborhood, Ninkasi Brewing Company has made a huge splash in the Northwest beer industry. Founded in 2006, the company has quickly grown into one of the largest producing breweries in Oregon. Ninkasi, which gets its name from the ancient Sumerian goddess of beer, is a production brewery with a focus on using a whole lot of hops. The beers are found all over the Northwest as well as in California, in both bottles and draft with their iconic branding. Gazing at a supermarket beer shelf, it's easy to recognize most Ninkasi beers, as they all have similar designs. The logo is generally heavily displayed, giving Ninkasi great branding and recognition in a crowded space.

Most known for their first brewed beer, **Total Domination IPA,** Ninkasi produces other year-round beers including **Believer Double Red Ale, Tricerahops Double IPA,** and **Oatis Oatmeal Stout.** The seasonal and special releases can often be found in stores along the West Coast. If you see the limited-release **Maiden the Shade IPA,**

Tricerahops Double IPA
Style: Double IPA
ABV: 8.8 percent
Availability: Year-round

Tricerahops is a mix of beauty and the beast. At a glance, it is a gorgeous hazy copper-orange color with an off-white head that leaves some nice lacing. The aroma is a bit delicate with orange, grapefruit, and some tropical fruits poking through with very little hoppiness. Take a sip, though, and it's all beast. The huge earthy yet some-what floral hop presence has a smooth caramel malt backbone strong enough to duel it out with the hops. It's a big beer that has a delicate side.

be sure to give it a try. The malts and 7 different hops balance together to make an easy-drinking beer that despite the abundance of hops isn't overly bitter. Another great beer worth seeking out is **Unconventionale,** a huge imperial stout brewed with lavender, tarragon, and heather. While it probably won't please everyone, it has bold flavors that will leave you almost chewing it.

The taproom, connected to the brewery, offers all of their year-round beers along with current seasonals. Specialty brewed beers are often available that can't be found elsewhere. Along with beer, the tasting room has a small food menu consist-ing of pasties, pretzels, and soups. If you're looking for a tour, they are offered Tues through Fri at 2 and 6 p.m. and Sat at 5 p.m. During the tour, you can check out the huge and updated brewhouse and get your Ninkasi questions answered.

Willamette Valley

OAKSHIRE BREWING

1055 Madera St., Eugene, OR 97402; (541) 688-4555; OakBrew.com; @Oakshire
Founded: 2006 **Founders:** Jeff and Chris Althouse **Brewer:** Matt Van Wyk **Flagship Beers:** Watershed India Pale Ale, Oakshire Amber Ale, Overcast Espresso Stout **Year-round Beers:** Watershed India Pale Ale, Oakshire Amber Ale, Overcast Espresso Stout
Seasonals/Special Releases: Ill-Tempered Gnome, O'Dark:30, Line Dry Rye, Harvest Ale, Hellshire, The Perfect Storm, Brewers' Reserve Series, Single Batch Series, and many more
Tours: Yes, Sat **Taproom:** Yes

Started in 2006 by brothers Jeff and Chris Althouse as Willamette Brewing, the Eugene production brewer was forced to change to Oakshire Brewing in 2008 after a legal dispute about the name. Fortunately for Oakshire, having a new name, along with landing one of the country's best brewers, helped create a growing brand

Beer Lover's Pick

Overcast Espresso Stout
Style: Oatmeal Stout
ABV: 5.8 percent
Availability: Year-round
Perfectly named for the dreary Oregon weather, Overcast Espresso Stout is an oatmeal stout with enough sweetness to make any day better. The dark black stout with a tan head is all about the espresso. Coffee, chocolate, and caramel give the aroma an almost iced coffee–type of smell. Following the nose, the flavor is full of roasted coffee, chocolate, roasted malts, vanilla, and a touch of bitterness in the finish. The creamy medium body makes it a real treat to drink, even on sunny days.

known for high-quality beers. The name comes from a combination of "oak," for its strength, and "shire," for a sense of community.

Oakshire offers 3 flagship year-round beers, which include **Watershed IPA, Oakshire Amber,** and **Overcast Espresso Stout.** Throughout the year, they also release a seasonal that corresponds with the current season. In the winter keep an eye out for **Ill-Tempered Gnome,** an American brown ale that has an added kick of hops and doesn't quite fit the winter warmer category, but could easily be enjoyed year-round. Where the brewery really flexes brewing muscle is the **Single Batch** and **Brewers' Reserve** series. The Single Batch series is a program where the brewers get to be creative and come up with new beers that are offered only on draft and often brewed in collaboration with other brewers, to mark anniversaries, or to be offered at festivals. Even rarer is the Brewers' Reserve series, a program using small batches that are aged in bourbon and pinot barrels. These beers are tough to find unless you visit the brewery or happen to come across them at a special event.

At the beginning, the brewery had limited distribution in Eugene and Corvallis, and has since expanded across the state as well as to some surrounding states with both draft and bottles. Their smaller batch beers, however, are much easier to find closer to the brewery. If you're in Eugene and want to stop by, make sure to give them a call, as the tasting room has limited hours. You can visit for a tour on Saturday; just be sure to confirm the time of the tour before heading over.

OREGON TRAIL BREWERY
341 SW 2nd St., Corvallis, OR 97333; (541) 752-8549; OregonTrailBrewery.com
Founded: 1987 **Founder:** Jerry Shadomy **Brewer:** Dave Wills **Flagship Beer:** Wit
Year-round Beers: Wit, Brown Ale, IPA, Ginseng Porter, Beaver Tail Ale **Seasonals/ Special Releases:** Barley Wine, Bourbon Barrel Porter, Smoke Signal, Hopgasm, Hop Doctor **Tours:** No **Taproom:** No

One of Oregon's oldest breweries and almost one of the least known is Oregon Trail Brewery. Founded in 1987 in Corvallis, the brewery has operated in a shared space with the Old World Deli since opening. Throughout the years the brewery has seen ups and downs, a change of ownership, and changes in beers, yet still keeps on chugging along supplying its beer to the college town. One interesting note is that the copper brew kettle was Full Sail Brewing's original brewing vessel. While the equipment may look old, in brewing you don't need a top-of-the-line brewery to make good beer. The deli where Oregon Trail Brewery is located has separate ownership but has been one of the brewery's main customers for years. It's also a great place to go if you're searching for a sample of their beer.

Bourbon Barrel Porter

Style: Robust Porter

ABV: 11 percent

Availability: Special release

If you enjoy a good bourbon, chances are you will get a kick out of Oregon Trail's Bourbon Barrel Porter. Just like the name leads you to believe, it's aged in Kentucky oak bourbon barrels, giving this huge porter a smooth and complex flavor. Lots of oak, bourbon, chocolate, coffee, dark fruit, and toffee malt combine to make a unique flavor. The body is a lot lighter than the 11 percent ABV leads you to believe, but it's best as a sipper. You can usually find it in a bottle with a label that looks like it was made for an Old West saloon.

While Oregon Trail doesn't brew a ton of beers, the regulars are clean and consistent. The lineup includes a **Wit** brewed with orange peel and coriander seed, an award-winning **Brown Ale,** a classic Northwest-style **IPA,** and a **Ginseng Porter.** One of the interesting seasonal brews is **Smoke Signal,** a German-style Rauchbier known for its smoky aromas and flavor. It's a bit of a subdued version, with a nice balance of smoke and sweet malts that has an almost bacon-like flavor. The brewery has a small room upstairs to store barrels for aging beers such as **Bourbon Barrel Porter** and other seasonals. While few of the beers are available outside of draft, you can find select brews around the state in 22-ounce bottles.

PALE HORSE BREWING

2359 Hyacinth St. NE, Salem, OR 97301; (503) 364-3610; PaleHorseBrewing.com; @palehorsebrewer

Founded: 2007 **Founders:** Dennis Clack and Sid Clack **Brewer:** Dennis Clack
Flagship Beers: Pale Horse Hillbilly Blonde, Pale Horse Stout **Year-round Beers:** Pale Horse Export Stout, Pale Horse Hillbilly Blonde, Pale Horse Hopyard Dog IPA, Pale Horse Mystic Wolf Amber, Ravens Roost **Seasonals/Special Releases:** Pale Horse Winter
Seasonal Tours: No **Taproom:** No

Pale Horse Brewing is one of the few production-only breweries in the state without a taproom. Located in Salem, the capital of Oregon, the brewery focuses on brewing great beer and getting it out to market. Owner Dennis Clack started

Beer Lover's Pick

Export Stout
Style: Foreign Stout
ABV: 6 percent
Availability: Year-round
Export stouts generally are brewed a little heftier than many other styles of stouts, and the Export Stout from Pale Horse is no exception, coming in at 6 percent ABV. It pours a dark black with a light mocha–colored head. There are subtle aromas of roasted malt, chocolate, dark fruit, and licorice, but you really need to focus to smell them. Most of the aromas transfer into the taste with the addition of some smokiness blasting through the carbonation. Smooth and mellow, this is a great everyday type of stout.

homebrewing years before opening up shop with his brother Sid. Their hard work has paid off enough that their beers are now found throughout the state as well all the way up through Washington in both bottles and kegs.

Their brewing philosophy is to simply brew beer. This has resulted in a lineup that includes **Export Stout, Hillbilly Blonde, Hopyard Dog IPA, Mystic Wolf Amber, Ravens Roost** double IPA, and a single seasonal simply called **Pale Horse Winter Seasonal.** Hillbilly Blonde was the first beer brewed and came from Dennis's homebrewing days. It's a light blonde ale with a grassy flavor and a touch of honey that would be a good crossover beer for those macro drinkers out there. For hop-heads, the Hopyard Dog IPA is a citrusy brew with a pretty decent bite of bitterness. With 7.6 percent ABV, the beer hides the alcohol pretty well with some nice help from the caramel malt finish that also works well at taming the bitterness. During the winter look for the seasonal heavy scotch ale. It's warming with 9.5 percent ABV and a chewy and heavy body. There are lots of flavors going on including caramel, chocolate, roasted malts, dark fruit, and licorice.

In Salem, many bars and restaurants carry Pale Horse, which can't be bought on site unless you're buying a keg. Throughout the Northwest the brewery is gaining traction and the beers are showing up in more and more places.

SEVEN BRIDES BREWING

990 N. 1st St., Silverton, OR 97381; (503) 874-4677; SevenBridesBrewing.com; @7bridesbrewing

Founded: 2008 **Founders:** Josiah Kelley, Phill Knoll, Karl Knoll, Ken DeSantis, and Jeff DeSantis **Brewer:** Phill Knoll **Flagship Beer:** Frankenlou's IPA, Becky's Black Cat Porter **Year-round Beers:** Lauren's Pale Ale, Emily's Ember, Oatmeal Ellie, Weezin-ator, Lil's Pils **Seasonals/Special Releases:** Abbey's Apple Ale, Maggie's Marzen, BrideZilla, Frankenlou's IPA, Becky's Black Cat Porter, Rose's Imperial Pilsner, Kili's Kolsch, Bea's Black Walnut Ale **Tours:** No **Taproom:** Yes

Silverton, Oregon, is well known for being home to the Oregon Garden as well as Silver Falls State Park. The picturesque town had been home to multiple coffee shops, antiques stores, and a restaurant, yet had no breweries up until 2008. At the time, five guys got together and talked about opening up the brewery. Between them were three dads and two uncles with a combined seven daughters. Discussing how they could pay for their daughters' future weddings, they figured it'd be best to start up the brewery. It was also how they got the name Seven Brides Brewing. Since opening up, they have named a beer after each of the seven daughters. Starting at the production brewery and taproom, the beers have started to find their way around the state.

Becky's Black Cat Porter
Style: Baltic Porter
ABV: 7 percent
Availability: Fall

The original bottles of Becky's Black Cat Porter had a mysterious Halloween-like label. A black cat's silhouette against a full moon and a haunted house gave this Baltic porter a spook factor. It has since been changed, but the beer has remained the same. Despite the name, the beer pours a deep, dark brown with a creamy tan head. Beautiful aromas of chocolate, coffee, toasted malts, and vanilla swirl around and lead into the creamy dark chocolate and coffee flavor with a huge malt backbone. At 7 percent ABV, this porter goes down all too easy.

Most of what they brew is traditional-style beers using local ingredients. Their malts come from Vancouver, Washington, a city just north of Portland, and their hops come from Odell, Oregon. Originally the brewery didn't offer an IPA, which those in the Northwest consistently requested. They listened and soon brewed **Frankenlou's IPA,** a fairly clear beer with a nice malt backbone and pine resin filled with hop bitterness in the finish. Another easy-drinking brew is **Lauren's Pale Ale.** Toasted malt and citrus fill the aroma, which leads to sweet malt and a citrusy hoppy flavor, perfect on a hot day.

Their beers are distributed throughout the state mainly in 22-ounce bottles as well as on draft. The brewery itself is located right next to Vitis Ridge Winery and the two businesses share a taproom. It's a great place to visit, especially if you bring along a wine lover, as you'll both be satisfied. A full pub food menu is offered along with live music, making it a fun place to visit, especially if you're seeing the Oregon Garden. Make sure to bring a growler or two, as there aren't any other breweries in the area.

Brewpubs

BREWERS UNION LOCAL 180

48329 E. 1st St., Oakridge, OR 97463; (541) 782-2024; BrewersUnion.com
Founded: 2008 **Founder:** Ted Sobel **Brewer:** Ted Sobel **Flagship Beer:** None **Year-round Beers:** None **Seasonals/Special Releases:** Frost on the Bumpkin, Tanninbomb, Union Dew, Wotcha, Good with Bacon, 3 Sigma Out, Cumbrian Moor, Mutant Dew IV, Black Wooly Jumper, Oh, the Humanities, Bona Fide Best Bitter, This Time For Sure, and many more

Oakridge, Oregon, and its neighboring city of Westfir are the only two cities in the state completely surrounded by a national forest. With the rise of mountain biking and hiking in the area, Oakridge has grown into a great little town for outdoor enthusiasts to stop in and relax after spending time enjoying one of the most scenic areas of the state. It's also an interesting, but fitting spot to find Oregon's only real ale public house. Brewers Union Local 180 is a mix of a British public house and Northwestern hospitality. Although owner Ted Sobel is from the US, he put in some time at a pub in England and brought back some of the traditions that have made public houses more than just a place to drink beer. At Brewers Union Local 180 you can feel free to stay as long as you want, as there's ample space to lounge, read books, play pool, listen to live music, and just enjoy the community feel. You won't, however, find TVs, piped-in music, or the wimpy 16-ounce pints you find most places around the country.

The small brewery bases all measurements off British standards. They serve imperial pints (20 ounces) of the house-made beer that's brewed on an imperial 2-barrel system (just about 2.8 barrels in the US). Once brewed and fermented, the beer is then cask conditioned in firkins, also used to dispense the beer without the need for carbon dioxide or nitrogen. They generally have 3 to 5 of their own "real ales" on cask in the pub, along with a handful of beers, ciders, and meads from other breweries being served with CO_2. They have a full food menu, although it is mostly American-style food. Brewers Union Local 180 is a great destination to visit and even better if you make a day out of it and really spend some time enjoying the experience.

CHEHALEM VALLEY BREWING COMPANY

2515 B Portland Rd., Newberg, OR 97132; (971) 832-8131; CVBrewing.com; @cvbrewing
Founded: 2011 **Founders:** John Price and Paul Looney **Brewers:** John Price and Paul Looney **Flagship Beer:** None **Year-round Beers:** Citra Blonde, Blackridge Stout,

Northern Porter, Summit Amber, Hop on Pop Double IPA, Broken Bottle IPA, Pacifica IPA, Blackridge Stout, Northern Porter, Wheat Free! **Seasonals/Special Releases:** Chocolate Cream Stout, Fresh Hop, and more

Up until 2011 when Chehalem Valley Brewing Company opened, residents in Newberg needed to drive into Portland or McMinnville if they wanted good beer fresh from a brewery along with pub food. The small brewpub filled the need and has been supplying locals and those passing through ever since. On the outside the building doesn't look like much. What was once a glass repair shop is now home to Newberg's only brewpub. Upon entering you get a feeling this is a great place to hang out if you're of legal drinking age. With 2 bay doors that open up and nicely colored walls, there is quite a bit of light, perfect for drinking beer on nice days. They also have multiple TVs around for watching games, free Wi-Fi if you want to catch up on some work or watch Internet videos, and a dartboard that's used for game nights.

Although it's a great local hangout spot, the beer selection is the real reason to visit. At any given time they offer 8 to 12 of their own beers on tap with up to 12 guest taps from other Oregon and Washington breweries. Their own beers focus on American ales, including a blonde ale, pale ale, amber, multiple IPAs, stout, porter, and even a gluten-free beer made with sorghum. This is still a small brewery, so knowing when each of the house beers will be on draft can be hit-or-miss. They don't distribute, so you will need to make a visit if you want to give Chehalem Valley beer a try. If you're hungry, you have a few options. They allow you to bring food in and you can even have them order from Ye Old Pizza, which is next door. In-house they have a small menu consisting of a few burgers, salads, and fish tacos.

FALLING SKY BREWING
1334 Oak Alley, Eugene, OR 97401; (541) 505-7096; FallingSkyBrewing.com; @FallingSkyBrew
Founded: 2012 **Founders:** Jason Carriere and Robert Cohen **Brewer:** Jason Carriere
Flagship Beer: None **Year-round Beers:** None **Seasonals/Special Releases:** Bare Hands NW Bitter, Blue Balloon Belgian Pale, Cloud Break Unfiltered Munich Helles, Dark Heart Munich Dunkel Lager, Doctor Optic Standard Bitter, Fallen Sky Juniper Rye, Leadbelly Oatmeal Stout, Oregon Logger, Treeline Pale Ale, Trouble Everyday ISA, Zig Zag Smoke Ale, Gluten Free at Last, and many more

Eugene has quickly become one of the great beer cities the state has to offer. With Ninkasi, Oakshire, and a handful of brewpubs in the town all doing very well, it made sense for the founders of Falling Sky Brewing to open up shop in the beer-loving city. Although the pub itself opened in 2012, cofounder and head brewer

Jason Carriere has been running a homebrewing-supply shop in the city since 2002. Located right by the pub, Valley Vintner & Brewer got a name change to Falling Sky Fermentation Supply Shop when the brewpub opened, and continues to serve the homebrewing community in Eugene. Taking experience from homebrewing and building a great team, Falling Sky Brewing has quickly become one of the city's most exciting pubs.

Inside the pub you'll find long tables, bay doors, high ceilings, and a beautiful wall with wood beams and glass windows that give you a fantastic view of the brewery and the large copper kettles. The owners have taken the approach of being a really good brewpub and not focusing on bottling the beer. This has allowed them to make a wide variety of beers ranging from traditional IPAs to a smoked ale. One of their original beers from the brewing-supply shop days is the **Fallen Sky Juniper Rye,** which is where they got the current name of the brewpub. Brewed with organic juniper berries, 4 hop varieties, and rye malts, it's like drinking a fresh-baked rye bread and a fruit orchard.

Along with the beer, they have a very well-crafted yet somewhat small food menu that includes specialty sandwiches, salads, plates to share, and snacks. Whenever possible, the food is local and made with organic ingredients.

THE RAM RESTAURANT & BREWERY/BIGHORN BREWERY
515 12th St. SE, Salem, OR 97301; (503) 363-1905; TheRam.com/Oregon/Salem.html; @theram
Founded: 1971 **Founder:** Jeff Iverson Sr. and Cal Chandler **Brewer:** Mike Paladino
Flagship Beers: Big Horn Blonde, Big Horn Hefeweizen, Big Red Ale, Buttface Amber Ale, Total Disorder Porter **Year-round Beers:** Big Horn Blonde, Big Horn Hefeweizen, Big Red Ale, 71 Pale Ale, Buttface Amber Ale, Total Disorder Porter, 71 Pale Ale, Oregon Blonde **Seasonals/Special Releases:** S'no Angel, Marion Monk IPA, Pooka Mocha Porter, Oktoberfest, and many more

The Ram is one of the few larger chain brewpubs the state has to offer. With locations in Idaho, Illinois, Indiana, Oregon, and Washington, the Ram empire has slowly been growing since 1971. In Oregon, they offer 3 locations: Clackamas, Wilsonville, and Salem. Each location has its own on-site brewery that produces year-round beers along with a handful of seasonal and special-release beers that are often unique to each location. The atmosphere has the chain-restaurant feel to it, yet is a fun place to grab some dinner or watch a game on one of the many TVs.

The beer is a fairly standard lineup made with nonoffensive recipes that exist to please a lot of people. Luckily they have some really good recipes and are making some solid beers. **Total Disorder Porter** is the award-winning porter with plenty of coffee, chocolate, and roasted flavors with a slightly bitter yet sweet finish. A favorite of many is the **Big Red Ale.** While not up to the hop levels of many Northwest IPAs, Big Red has a nice balance of citrus and piney hops along with sweet malts that is easy to knock back along with a good meal.

The food menu is pretty massive, with everything from steak and burgers to salads and desserts. If you can eat more food than any human should, take the challenge and eat the BeHemoth. Those who can eat the 5-pound burger, bursting at the seams with all of the fixings, walk away with a T-shirt and most likely heartburn.

STEELHEAD BREWING COMPANY
199 E 5th Ave., #1, Eugene, OR 97401; (541) 686-2739; SteelheadBrewery.com
Founded: 1991 **Founder:** Cordy Jensen **Brewer:** Ted Fagen **Flagship Beers:** Hairy Weasel Hefeweizen, Raging Rhino Red, Bombay Bomber IPA **Year-round Beers:** Hairy Weasel Hefeweizen, Barracuda Blonde, Raging Rhino Red, Bombay Bomber IPA **Seasonals/Special Releases:** Rurik Imperial Stout, Twisted Meniscus IPA, Orange Wheat, Break-Action Porter, Hopasaurus Rex

Since 1991, Steelhead Brewing Co. has been serving craft beer and a nice selection of pub food in its Eugene location. Over the years the owners opened up 4 other locations in California, though only 2 of those remain in operation today, in Burlingame and Irvine. The Eugene location is the original and has stood the test of time mainly because they brew some pretty decent beer. Although the brewery is named Steelhead Brewing Co., you get the feeling that you're in an English restaurant. While there are fish on the logo and a few other places, the place is decked out in English pub–style furniture along with a British phone booth inside. Outside you can sit at one of the tables on the sidewalk, or head on into the restaurant. Inside, the bar is decked out with a couple of TVs that can easily be missed because a huge window looks into the brewery. Beer geeks will enjoy sitting at the bar and watching beer being brewed right in front of them.

IPA lovers will appreciate the **Bombay Bomber IPA.** It punches you in the face with a blast of citrus in the aroma and then eases into a nice malt and grapefruit flavor with a piney finish. For those who enjoy even more hops, keep an eye out for **Hopasaurus Rex.** Just like the name implies, it is a beast of an imperial IPA, yet fruity enough that those who aren't hopheads may enjoy it. They also make 2 flavors of root beer—honey vanilla and original spicy draft—that you can order there or buy to go.

The food selection is an array of pub food including pizza, burgers, sandwiches, salads, and entrees. If you visit, you might be able to arrange a quick tour of the brewery if they have time; just make sure to call ahead.

Beer Bars

THE BIER STEIN

345 E. 11th Ave., Eugene, OR 97401; (541) 485-2437; TheBierStein.com;
@biersteineugene
Draft Beers: 12 **Bottled/Canned Beers:** Over 1,000

If you're south of Portland and are looking for a huge selection of local, national, and imported craft beers, the Bier Stein in Eugene will offer you the most options. The small building packs a ton of beer goodness in a very comfortable way. The inside feels less like your typical bottle shop and more like a friendly neighborhood pub. While there are coolers housing the over 1,000 bottles to choose from, multiple tables and a bar make it a fun place to hang out. Being located not too far from the University of Oregon, it does tend to get packed in the evening, especially on the weekend, by good beer-loving college students and locals. For the beer geeks, plenty of tastings and events take place throughout the year. You can even try to squeeze your way in when Russian River's triple IPA, named Pliny the Younger, makes its extremely limited annual appearance.

The 12 rotating taps come from breweries all over the world. While heavily weighted toward West Coast breweries, the place often has imports on tap. The Bier Stein is also where to go if you're looking for special beers from Belgium or Germany. In addition to the huge selection, the staff is very knowledgeable about beer and will give advice if you're trying to figure out what to order.

They also offer a great selection of salads, sandwiches, and soups, many with some pretty interesting names. Try not smiling as you order Yo Mama Likes Our German Sausage or Love Me Tenderloin. There are also multiple options for vegetarians, so it's a great place for anyone to grab lunch, dinner, or an after-dinner snack. If you're visiting Eugene, the Bier Stein needs to be on your must-visit list.

CAPPIES BREWHOUSE

211 1st Ave. W, Albany, OR 97321; (541) 926-1710; CappiesBrewhouse.com;
@cappiesbrew
Draft Beers: 24 **Bottled/Canned Beers:** Over 140

Located in historic downtown Albany lies a beacon of good beer and delicious food. Cappies Brewhouse, which opened in 2010, offers a full restaurant experience with a separate room for the bottle shop. As you walk inside, one of the first things you'll notice is the brick walls with exposed mortar. The place has somewhat of a saloon-type feel, but is a little more neighborhood-like. Downstairs is filled with tables and a bar. Head on up to the second floor and you can relax at a table that overlooks the rest of the restaurant. The laid-back atmosphere makes it great for ordering just a beer, or a full meal—it's up to you.

The brewhouse offers 24 beers on tap, with half of those being filled by Calapooia Brewing, a brewery located just under a mile away. The other 12 taps are a selection of great craft beers from Oregon breweries as well as others throughout the country, such as Dogfish Head, Firestone Walker, Anderson Valley, and Lost Coast. If that isn't enough, Cappies offers a small bottle shop with over 140 beers that can be either drunk on site or taken home.

If you're looking for food, there's a full menu with plenty of options. If you're in the mood for steak, the Cappies Hop Steak is a 10-ounce Angus New York strip dusted with peppercorns and topped with locally grown hop butter. If hops can make beer better, why not put them on a steak? Other options include a mix of appetizers, salads, sandwiches, and other entrees. If you're a regular, you can become a member of the mug club. You get your own 20-ounce Cappies mug that you can get filled for the price of a pint as well as receive members-only discounts.

16 TONS TAPHOUSE
265 E. 13th Ave., Eugene, OR 97401; (541) 345-2003; SixteenTons.biz; @16TonsBeer
Draft Beers: 18 **Bottled/Canned Beers:** 350

16 Tons Taphouse is a beer shop that takes its taps very seriously. Not so much in the beer-snob sense, but from a selection standpoint. On the corner of 13th and High Street in Eugene sits the fairly plain brick building that houses the Taphouse. Inside you'll find shelves of beer and wine that have been masterfully selected to best utilize the small space. It can be a bit cold at times because the temperature is set fairly low to ensure the best bottling conditions; their bottled beer isn't stored in coolers. Though it's more of a bottle shop atmosphere, you can consume the beer on site. For the bottled beers, they do charge a corkage fee, so it might be worthwhile to check out what's on tap; you'll be glad you did, because the tap selection is what makes 16 Tons a gem in a city bursting with quality beer. Unique beers from all over the West Coast and the world rotate through the taps, giving drinkers 18 options to choose from. Many smaller brewers from outside Eugene can be found, along with the best Oregon has to offer. As this is just a tap house, they don't offer food, but the location is surrounded by a lot of great options

if you're hungry. They offer plenty of tastings and special events ranging from "meet the brewers" to special food-pairing events.

As well as the Taphouse, there's a 16 Tons Cafe in Woodfield Station at 29th and Willamette. The cafe offers a range of your favorite coffee drinks along with crepes, sandwiches, and other snacks. What sets it apart from your typical coffee shop is the 12 rotating beer taps, featuring some great beers from around the country.

VENTI'S CAFE + TAPHOUSE

2840 Commercial St. SE, Salem, OR 97301; (503) 391-5100; VentisCafe.com; @ventiscafe
Draft Beers: 24 **Bottled/Canned Beers:** 100

Serving downtown Salem since 1996, Venti's Cafe + Basement Bar became a great local place for food and great beer. After many successful years, the restaurant decided to open a new location that was more focused on beer. The new Venti's Cafe + Taphouse is located on Commercial Street and Fairview Avenue in south central Salem in what was once a Buster's BBQ. If you're looking for great beer in Salem, Venti's is the place to go. With 24 rotating taps, 2 of which are nitro and 2 are cask, Venti's always has something a beer lover will enjoy. One of the taps is usually a rotation of hard cider and one generally carries Ninkasi Tricerahops Double IPA. All others rotate as soon as the kegs empty. Most of the beers are from Oregon and Northwest breweries, although Venti's throws in a few other options every so often. Along with a huge tap list, they carry 100 rotating bottles to make sure there is a wide variety of options to choose from.

Make sure to bring the children, as they have a kids' space and menu. There's a rather large menu, with chicken teriyaki being the star of the show. Along with a selection of Asian cuisine, you can also find curries, Moroccan chicken, specialty sandwiches, burgers, and multiple vegetarian options as well as a full dessert menu.

Multiple times throughout the month, the Taphouse offers live music for local acts. Make sure to check the website, as there is no set schedule for live music. If you want to learn more about beer, they also offer beer-geek training periodically. They teach you about beer history, styles, food pairings, and anything else related to beer you're interested in.

Southern Oregon

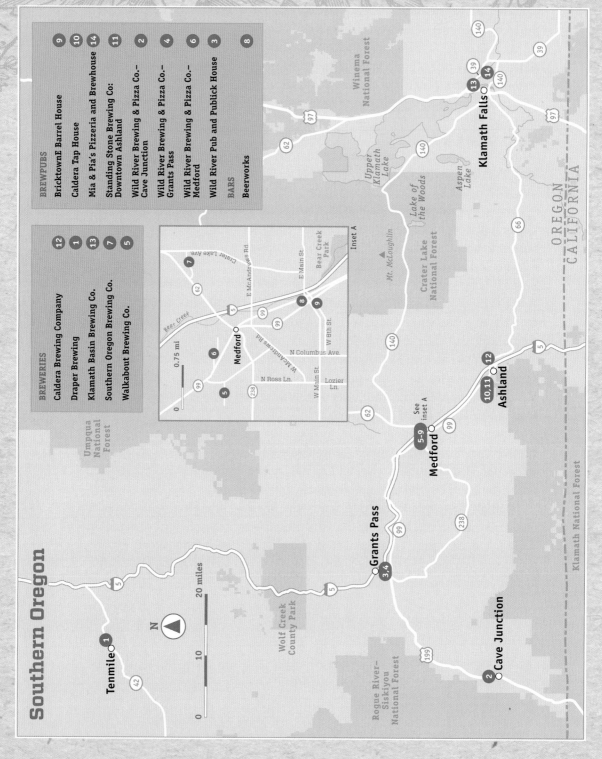

BREWERIES

12 Caldera Brewing Company
1 Draper Brewing
13 Klamath Basin Brewing Co.
7 Southern Oregon Brewing Co.
5 Walkabout Brewing Co.

BREWPUBS

9 BricktownE Barrel House
10 Caldera Tap House
14 Mia & Pia's Pizzeria and Brewhouse
11 Standing Stone Brewing Co.: Downtown Ashland
2 Wild River Brewing & Pizza Co.—Cave Junction
4 Wild River Brewing & Pizza Co.—Grants Pass
6 Wild River Brewing & Pizza Co.—Medford
3 Wild River Pub and Publick House

BARS

8 Beerworks

Inset A

0.75 mi

E McAndrews Rd
Crater Lake Ave.
E Main St
Bear Creek Park
62
5
99
99
7
8
9
Medford
6
N Columbus Ave.
W McAndrews Rd
N Ross Ln.
W Main St
Lozier Ln.
W 8th St.
5
99
238
0

Umpqua National Forest

Winema National Forest

Upper Klamath Lake

Lake of the Woods

Aspen Lake

Mt. McLoughlin

Crater Lake National Forest

Klamath Falls 13 14
39 140
39
140
97
140

OREGON
CALIFORNIA

66

5

140

Ashland 12
10,11
99

See Inset A

Medford 5–9

62

99

Grants Pass 3,4
5
99
238

Klamath National Forest

Wolf Creek County Park

Rogue River–Siskiyou National Forest

Cave Junction 2
199

5
42
Tenmile 1

N

0   10   20 miles

Southern Oregon

Although southern Oregon isn't known for a huge beer culture, the area is producing some great beer. With breweries such as Caldera Brewing, Southern Oregon Brewing, and Walkabout Brewing distributing throughout the state, more people are starting to take notice. Southern Oregon is also home to some great brewpubs, such as Standing Stone Brewing in Ashland and Mia & Pia's Pizzeria and Brewhouse in Klamath Falls. Smaller breweries, such as BricktownE Brewing and Draper Brewing, have recently opened up, making for a more diverse and exciting area for beer lovers to live and visit. With new beer festivals in the area, more people are being exposed to great craft beer.

Breweries

CALDERA BREWING COMPANY

540 Clover Ln., Ashland, OR 97520; (541) 482-4677; CalderaBrewing.com; @calderabeer

Founded: 1997 **Founder:** Jim Mills **Brewer:** Jim Mills **Flagship Beer:** IPA **Year-round Beers:** Lawnmower Lager, Pale Ale, IPA, Hopportunity Knocks, Hop Hash, Ashland Amber, Ginger Beer **Seasonals/Special Releases:** Pilot Rock Porter, Mogli, Helles Lager, Rose Petal Imperial Golden Ale, Vanilla Wheat, Cauldron Brew, Rauch Ür Bock, Vas Deferens Ale, Toasted Coconut Chocolate Porter, South Side Strong, Oatmeal Stout, Old Growth Imperial Stout, Hemp Brown Ale, Dry Hop Ale, Dry Hop Red, Against the Grain **Tours:** No **Taproom:** Yes

Interestingly enough, the first beer brewed at Caldera Brewing Company was brewed on the Fourth of July in 1997. For the first 8 years, the Ashland-based production brewery was draft only and you could find their beers only on tap throughout the state. In 2005 things changed when Caldera canned their **Pale Ale,** becoming the first microbrewery in Oregon to can its own beer. Since then they have also canned their **Ashland Amber** and **IPA,** which have shown up all across the country as well as in England and Japan. Cans have had a bad reputation over the years, mainly due to their affiliation with cheap beers. The benefits of canning beer often outweigh bottling it in glass. Cans are portable, 100 percent recyclable, eliminate light (which is the leading cause of beer going bad), and, unlike cans from years ago, today's versions don't impart any metallic flavors to beer.

Along with cans, multiple Caldera beers also come in 22-ounce bottles. One bottled beer in the **Kettle Series** is the award-winning **Rauch Ür Bock,** a Rauchbier brewed with 2 different smoked grains. Huge smoke flavors come from the cherrywood- and beachwood-cured grains that linger long after you take a drink. **Mogli** is a special-release oak-aged imperial porter brewed with chocolate and named after a black Lab owned by brewer Jim Mills's girlfriend that would often accompany her to the pub. He's featured on the label and stares at you while you drink the beautiful chocolaty brew.

For years the brewery was production only, but a few years back they opened up a tap house at 31 Water St. in Ashland. The deck is huge and they claim it's Ashland's largest. They have also expanded into a much larger building, allowing them to brew more beer and ramp up distribution.

Old Growth Imperial Stout
Style: Imperial Stout
ABV: 8.8 percent
Availability: Winter

On cold winter nights not much else warms you up like a huge beer does. Sitting around a fire and drinking Caldera's Old Growth Imperial Stout will definitely make a cold night much more enjoyable. The dark black stout is a hefty beer with strong aromas of roasted malt, chocolate, licorice, and coffee. Take a sip and the warming beer is filled with the same flavors that were in the nose, with the addition of some dark fruits, bitter hops, and a fairly strong alcohol presence. It's a sticky yet dry finish that is very enjoyable just about any time of the year.

Southern Oregon

DRAPER BREWING

7752 OR 42, Tenmile, OR 97481; (541) 482-4677; DraperBrewing.com
Founded: 2010 **Founder:** Sam Eslinger **Brewer:** Sam Eslinger **Flagship Beer:** Draper IPA **Year-round Beers:** India Pale Ale, Cream Ale, Chocolate Porter, Barrel Aged Stout **Seasonals/Special Releases:** Strong Ale, Blueberry Saison **Tours:** No **Taproom:** No

Draper Brewing started off as one of the smallest running breweries in the state in 2010. On a small 1-barrel system in Tenmile, owner Samuel Draper Eslinger set out to create great beer. What started as a homebrewing hobby turned into a small business. After picking up sales throughout the area, he since has upgraded

IPA

Style: IPA

ABV: 6.0 percent

Availability: Year-round

Draper Brewing's simply named IPA is a unique and different IPA in an area swimming with West Coast–style beers. The soft-bodied beer has some interesting malt complexities with grassy and citrus hoppy flavors that are light on bitterness. It's bottle conditioned and unfiltered, so you get a hazy amber color with a slight white head and some nice lacing on the glass. With such a mild bitterness, you could pair this with many different foods. Try it with a meat lover's pizza, as it works perfectly with Italian sausage and pepperoni.

to a slightly larger 5-barrel system, allowing distribution to expand. His beer is fermented in an open primary fermenter. It's then bottle conditioned, giving the beers a hazy look. The brewery itself is a production-only facility; however, in 2012 Eslinger opened up Draper Draft House in Roseburg, where his beers are offered on draft along with other craft beers from around the area.

The year-round lineup includes a cloudy **India Pale Ale,** a sessionable **Cream Ale,** a dessert-like **Chocolate Porter,** and a robust **Barrel Aged Stout** that's full of chocolate with hints of vanilla and roasty malts. Draper's beers are available in 22-ounce bottles and can be found in southern Oregon and all the way up to Portland at times.

KLAMATH BASIN BREWING COMPANY

1320 Main St., Klamath Falls, OR 97601; (541) 273-5222; KBBrewing.com
Founded: 2001 **Founders:** Lonnie Clement and Del Azevedo **Brewer:** Corey Zschoche
Flagship Beer: Crater Lake Amber Ale **Year-round Beers:** Crater Lake Amber Ale,
Crystal Springs IPA, Bare Island Blonde Ale, Hogsback Hefeweizen, Drop Dead Red, Pelican
Butte Pale Ale, Buttcrack Brown, Cabin Fever Stout, Vanilla Porter **Seasonals/Special
Releases:** Linkville Lager, Summer Squeeze, Migration Destination, McLoughlin Scottish
Ale **Tours:** No **Taproom:** Yes

Klamath Basin Brewing Company is a great example of a couple of guys with
an idea to open a brewery and build up a business, even if it means starting
small. Friends and founders Lonnie Clement and Del Azevedo started the brewery

Beer Lover's Pick

Vanilla Porter
Style: American Porter
ABV: 6.7 percent
Availability: Fall and winter

Don't let the somewhat boring label on the bottle fool you; Klamath Basin's Vanilla Porter is a very flavorful beer. Brewed with a blend of vanilla beans, it's a well-balanced porter with vanilla dominating both the aroma and the flavor. It pours a deep black with a beautiful tan head. Along with vanilla, you can smell chocolate, coffee, and a touch of smokiness. The flavor follows the nose with a touch of coffee bitterness and a tasty chocolate aftertaste. This would be an excellent beer to pair with a dessert or just drink on its own as a dessert.

in Lonnie's garage. After getting the licenses they needed, the two ran the commercial brewery out of the garage for four years until it was time to upgrade to a larger facility. They purchased the historic Crater Lake Creamery building, which was built in 1935 in downtown Klamath Falls. Leaving the infamous "Blue Cow" sign on the building, they renovated it and opened up the Creamery Brewpub and Grill and Klamath Basin Brewing Company in 2005. Since then they have been serving the southern Oregon town both great beer and delicious food.

Catering to the local market, most of the Klamath Basin beers are light and easy-drinking styles. **Crater Lake Amber Ale** is the brewery's flagship beer, named after the nearby national park. It's light but packed with caramel and bready flavors that are balanced by earthy hops. While naming a brown ale **Buttcrack Brown** is a bit unappealing, the dark ale has a nice malt body that's mixed with toffee and a slight taste of hops. Don't think about the name and just give it a try. While most of the beers are available at the pub and around town on draft, you can find a handful of them in 22-ounce bottles at select bottle shops in the state.

One of the advantages they have being located in Klamath Falls is that they use natural geothermal resources for heating the building as well as in their brewing process. If you visit the pub, make sure to come hungry. The pub food is made from scratch, including the pasta. The menu also helps you decide what beer to pair with your meal, and shows that they have put a lot of thought into their food and beer pairings.

SOUTHERN OREGON BREWING COMPANY

1922 United Way, Medford, OR 97504; (541) 776-9898; SOBrewing.com; @SOBMedford

Founded: 2006 **Founder:** Tom Hammond **Brewer:** Anders Johansen **Flagship Beers:** Pin-up Porter, Na Zdravi Czech Style Pilsner **Year-round Beers:** Na Zdravi Czech Style Pilsner, Pin-up Porter, Nice Rack IPA, Gold Digger Northwest Lager, SOB Pale, Mrs. Claws Barley Wine **Seasonals/Special Releases:** Old Humbug Winter Ale, Black Heart Imperial Stout, Holy Water Maibock, Woodshed Red, Extra Special Britt **Tours:** Yes, 4 p.m. Sat **Taproom:** Yes

Medford's Southern Oregon Brewing Company is another great story of how a homebrewer turned his passion and dream into a commercial brewery. Dr. Tom Hammond, an anesthesiologist, dreamed of the day he could open up a brewery in the city. In 2006 the 20-barrel brewery was opened and his dream was born. Starting out as a production-only facility, the brewery distributed its beers around southern Oregon. In an area that doesn't have a huge concentration of breweries, they were welcomed with open arms and locals requested that the owner open up a taproom.

Holy Water Maibock
Style: Maibock
ABV: 7.1 percent
Availability: Spring

Maibocks aren't the most popular style of beer in the Northwest, and the breweries that do brew them in the region often do so with a local twist. Holy Water Maibock, however, was brewed true to style by exclusively using German specialty malts. Aromas of sweet malt, bread, lemon, and a touch of oak give the clear, bright amber beer a light yet refreshing smell. With fruity sweetness up front and lots of malt and bready flavors, Holy Water finishes with slightly bitter hops yet leaves you with a sweet aftertaste.

Today you can visit the taproom, located on the other side of a huge glass window from the brewery so you can watch beer being made as you sip on their beers.

You won't find a huge number of beers being brewed, yet the company takes great pride in brewing quality ales and lagers. **Na Zdravi** is a Czech-style Pilsner that is one of the more popular beers. The clear golden lager has a nice balance of sweet malts and floral hops that produces a refreshing and easy-drinking beverage. The **Pin-up Porter** is dry with a coffee, chocolate, and smoky flavor combined with a tantalizing sweet malt and chocolate aroma. Southern Oregon Brewing stands out in a somewhat crowded market with great use of both beer names and labels. For example, the **Nice Rack IPA** features the antlers from an elk, while **Gold Digger** shows an actual old gold digger and not the type of woman Kanye West raps about.

SOB beers can be found across Oregon and southwest Washington at multiple bars, restaurants, and retail locations, both on draft and in 22-ounce bottles. If you're in Medford you can visit the taproom most days of the week for a drink or to fill up a growler. Local food trucks often provide food; just call ahead to make sure they'll be there if you're hungry. Plan your visit on a Saturday and you can catch a tour of the brewery at 4 p.m. most of the time.

WALKABOUT BREWING COMPANY

921 Mason Way, Medford, OR 97501; (541) 858-5723
Founded: 1997 **Founder:** Ross Litton **Brewer:** Ross Litton **Flagship Beer:** Worker's Pale Ale **Year-round Beers:** Jabberwocky Ale, Redback IPA, Worker's Pale Ale, Wallaby White, Aussie Amber, Point the Bone **Seasonals/Special Releases:** Crocktoberfest, Hops Away Imperial IPA **Tours:** No **Taproom:** Yes

Although Walkabout Brewing Company has been making beer since 1997, most people outside of southern Oregon most likely had never heard of them until the past few years. Started by Australian-born Ross Litton in Central Point, the small production brewery took the path of slow growth. Taking things easy has paid off—the company moved to a new facility in an industrial area of Medford, broadened distribution across the state, and opened a taproom in 2012 where customers can come try the beer fresh.

The beers, available in 22-ounce bottles and on draft, have a range of styles, many with Aussie-themed names. The flagship **Worker's Pale Ale** has a beautiful white head with lots of caramel malt and citrusy hops. It's a true Northwest-style ale. **Point the Bone IPA** started off as a seasonal beer but had a great following, so you can now find it outside of the Halloween season it was originally created for. A Northwest-style IPA, it's got a beautiful dark amber color with a very floral and piney hoppy flavor without a lot of bitterness. Each bottle features the logo in a way that makes it look like a street sign.

Luckily for those outside of southern Oregon, distribution is increasing across the state, so those up north are more easily finding Walkabout beers. If you're in Medford, stop by the taproom for pints of beer along with a selection of food. Fill up your growler or order a full keg if needed.

Jabberwocky Ale
Style: English Strong Ale
ABV: 7 percent
Availability: Year-round

Looking at the Walkabout Jabberwocky bottle, you'll notice
a logo that looks much like a
caution sign. It's subtle, but it
stands out and almost tempts
the drinker with the message,
"Caution, you're about to drink
a well-brewed beer." The dark
amber ale is brewed with lots
of specialty grains and four hop
varieties, which give it a well-
crafted balance of sweet fruit,
malt, and a somewhat bitter
bite. It's light bodied, smooth,
and easy to drink, yet the 7
percent ABV makes its presence
known. Pair Jabberwocky with
some fish and chips for an excellent meal.

Southern Oregon

Brewpubs

BRICKTOWNE BARREL HOUSE

111 E. 8th St., Medford, OR 97501; (541) 973-2377; BricktowneBeer.com; @bricktowne
Founded: 2011 **Founders:** Jamie, Denny, and Craig McPheeters **Brewer:** Craig
McPheeters **Flagship Beer:** Rogue Trail Barrel Hopped India Ale **Year-round Beers:**
Blue Collar Cream Ale, Applegate Pale Ale, HopJaw West Coast IPA, Table Rock Red, Rogue
Trail Barrel Hopped India Ale, Barrique Black Ale, Siskiyou Pass ESB **Seasonals/Special
Releases:** Calcommon, Summer Swelter

Located in downtown Medford's historic district in the old Halley's Palace Hotel, BricktownE Barrel House is the tasting room of BricktownE Brewing Company. (They use a capital "E" at the end of their name to reference that they typically brew English-style beers.) What started out as a nanobrewery, a few upgrades later has the small brewery brewing up beer for the southern Oregon town. Inside, the pub is pretty small, yet cozy. Tables made with barrels and taps coming out of barrels help add to the name. Not just for show, many of their beers are aged in locally sourced wine barrels. The majority of their beers, however, are English-style ales.

Their best-selling beer is the **Rogue Trail Barrel Hopped India Ale.** It's an English-style IPA packed with hops and aged in oak barrels, giving it a hoppy yet distinct flavor. **Barrique Black Ale** is a smooth, robust porter fermented in French oak barrels and infused with curacao vanilla beans, perfect for dessert. **Table Rock Red** is another popular beer that's pretty hopped up with noble hops, yet is well balanced with plenty of malts.

BricktownE's beers are very reasonably priced, with a 6-beer sampler of 4-ounce pours starting at just $6. Order that along with the artisan paninis, soups, and salads for an inexpensive meal paired with some great beer. Each year the pub puts on a BeerZilla homebrew competition giving local homebrewers a chance to win ribbons and bragging rights.

MIA & PIA'S PIZZERIA AND BREWHOUSE

3545 Summers Ln., Klamath Falls, OR 97603; (541) 884-4880; MiaPia.com
Founded: 1997 (restaurant opened in 1987) **Founders:** Don and Nancy Kucera
Brewer: Rod Kucera **Flagship Beer:** Improvisor IPA **Year-round Beers:** Screamin'
Eagle American Lager, Merrill Marzen, Henley Hayfeweizen, Applegate Trail Pale Ale,
Spencer Creek Amber Ale, Improvisor IPA, Rod's Rodeo Red, White Pelican Porter
Seasonals/Special Releases: ND Dairy Golden Ale, Flash Flood ESB, Otto Mulligan's
Irish Stout, Emmett & Anna's Pivo (Czech Pilsner), Spring Lake Amber Lager, Irrigator
Dopplebock, Blast Off Barley Wine, Sweetheart's Double Chocolate Stout

In 1987 Don and Nancy Kucera, who owned a dairy operation, opened a small pizza business in Keno, Oregon. A year later they moved it into Klamath Falls, serving up delicious pizzas in the new location. By 1997 head brewer Rod Kucera, Don and Nancy's son, converted the former dairy into a brewery and the pizza place became known as Mia & Pia's Pizzeria and Brewhouse. Prior to starting up the brewing operation, Rod spent time traveling the rodeo circuit as a bull rider. Although at the time he didn't have much professional experience in brewing, he has spent plenty of time creating some delicious beers for the brewhouse.

Among the 13 beers on tap, you can always find a year-round beer or seasonal to match your mood. The majority of the selection is meant to pair well with the pizza, and most have under 6 percent ABV. One exception is the **Blast Off Barley Wine,** which boasts a hefty 10.5 percent ABV and is often aged in Jack Daniels whiskey barrels. It's a complex brew with plenty of caramel malts, spices, a touch of hops, and a nice alcohol bite. One of the most popular beers with the locals is the **Applegate Trail Pale Ale.** Named after the area trail that was used as a less dangerous route than the Oregon Trail, the pale ale lives up to its less-than-dangerous name. It's a great beer to eat with pretty much any of the house-made pizzas. If you're in the area, bring the kids, as the place is very family friendly with plenty of entertainment for the little ones while you relax with a beer.

STANDING STONE BREWING COMPANY

101 Oak St., Ashland, OR 97520; (541) 482-2448; StandingStoneBrewing.com; @ssbc
Founded: 1996 **Founder:** Alex Amartico **Brewer:** Larry Chase **Flagship Beer:** Double IPA **Year-round Beers:** I Heart Oregon Ale, Amber Ale, Double IPA, Oatmeal Stout, Noble Stout **Seasonals/Special Releases:** 350 Ale, Backyard Brew, Barley Wine, Benefit Bock, Butternut Brown, Farmer Brown, Hefeweizen, Hop Night, Indie Pilsner, Jefferson Common, Madrone Red, Midsummer Dream, Milk and Honey, NPK, Oktoberfest, Peace Ale, Pacific Crest Ale, Pints for a Purpose Ale

Standing Stone Brewing Company has been making a name for itself in Oregon, and not just because of the beer. The Ashland-based brewpub is located in a renovated historic building in downtown just a block from the Oregon Shakespeare Festival. The company has received recognition from around the state with multiple awards for the sustainability-focused business model. The company also has been recognized as a leader in restaurant energy conservation. Multiple steps have been put into place to conserve energy, including solar panels and a variable-speed hood in the kitchen that reduces energy. The owners have also implemented the RPM program, which gives employees a free bike if they commit to commuting to work 45 times a year on two wheels. Along with energy and resource conservation, they

Southern Oregon

raise their own chickens, cows, and sheep while even using an electric motorcycle to get eggs from the farm and transport them to the pub.

Along with all of these sustainable practices, the beer also contains 90 percent organic grains. The **Pints for a Purpose Ale** is a light golden summer ale, and for each pint ordered, Standing Stone donates 25 cents to a local nonprofit organization. One of the most popular beers is the simply named **Double IPA.** With a nice citrus aroma coming from the dry hopping, it has a solid caramel malt backbone beautifully balanced with pine and citrusy hops. Make sure to bring a growler to fill up on your visit.

WILD RIVER BREWING & PIZZA COMPANY

595 NE E St., Grants Pass, OR 97526; (541) 471-7487; WildRiverBrewing.com; @WRBrewing
Founded: 1975 (brewing started 1990) **Founders:** Jerry and Bertha Miller **Brewer:** Scott Butts **Flagship Beer:** India Pale Ale **Year-round Beers:** India Pale Ale, Harbor Lights Kolsch Style, Bohemian Pilsener, Nut Brown Ale, Extra Special Bitter, Double Eagle Imperial Stout **Seasonals/Special Releases:** Blackberry Porter, Oktoberfest, Snug Harbor Old Ale, Cave Bear Barley Wine

Wild River Brewing & Pizza Company as it stands today is the result of many changes and years of refining who the company is and what it offers its customers. Owners Jerry and Bertha Miller started the restaurant in 1975 in the southern Oregon town of Cave Junction as Miller's Shady Oaks Pizza Deli. Five years later they expanded by adding a location in Brookings-Harbor that was headed up by their son and his wife. After years of running the two restaurants, they decided to enter the brewing business and began brewing in 1990 under the name Steelhead Brewery. When it came time to open their third location in Grants Pass, they ended up adding a 15-barrel brewhouse and rebranding the entire operation as Wild River Brewing & Pizza Company to reflect that beer was a big part of who they were. Today the company has 5 total locations: Medford, Brookings-Harbor, Cave Junction, and 2 in Grants Pass.

They offer a fairly standard lineup of beers with a handful of seasonals brewed throughout the year. Their **India Pale Ale** is a favorite. Packed with lots of citrus and pine flavors, it pairs well with just about any pizza. **Harbor Lights Kolsch Ale** is a traditionally brewed Kolsch using yeast from Cologne's renowned Paffgen Brewery.

Both the Grants Pass and Cave Junction locations have a brewery on site, and you may be able to snag a quick tour if the brewer has time. Just give them a call if interested.

Beer Bars

BEERWORKS
323 E. Main St., Medford, OR 97501; (541) 770-9100
Draft Beers: 6 **Bottled/Canned Beers:** Over 450

Beerworks is the beer shop that southern Oregon has needed for quite some time. Opened in 2011, the bottle shop and bar supplies craft beer to Medford, a city with few options when it comes to good beer. Making use of a not-so-large space, it's a very comfortable place to drink beer. Walking in, you'll notice multiple round tables where you can mingle with other beer geeks. The side of the building the bar is on is an old brick wall, which adds to the atmosphere quite a bit, giving it an almost underground feel. On the other side is a beautiful wall of beer fridges. Comparing the selection to places in Portland, it's not huge. However, compare it to southern Oregon and it is most likely the largest selection of beers you'll find for miles. Over 450 bottles and cans fill the fridges while 6 beers flow through the rotating taps. With the 6 taps, they do a great job of picking unique and rare beers that come from all over the state and country from breweries such as Russian River, Firestone Walker, Boneyard, Lagunitas, Oakshire, and Mad River. You can also attend "meet the brewer" nights, where representatives from different breweries come for tastings and discuss their beers.

While they don't serve food, it can be brought in or you can have it delivered. If you're looking at getting beer to go, make sure to bring in your growler and get it filled with one of the beers they have on tap.

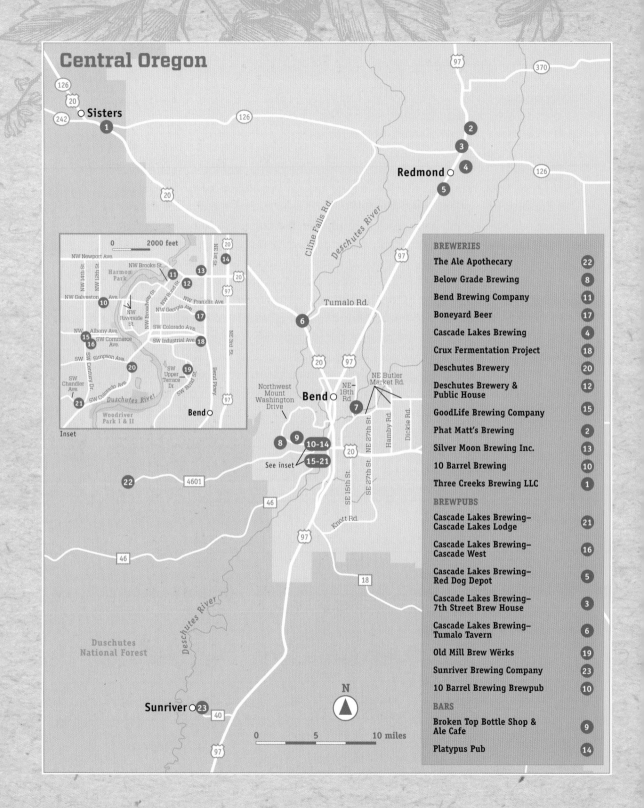

Central Oregon

126
20
242
○ Sisters
1

97
370
126
2
3
Redmond ○
4
5

Cline Falls Rd.
Deschutes River
126
97

Inset

0   2000 feet
NW Newport Ave.
NW Brooks St.
NW 14th St.
NW 12th St.
NW 9th St.
Harmon Park
11
13
NE 1st St.
NE 1st St.
20
14
12
20
97
NW Galveston Ave.
10
NW Broadway St.
NW Bond St.
NW Wall St.
NW Franklin Ave.
NW Georgia Ave.
NW Riverside Ct.
17
SW Colorado Ave.
NW Albany Ave.
15
SW Commerce Ave.
18
NE 3rd St.
16
SW Industrial Ave.
SW Simpson Ave.
20
SW Century Dr.
SW Upper Terrace Dr.
19
SW Bond St.
Bend Pkwy.
SW Chandler Ave.
21
Deschutes River
SW Colorado Ave.
97
Woodriver Park I & II
Bend ○

Tumalo Rd.
6

Northwest Mount Washington Drive
NE Butler Market Rd.
NE 18th Rd.
20
97
Bend ○
7
NE 27th St.
SE 27th St.
Hamby Rd.
Dickie Rd.

8   9
10-14
15-21
See inset

22
4601
46
SE 15th St.
SE 27th St.
20
46
97
Knott Rd.
18

Duschutes National Forest
Deschutes River

Sunriver ○ 23
40
97

N ▲

0   5   10 miles

Central Oregon

It's no secret that Central Oregon is a hotbed of brewing. In the past few years a whole wave of new breweries producing some of the best beer the state has to offer has taken the area by storm. While Deschutes Brewery is still anchoring the area in terms of production, many of the smaller breweries have been set up by former employees of the giant craft brewery or those moving to the area because of the growing beer culture. Between Bend and Redmond breweries, brewpubs, and beer bars are opening up shop just about every other month, creating an amazing place to be if you're a beer lover. With breweries such as 10 Barrel Brewing, Boneyard Beer, Crux Fermentation Project, GoodLife Brewing, Bend Beer, and others making such great beer, it's easy to see why anyone would want to live here.

For those seeking a unique vacation, the Bend area is a must-visit location. With wonderful outdoor activities, beautiful scenery, a thriving restaurant scene, and a strong yet growing beer culture, central Oregon has quickly become one of the best regions in the state for beer lovers.

Breweries

THE ALE APOTHECARY

61517 River Rd., Bend, OR 97701; (541) 318-9143; TheAleApothecary.com
Founded: 2012 **Founder:** Paul Arney **Brewer:** Paul Arney **Flagship Beer:** Sahalie
Year-round Beers: Sahalie **Seasonals/Special Releases:** The Beer Formerly Known as
La Tache, Sahalien, Sahati, El Cuatro **Tours:** No **Taproom:** No

Located in the mountain woods outside of Bend, the Ale Apothecary brews beer using a mix of ancient art with traditions of wine and champagne. In other words, they do things a lot differently than most other breweries. Started by Paul

Beer Lover's Pick

Sahalie
Style: Wild Ale
ABV: 8.75 percent
Availability: Varies
Sahalie is the Ale Apothecary's flagship beer that is shrouded in experimentation. Aged in wine barrels, the wild ale is meant to change with time. Every bottle you get may have different aromas, flavors, and complexities, and that is just what brewer Paul Arney is going for. It's sour and mildly tart with an almost champagne-like acidity that evolves and changes with time. You're not going to be able to find Sahalie all over, but it's a beer experience that is definitely worth seeking out.

Arney, a former Deschutes brewer, the small operation produces a limited amount of beer distributed mainly in 750-milliliter bottles. Customers can sign up and pay to become Ale Club members, which allows them to receive free beer each quarter as well as gain access to special events and other perks. While it sounds a bit unusual, it's a great deal, as Ale Club members get first crack at the beer, which is very limited.

The beers are all unusual styles brewed with many techniques uncommon today. One of the most interesting is the **Sahati.** It's an ancient Finnish ale that's spiced with fresh spruce tips. Instead of brewing it in a modern-day mash tun, they make a kuuma by taking an 85-foot spruce tree that is hollowed out like a canoe and using the boughs as a mash filter. Another notable beer is **El Cuatro,** a specialty ale brewed without hops and aged in brandy barrels.

Because this is still a very new brewery, the beer is very limited. To get your hands on some to try, either join the Ale Club or give them a call to set up a tour and buy some bottles if any are available. The Ale Apothecary is a brewery you'll want to keep an eye on, as it'll be producing some uncommon beers you won't find at your local grocery store.

BELOW GRADE BREWING

1362 NW Fort Clatsop St., Bend, OR 97701; (541) 280-5704; BelowGradeBrewing.com; @bgbdean
Founded: 2010 **Founder:** Dean Wise **Brewer:** Dean Wise **Flagship Beer:** Validation Imperial IPA, Dangerous Kate Imperial Cascadian Black Ale **Year-round Beers:** Validation Imperial IPA, Old School Ale, Volksvitzen South German Weissbock, Dangerous Kate Imperial Cascadian Black Ale, Jack A Boy Pale Ale, Nevermind White IPA
Seasonals/Special Releases: Identity Crisis, RB/X Red/Brown Experimental **Tours:** No
Taproom: No

Founder Dean Wise of Below Grade Brewing is proof that you don't have to have the largest brewery on the block to make really tasty beers. In his case, he didn't even need a traditional brewhouse to get his startup brewery up and running. Starting out as a homebrewer in his basement, he decided to open up his own brewery. Instead of seeking out a facility to lease, he was able to get approved to run the brewery from the basement of his house, where he was already brewing. The name Below Grade comes from this basement, although the beer is anything but below grade. Starting out, the brewery sold its beer through the Northwest Crossing Farmers' Market in Bend and has since expanded to offering bottles around town.

The 1-barrel brewing system cranks out a handful of beers ranging from a German-style **Weissbock** and old ale to an imperial IPA and imperial Cascadian black ale. As part of the philosophy, the brewery has limited itself to the 4 basic

Old School Ale
Style: Old Ale
ABV: 8.5 percent
Availability: Year-round

Below Grade Brewing's Old School Ale is an English-style old ale that will have fans of big, malty beers hooked at the first sip. Brewed with eight different malts and three hop varieties, it pours a beautiful dark reddish brown color. Caramel sweetness fills the aroma and chewy sweet malt, chocolate, and coffee flavors hide the 8.5 percent ABV extremely well. The red label falls in line with the rest of Below Grade's labels, so keep an eye out for it if you're around Bend.

ingredients of beer: malt, hops, yeast, and water. They also use a multistep mash, open fermentation, and whole hops in both the boil and for dry hopping, all of which help produce some solid beers.

The **Old School Ale** is an English-style old ale made with 3 hop varieties and 8 different malts, giving it some pretty complex flavors. The dark brown and red ale has rich caramel, coffee, and chocolate flavors with very low bitterness. At 8.5 percent, this malt masterpiece is a great beer. **Dangerous Kate,** the brewery's dark imperial Cascadian black ale, packs an 8.5 percent ABV punch as well. It's not for the faint of heart, as it's hopped up and bitter, but the roasted malt gives it some tasty flavors that balance out the hops.

The small brewery doesn't offer any public hours for visits, and distribution is small. Draft and bottle sales are available at select Bend locations.

BEND BREWING COMPANY

1019 NW Brooks St., Bend, OR 97701; (541) 383-1599; BendBrewingCo.com
Founded: 1995 **Founder:** Wendi Day **Brewer:** Ian Larkin **Flagship Beers:** HopHead
Imperial IPA, Ching Ching **Year-round Beers:** High Dessert Hefeweizen, Metolius Golden
Ale, Elk Lake IPA, Outback Old Ale, Pinnacle Porter **Seasonals/Special Releases:** Big
Eddy Bitter, Paulina Pale Ale, Hop-Head Imperial IPA, Scottish Heart, Dopplebock, Ching
Ching, Outback X, Lovely Cherry Baltic, and many more **Tours:** No **Taproom:** Yes

As the second brewery to open in town, Bend Brewing Company has been serving both locals and tourists great beer and food since 1993. The company feels more like a brewpub than a production brewery, although the brews are available around the state in 22-ounce bottles. Located on the Deschutes River at Mirror Pond in downtown Bend, this is arguably the best spot in town. In the summer months you can sit on the outdoor patio with a view of the river and sip on some award-winning beers. The space inside is small yet cozy, with block walls, hardwood floors, and local photography lining the walls. Sitting in the main part of the restaurant, you can look upstairs and see the brewhouse and get a taste of where the magic happens.

Outback X
Style: Old Ale
ABV: 9.5 percent
Availability: Seasonal

Oftentimes you'll find big, heavy old ales that while tasty are not super drinkable. Half a pint in, your palate gets tired. Outback X is one of those old ales that doesn't fit that mold. As far as beers in the style, it's one of the best and most drinkable you'll find in Oregon. Its deep amber brown semitransparent body sparkles with a small tan head. The aroma is faint, consisting of caramel malts, sugary fruit, and floral hops. Take a sip and the balanced, complex flavors jump out and play a symphony in your mouth. At 9.5 percent ABV it's almost too drinkable.

In the years since it opened, the brewery has crafted a wide range of high-quality beers winning awards at the World Beer Cup and Great American Beer Festival. With 5 beers in the year-round lineup and multiple seasonal and special releases, there is always something new to try. The **Hop-Head Imperial IPA** is one of the brewery's most sought-after seasonal releases. Sweet citrus plays behind the star of the show, delicious piney hops. For the year-round hop lover, **Elk Lake IPA** is always a solid choice. As the brewery's most popular offering, this IPA is a very approachable beer: piney hops with a touch of malt in the background and a dry finish.

BBC, which is what locals call the place, offers a full lunch and dinner menu consisting of comfort foods, salads, seafood, pastas, and steaks. The fish and chips are made with **Metolius Golden Ale** batter and are always a great choice. If you really like seafood, the calamari is the best in town and is served with hot mustard. The nachos are one of the most ordered items on the menu for a reason: They are delicious. If you are in town on Tuesday night, make sure to head in for locals night to get discounted pints.

BONEYARD BEER

37 NW Lake Place #B, Bend, OR 97701; (541) 323-2325; BoneyardBeer.com; @boneyardbeer

Founded: 2010 **Founders:** Tony Lawrence, and Clay and Melodee Storey **Brewer:** Tony Lawrence **Flagship Beer:** RPM IPA **Year-round Beers:** Bone-A-Fide Pale Ale, Black 13, Girl Beer ALA, RPM IPA, Diablo Rojo **Seasonals/Special Releases:** Wit Shack Wit, The Backbone, Femme Fatale, Hop Venom Double IPA, Armored Fist, Notorious Triple IPA, Skunkape IRA, Suge Knite Imperial Stout **Tours:** No **Taproom:** Yes, Mon–Sat 11 a.m.– 6 p.m.

Boneyard Beer has shown that it doesn't take obscene amounts of money to open up a quality craft brewery that produces some of the best beer in the state. As you look inside the brewery, it doesn't seem as impressive as other brewers with huge budgets, but once you take a drink you'll quickly realize brand-new brewing equipment doesn't equate with good beer. Instead of buying all new vats and fermenters, Boneyard's owners opted to scrounge around other breweries and piece together a setup that works for them, using old and run-down devices. Just like their creativity with producing quality beer, they have masterfully created a brewhouse that works for them using secondhand equipment.

What separates Boneyard from most of the breweries in the country isn't the equipment, but the quality of beer. For those who like light and fruity beers, Boneyard offers **Girl Beer ALA,** made with Oregon cherries. At only 4.3 percent ABV, it's perfect for a summer day. The label, however, looks tough and it's definitely not a girl you'd mess with. If you like beer with a little more alcohol and bitterness, seek out the **Hop Venom IPA.** At 10 percent ABV, this double IPA is well balanced, hoppy, and not as bitter as other double IPAs. In a state known for creating some amazing IPAs, both the Hop Venom IPA and **RPM IPA** rank among the best.

Aside from the beer itself, the labels look as though they could be posters for a punk band. Each utilizes white, black, and the occasional red, giving them a very tough and in-your-face look. The punk flair transfers over to the taproom, which is covered in stickers, skulls, and bones. Inside you can fill up your growlers or have a taste of a few brews. There's no food or tables inside and the place is pretty small, but is definitely worth a visit.

Hop Venom Double IPA
Style: Double IPA
ABV: 10 percent
Availability: Occasional
While many double IPAs immediately give you the bitter-beer
face, Hop Venom isn't overly bitter. In fact, it's an almost perfect blend of hops and malt that
leaves you smiling. Pouring it
into a glass is a thing of beauty.
Dark glimmering orange in color
with an almost white head, this
classic West Coast–style double
IPA screams "drink me." It has
a blast of pine, grapefruit, and
oranges in the aroma, with a
similar fruity and piney flavor
and a solid malt backbone. Be
careful; the 10 percent ABV can
sneak up on you.

CASCADE LAKES BREWING

2141 SW 1st St., Redmond, OR 97756; (541) 923-3110; CascadeLakes.com; @Cascade
LakesAle
Founded: 1994 **Founder:** Steve Gazley **Brewer:** John Van Duzer **Flagship Beer:**
Rooster Tail Ale **Year-round Beers:** Blonde Bombshell, Rooster Tail Ale, Monkey Face
Porter, 20" Brown, Cyclops IPA **Seasonals/Special Releases:** Paulina Lake Pilsner,
Skookum Creek Ale, Slippery Slope, Riverside Red, Waste Deep Weiss, Harvest Ale, India
Red Ale (IRA), Project X, Santa's Little Helper **Tours:** By appointment only **Taproom:**
Multiple pubs

When you think of Redmond, Oregon, Cascade Lakes Brewing may be one of the
first things to pop into your mind. Brewing beer since 1994, the Redmond-based

Monkey Face Porter
Style: American Porter
ABV: 5 percent
Availability: Year-Round

Monkey Face is a chocolate lover's porter, yet it's not too heavy. It pours a dark brown with a thin, light brown head. Chocolate, coffee, nuts, roasted malt, and earthy hops rise out of the glass in the aroma. The flavor follows the nose but is a bit light. It's a well-balanced porter that is very sessionable. If you look at the logo on the bottle, you might be a little surprised to see a rock climber instead of a monkey. The name, however, comes from a popular rock climbing formation named Monkey Face found in Smith Rock State Park in the Oregon Cascades.

brewery has seen steady growth over the years and has made a solid name for itself on the central Oregon beer scene. What started off as a small brewing facility near the Redmond airport has become a much larger brewing system and a chain of pubs located throughout central Oregon. Now you can also find the beer throughout the state as well as in Washington and Idaho. The brewery offers 5 year-round beers as well as a few seasonal and special releases in 12- and 22-ounce bottles.

The **20" Brown** is packed with healthy doses of malt, nuts, and roasted flavor, and is a smooth, easy drinker. It's even better on nitro if you can find it. The rest of the lineup includes fairly solid beers such as **Blonde Bombshell Ale, Rooster**

Tail Ale, and **Cyclops IPA,** which are all brewed to please the masses and are very drinkable. During the winter they brew **Santa's Little Helper,** a winter warmer that is pretty tasty and easy to drink. At 6.4 percent ABV, it's a little lighter than other winter warmers out there, so you can have more than one around a nice fireplace.

Cascade Lakes runs 5 pubs besides the brewery where you can try these beers. Two are in Redmond, at the 7th Street Brew House and Red Dog Depot. Cascade Lakes Lodge and Cascade West are located in Bend, while the Tumalo Tavern is a small-town pub between Bend and Sisters. Each pub has a unique feel to it, but all make you feel like you're part of the neighborhood. The flagship pub in southwest Bend, Cascade Lakes Lodge, is on the way to Mt. Bachelor and attracts a lot of winter sports enthusiasts on their way home from the mountain. It's a great place to warm up after a day skiing. Don't forget to bring the kids on Sunday, when they eat free all day.

CRUX FERMENTATION PROJECT

50 SW Division St., Bend, OR 97702; (541) 385-3333; CruxFermentation.com; @CruxFP
Founded: 2012 **Founders:** Larry Sidor, Paul Evers, and Dave Wilson **Brewer:** Larry Sidor **Flagship Beer:** None **Year-round Beers:** On the Fence NW Pale Ale **Seasonals/Special Releases:** Just In Time NW Pale Ale, Outcast IPA, Sugar Daddy Sweet Pale, Off Leash NW Session Ale, and many more **Tours:** No **Taproom:** Yes

One of Bend's newest breweries, Crux Fermentation was launched in the summer of 2012 with former Deschutes brewmaster Larry Sidor and his partners Dave Wilson and Paul Evers. The team turned an old transmission shop into a beautiful brewery with exposed beams, concrete flooring, reclaimed wood from a 100-year-old house, and the beautiful copper kettle brewhouse. It's anything but your typical brewery. With a room for open fermentation that you can view behind glass and a taproom experience that almost makes you feel as if you're part of the brewing process, this brewery is best enjoyed by being there.

Crux likes to do things a little differently than a lot of breweries. Things are measured metrically, so if you're from most places outside the US, you will know what they're talking about. If you visit, you'll be poured either a 500- or 300-milliliter glass. Once the brewery starts bottling, 375-, 500-, and 750-milliliter bottles will be available, depending upon the beer. The owners also are content with staying small and producing small batches. This means that the beers have a lot of variety, from sour barrel-aged beer to those using experimental hops or crazy yeast varieties. While the brewery has a couple of traditional styles of beer, the pub carries a wide range of styles that are constantly changing.

Beer Lover's Pick

On the Fence NW Pale Ale
Style: American Pale Ale
ABV: 6.4 percent
Availability: Year-round
In true Northwest style, On the Fence is a pale ale that's hopped up, making it not really a pale ale, yet not an IPA. It's "on the fence." Lots of citrus and tropical aromas fill the nose, and flavor comes from the Citra and Centennial hops. Balanced with pale malts, the beautiful orange beer is still a bit hoppy, yet not overly bitter. While this is a fairly new beer, it already ranks as one of the state's best pale ales and will make you want more.

If you're visiting Bend, Crux Fermentation Project needs to be on your must-visit list. With a well-crafted food menu and an interesting beer selection, it's a great place to grab a brew, relax, and watch the brewers work. As the brewery expands, keep an eye out for its beers across the Northwest.

DESCHUTES BREWERY
901 SW Simpson Ave., Bend, OR 97702; (541) 385-8606; DeschutesBrewery.com; @DeschutesBeer
Founded: 1988 **Founder:** Gary Fish **Brewers:** Cam O'Connor and Brian Faivre
Flagship Beer: Black Butte Porter **Year-round Beers:** Black Butte Porter, Mirror Pond Pale Ale, Inversion IPA, Green Lakes Organic Ale, Obsidian Stout, Chainbreaker White IPA **Seasonals/Special Releases:** Red Chair NWPA, Twilight Summer Ale, Jubelale, Hop Henge, Hop in the Dark, Hop Trip, Fresh Hop Mirror Pond, The Abyss, The Stoic, The Dissident, Mirror Mirror, and many more **Tours:** Yes, 1, 2, 3, and 4 p.m. daily, limited to 15 guests **Taproom:** Yes

As one of the Northwest's most well-known breweries nationwide, Deschutes Brewery has grown into one of the largest craft breweries in the US. Founded by Gary Fish in 1988 as a small brewpub in Bend, Deschutes has focused on quality ingredients and products since day one. By 1993 the pub was growing so fast, the owner expanded it to a much larger production facility, allowing the beer to be distributed throughout the West Coast. Throughout the years the brewing facilities have been upgraded to offer beer in at least 18 western and midwestern states. The

Central Oregon

brewery still operates and brews at a brewpub in Bend, although it has changed locations, as well as operating a brewpub in Portland's Pearl District.

Deschutes is well known for the **Black Butte Porter,** the nation's top-selling craft porter. Black Butte, which is named after an extinct volcano in the Deschutes National Forest, is a creamy porter booming with complex roasted malt, coffee, and chocolate flavors that's balanced with a gentle presence of hops. It's a great beer to pair with a nice grilled burger packed with vegetables. One of the most interesting beers that has been brewed only a few times is **The Dissident.** It's an Oud Bruin, a Flanders-style sour brown ale that uses wild yeast to help give it a unique flavor. The beer has to be fermented in isolation from other beers for 18 months, partly in Pinot and Cabernet wine barrels. If you find it, order it.

The brewery itself is pretty massive and impressive to tour. Free guided tours take place on the hour from 1 to 4 p.m. daily. Inside they also have a tasting room, but it has somewhat of a cafeteria feel to it, so try to visit one of the pubs if you're looking at making it a relaxed tasting, or want some good food along with your beer. Plus the pubs offer beers you can't find anywhere else that are pretty outstanding.

See Jill Ramseier's recipe for **Apricot Jubelale Scones** on p. 215 and for **Yellow Belly Burger** on p. 219.

Beer Lover's Pick

The Abyss
Style: Imperial Stout
ABV: 11 percent
Availability: Released once a year in winter
Some beers such as The Abyss have a lot of hype surrounding them. While some don't live up to it, The Abyss deserves recognition for the fact it is one awesome brew. Brewed once a year since 2006 and aged in oak and bourbon barrels, the imperial stout is worth seeking out. With its many complex flavors and aromas consisting of molasses, oak, licorice, nuts, chocolate, vanilla, coffee, and dark fruit, you'll be spending your time enjoying all of the intricacies that make this such an amazing beer.

GOODLIFE BREWING COMPANY

70 SW Century Dr. 100-464, Bend, OR 97702; (541)728-0749; GoodLifeBrewing.com; @GoodLifeBrewing

Founded: 2011 **Founders:** Ty Barnett, Pratt Rather, and Curt Plants **Brewer:** Curt Plants **Flagship Beer:** Mountain Rescue Dry Hop Pale Ale **Year-round Beers:** Mountain Rescue Dry Hop Pale Ale, Descender IPA **Seasonals/Special Releases:** Pass Stout American Stout Ale, 29'er India Brown Ale, Sweet as Pacific Ale, Comatose Imperial IPA, Scottish Heart Scotch Ale, Good & Worthy—Belgian rye **Tours:** Yes, 4 p.m. Tues–Sat **Taproom:** Yes

As one of the new kids on the block, GoodLife Brewing Company has taken an already amazing beer city and made it just a little bit better. Founded in 2011, the brewery was set up with growth in mind while not sacrificing the quality of the beer. Located in the Century Center Complex of SW Century Drive, the brewery has plenty of room to brew and to be a great destination for beer lovers to gather. The brewery itself is a 30-barrel system located in a massive warehouse with room to add

more equipment. Inside there's plenty of space for people to hang out and play at the pool table, listen to live music, and marvel at the shining brewhouse. A window separates the brewery from the bier hall, which is where you go when you want some food or to belly up to the bar to try some of the mostly hoppy brews. While the bier hall itself isn't that large (and has only a single bathroom), it has 2 bay doors that open up, making it feel a lot larger. While watching the brewing process through the window, grab some food. The menu consists of salads, wraps, and panini. Whatever you decide on, make sure to start out with the Bacon2 if you like spicy food. Cream cheese and thick-cut-bacon–stuffed jalapeños are a perfect pairing for the hoppy beers.

Beer Lover's Pick

Descender IPA
Style: IPA
ABV: 7 percent
Availability: Year-round
Breaking into the IPA market in Oregon isn't the easiest thing for a new brewery to do. Good-Life, however, hit a home run with the release of Descender IPA. With a glowing orange body and beautiful lacing, it's a pretty beer, with lots of citrus in the nose with caramel and pine in the background. They use five hop varieties in brewing, giving it a very nice hoppy flavor that's not overpowering. The malt backbone keeps it grounded. A creaminess in the mouthfeel makes it go down way too smoothly.

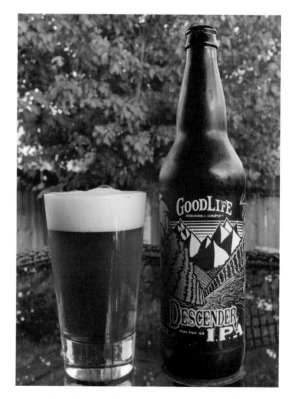

Speaking of beers, the brewery specializes in making some really excellent Northwest-style brews that aren't overly bitter. The flagship **Mountain Rescue Dry Hope Pale Ale** is a very hoppy pale ale that is incredibly balanced. It is dry hopped, so it has an excellent floral aroma yet leaves you without the bitter-beer face. The **29'er India Brown Ale** is definitely unique. It has the nutty and somewhat chocolate and coffee flavors found in a lot of brown ales, yet it is slightly hoppier than most. The flavors play really well together and it's definitely worth seeking out.

In the summer months, make sure to stop by the beer garden. There is plenty of room on the lawn to spend the evening in the fresh air, listening to good music and drinking beer.

PHAT MATT'S BREWING COMPANY
580 NE Hemlock, Ste. 105, Redmond, OR 97756; (541) 316-5551; PhatMattsBrew.com
Founded: 2011 **Founders:** Matt Mulder, John Foran, Mike Johnson, and Paul Mercer
Brewer: Josh Riggs **Flagship Beer:** Phat Matt's Red **Year-round Beers:** Phat Matt's IPA, Phat Matt's Kölsch, Phat Matt's Red, Phat Matt's Golden Ale **Seasonals/Special Releases:** Phat Snowman **Tours:** No **Taproom:** Yes, 3–7 p.m. Fri and Sat

Just 15 miles north of Bend lies the small but beer-friendly town of Redmond, home to Phat Matt's Brewing Company. Founded in 2011, the small but growing production brewery supplies clean, quality beer all over Oregon. Currently the beer is offered in 22-ounce bottles, on tap around town, or in the tasting room at the brewery in Redmond. The labels take a no-nonsense approach, and all sport the same look with only their name and colors differing. Looking at the bottles sitting on the shelf in the store, you almost feel like you've seen them before. Aesthetically they are very approachable beers.

Phat Matt's Red is a classic red ale that has a balanced mixture of bitterness and sweetness from the caramel malt flavors. Add to that a thick and creamy head and you get a pretty smooth beer that would pair nicely with a grilled burger or chicken breast. The **Phat Matt's IPA** is pretty mellow for the hop-loving palates of Northwesterners. It has light malt aroma and flavor with just a touch of hops. With so many IPAs in the region, it does very little to stand out, yet is very delicious. If you want to try out all of the beers and happen to be in Redmond, the small tasting room is open Fri and Sat from 3 to 7 p.m. The place does have some killer prices on growler fills, so make sure to bring yours.

If you attend any of the same events as the brewery, keep an eye out for the "Phat Mobile." The owners restored an old Volkswagen bus, painted it up with their logo, and of course added 4 taps to the side to pour beer. It is the ultimate van, for sure.

Phat Matt's Kölsch
Style: Kölsch
ABV: 6.5 percent
Availability: Year-round
Perfect for hot summer days, Phat Matt's Kölsch delivers a refreshing beer that does a great job at capturing the style. With a nice, clean straw-yellow hue, the carbonation bubbles are evident as they dance their way toward the beautiful white head. A light and slightly bready nose eases into a bread-like malt flavor balanced with grassy yet somewhat spicy hops. A touch of fruit in the finish of this easy-drinking brew adds to its appeal. It's easy to drink all 22 ounces without realizing you started.

SILVER MOON BREWING

24 NW Greenwood Ave., Bend, OR 97701; (541) 388-8331; SilverMoonBrewing.com; @silvermoonbeer
Founded: 2000 **Founder:** Tyler Reichert **Brewer:** Brett Thomas **Flagship Beer:** Snake Bite Porter, Hop Nob IPA **Year-round Beers:** Badlands ESB, Amber Ale, Hop Nob IPA, Bridge Creek Pils, Snake Bite Porter **Seasonals/Special Releases:** Purgatory Shadow, Epic Trail Ale, HOPpopotamus, Hop Fury IPA, Getsum Pale Ale, Hoptagon Imperial IPA, Dark Side Stout, Asmodeus Dark IPA, Lincoln Lager, Bone Crusher Red, Snoegaarden Belgian Wit, Hounds Tooth Amber Ale, and many more **Tours:** No **Taproom:** Pub

Silver Moon Brewing is a good mix of a brewery and brewpub. Founded in 2000 by Tyler Reichert, Silver Moon started out brewing on a small 1.5-barrel system. Five years later, the brewery moved into the current location with a new upgraded

Snake Bite Porter

Style: Robust Porter

ABV: 5.5 percent

Availability: Year-round

When a beer has a name like Snake Bite, you expect it to have a bit of a bite. Silver Moon's Snake Bite Porter does a great job of providing that bite. The label has a snakeskin background with two silver fangs sticking down, inviting you to "Git bit!" The black porter has a beautiful mocha head that lasts awhile, leaving beautiful lace on the glass. Huge roasted layers give way to a touch of chocolate and plenty of coffee bitterness, giving it the bite. Make sure not to serve this too cold, as the beautiful flavors really show themselves as it warms.

Central Oregon

system that pumps out a range of beers for both the pub and to ship around Oregon and Washington in 22-ounce bottles. Focusing mainly on Northwest-inspired beers, the brewery offers 5 year-round brews and a rotating list of seasonals available in the pub. The year-round lineup includes an ESB, IPA, amber, Pilsner, and one of the highly awarded brews, **Snake Bite Porter.** In the fall during hop harvest, Silver Moon brews **HOPpopotamus,** an IPA made with fresh Oregon-grown Cascade hops. For the hop lovers who enjoy a good, fresh hop ale, this one stands up pretty well to the competition. If you're looking for a hoppy, high-alcohol double IPA, **Hoptagon Imperial IPA** is another great choice.

Of all the brewpubs in the Bend area, Silver Moon has the best live music scene. With both local and national acts coming to the pub weekly, it's a great place to go if you like live music. Unlike those at many other bars that offer live music, the sound system is fantastic, making for an enjoyable evening of dancing and beer. When there isn't music you can pull up a chair and watch games all day on the TVs while munching on some good pub food. Choose from a variety of pizzas, salads, sandwiches, and chili. The menu even gives you good beer pairing options for your meal selection. Before 8 p.m. kids are allowed in, so bring them and make sure to order some of the house-made root beer for them. You can also purchase beer to go with kegs, growlers, and bottles. If you like deals, there are growler power hours at certain times on Tuesday and Wednesday when you can fill a growler for only $5. That's probably the best deal in the state.

10 BARREL BREWING COMPANY

1135 NW Galveston, Bend, OR 97701; (541) 678-5228; 10Barrel.com; @10barrelbrewing .com

Founded: 2006 **Founders:** Chris Cox and Jeremy Cox **Brewer:** Jimmy Seifrit **Flagship Beer:** Apocalypse IPA **Year-round Beers:** Mike Saw a Sasquatch Session Ale, ISA, S1NISTOR Black Ale, Northwest Red, Apocalypse IPA, Hop Junkie **Seasonals/Special Releases:** Citron Kolsche, Oregon Brown, Saison de 10 Barrel, DITD Belgian, Pray for Bourbon, Bourbon Bitter, Black Bourbon, Precursor, One in the Sun Sour, Pray for Snow Strong Ale, Oatmeal Stout, Hop Junkie, Belgian Blonde, Duke, 11R Coffee Porter, plus many more **Tours:** No **Taproom:** Yes

It's no secret that Bend is known for its growing and vibrant beer culture. With so many breweries and more opening every year, the best way to stand out is to make incredibly good beer. Making great beer is exactly what 10 Barrel Brewing does. Started by two brothers who had little experience in the beer industry, 10 Barrel has become one of the most popular and fastest-growing breweries in the state. Founded as Wildfire Brewing, the brewery later was renamed 10 Barrel after the small brewing system. A year later the production brewing opened up a neighborhood pub in Bend's west side, helping expand into the food business and give both locals and tourists easy access to the growing list of high-quality craft beers. In addition to the brewpub and brewery in Bend, the company opened a new pub in Boise, Idaho, in 2012.

In the pub you can find the 6 year-round beers or choose from 9 or so seasonal and brewer's select brews. Variety is one of 10 Barrel's strengths. Outside the pub, you can find a handful of beers, such as **Apocalypse IPA, S1NISTOR Black Ale,** and **ISA** in 22- and 12-ounce bottles. If you visit, make sure to bring a growler as you

Oregon Brown Ale
Style: American Brown Ale
ABV: 7.1 percent
Availability: Seasonal
Just as the name implies, Oregon Brown Ale is an American brown ale with an Oregon twist. The state is known for lots of hops and that is exactly what 10 Barrel did. In fact they used five hop varieties including Cascade, Centennial, Northern Brewer, Simcoe, and Chinook, which gives this brown a unique citrus and piney aroma and flavor. The beautiful light tan head and brown caramel-looking color give this uncharacteristically hoppy beer a touch of class. It's a tad sweet, a bit citrusy, a little toasty, quite a bit hoppy, and 100 percent delicious.

Central Oregon

can get a fill on most of the 15 beers available. If you come during the summer, order a **Mike Saw a Sasquatch Session Ale.** It's an easy-to-drink session ale that is light and smooth, perfect to drink on the back deck. Speaking of the back deck, this is one of the best outdoor patios in the city, complete with a wood-burning fire pit. If you have a dog, bring him along as well, as dogs are welcome outside. You may have to wait most nights, as it does get busy with people there to drink great beer and eat the incredible pizzas.

THREE CREEKS BREWING CO.

721 Desperado Ct., Sisters, OR 97759; (541) 549-1963; ThreeCreeksBrewing.com; @threecreeksbrew

Founded: 2008 **Founder:** Wade Underwood **Brewer:** Zach Beckwith **Flagship Beers:** Knotty Blonde, Hoodoo Voodoo **Year-round Beers:** Knotty Blonde, Stonefly Rye, Old Prospector, Anvil Amber, Firestorm Red, Hoodoo Voodoo, Fivepine Porter **Seasonals/ Special Releases:** Rudolph's Imperial Red Ale, Oatmeal Porter, 8 Second IBA **Tours:** No **Taproom:** Yes

Located in the small tourist town of Sisters, about 20 minutes northwest of Bend, Three Creeks Brewing Co. has been brewing up beer that's being noticed by more than just the locals. Started out as just a brewpub, the brewery in the Old West–style town has been growing at a rapid pace, resulting in the need to open up a separate brewing facility. From the outside of the brewpub, the building fits into the western-style theme seen throughout the city. The wood-lodge feeling makes it a welcoming place to visit. You can eat in the main dining room, head outside to the patio, or make your way to the other side of the brewery, which is considered the bar. The bar is definitely the nicest part, with its hardwood floors, a relaxed layout, and a huge window to view the brewing facility. Unfortunately, kids aren't allowed in that area, but adults can enjoy watching the brewing process while drinking their beers and enjoying good pub-style food.

Three Creeks brews clean beers that are meant to please a lot of people. The brewery focuses on brewing solid lower-alcohol-content session-style beers that are easy to drink. **Stonefly Rye** is a crisp, light, and cloudy rye beer that has some slight grass-like flavors to it. It's an interesting, easy-to-drink beer to try that might not please everyone, but there are those who love it. The **Fivepine Porter** is dark in color with some nice dark roasted malts and hops in the aroma. The flavor follows the nose with considerable amounts of sweet chocolate, nuts, and coffee thrown into the somewhat thin mouthfeel.

In the pub you can order the beer in glasses, pints, pitchers, growlers, and even kegs at times. Currently they distribute 22-ounce bottles of select beers around the state. Like those of most breweries, however, the beer tastes even better on draft. Show up on Wednesday for the best deal on growler fills.

Hoodoo Voodoo IPA
Style: IPA
ABV: 6.2 percent
Availability: Year-round

With so many IPAs around Oregon, it's easy for good ones to fly under the radar. While Hoodoo Voodoo probably isn't the best the state has to offer, it's a well-executed and delicious beer with great drinkability. It's darker than a lot of IPAs, with a light tan head and excellent lacing. Toffee, grapefruit, and brown sugar dominate the sweet aroma with some floral hops present. The taste is a slightly less sweet version of the nose with more citrus and pine added. Overall it's a solid IPA that is worth a drink.

Central Oregon

Brewpubs

OLD MILL BREW WËRKS

384 SW Upper Terrace Dr., Bend, OR 97702; (541) 633-7670; OldMillBrewWerks.com; @OldMillBrewWerk

Founded: 2011 **Founders:** David and Teri Love **Brewer:** Michael McMahon **Flagship Beer:** Irreverence **Year-round Beers:** Audacious Amber Ale, Schizophrenic Stout, Rabble-Rouser Imperial Red Ale, Neurotic Blonde Ale, Irreverence IPA, Eccentric ESB **Seasonals/Special Releases:** None

In the upper section of the Old Mill District sits a building that looks more like an office than a brewpub. Enter through the doors and walk down a hall like you're about to go to a business meeting and you will find the entrance to Old Mill Brew Wërks. The brewpub occupies a space that has very little walk-by traffic and no street entrance, but people still show up for the beer selection. Inside, the pub is a bit crammed into the small space, with the bar taking up a good majority of the restaurant. There is a European flair that is evident in not just the decor, but also the beer. The floors are covered in brick, beer signs line the wall, no TVs are in sight, and it's tastefully painted to make it feel a bit cozy.

The brewing side of the business is technically called Brew Wërks Brewing, which also supplies kegs to a few restaurants around Bend. If you're looking for the full lineup of beers, however, you need to head to the brewery's own pub. In the pub's 12 tap lines, you will usually find 5 or 6 Brew Wërks beers flowing, with the rest filled out with guest taps from West Coast breweries. Among the qualities that stand out the most are the names and logos of the beer. For example, **Schizophrenic Stout** shows a woman who most certainly looks like a schizophrenic. **Irreverence IPA** shows a man flipping the bird, with a black circle censoring his middle finger. The IPA is a solid, easy-to-drink IPA with a mix of floral and citrus notes that shine through the hop bitterness.

If you're looking for some decent food, there's a pub-inspired menu of burgers, sandwiches, and salads. If you go for size, the burgers are pretty big and do a great job of filling you up. If it's nice outside, make sure to ask for a seat on the patio.

SUNRIVER BREWING COMPANY

57100 Beaver Dr., Building 4, Sunriver Village, Sunriver, OR 97707; (541) 593-3007; SunriverBrewingCompany.com

Founded: 2012 **Founders:** Brian, Marc, and Karol Cameron **Brewer:** Brian Cameron **Flagship Beers:** Amber, IPA, Pale Ale, Stout **Year-round Beers:** Amber, IPA, Pale Ale, Stout **Seasonals/Special Releases:** None right now, will brew some in the future

In recent years it seems just about every month a new brewery has opened up in central Oregon. One of the underserved towns for good beer in the area, however, was Sunriver, a place packed with vacation homes and tourists. That all changed in the summer of 2012 when the resort town got its first brewery in Sunriver Brewing Company. Like many newer brewpubs, Sunriver started off in small phases, slowly rolling out new parts of the business. The beer is brewed off site, although the owners plan to bring this operation in-house in the near future. Although they offer just 4 house-brewed beers, they also have a rotating tap list consisting of other local beers. In-house they offer a Northwest-style IPA, a dry stout, an amber, and an easy-drinking pale ale. Their beers aren't super adventurous but are brewed to please the average resort visitor. If you're visiting with a non–beer lover, there's also a small selection of well-chosen wines.

The pub's strongest feature is the food. The owners have taken typical pub fare and made it even better. You'll find entrees such as grilled steelhead, crab and artichoke melts, and rib eye steak. The menu contains quite a few gluten-free and vegetarian options along with certified natural Angus beef. Inside you'll find a lodge-type setting that fits in perfectly with the rest of the town's feel. If you're on vacation with the family, feel free to bring the kids.

Rise of the Nanobreweries

Throughout the country we are seeing a huge increase in the number of craft breweries opening each year. With the greater love of craft beer hitting the marketplace, homebrewers, entrepreneurs, and professional brewers are stepping out and opening new ventures just about every day. Many of these small breweries start off with equipment they can afford and limited capital, causing their production to be scarce, yet often they brew up some amazing beer. Over the years the term "nanobrewery" has been picking up steam as a way to classify these smaller breweries. Although there is no standard definition to the word, these breweries often are busting their butts to produce enough quantity on their smaller systems to pay the bills. Below are a few of the nanobreweries operating throughout Oregon. By the time this book is printed, there will be many more that could be added. At the same time, many of these breweries will have outgrown the nano status and expanded their operations.

(Continued on next page)

(Continued from previous page)

Conner Fields Brewing, *Applegate Valley, OR; ConnerFields.com*

Founded by two roommates from New York, the brewery sells its beer in growlers from a beer van at multiple southern Oregon farmers' markets. The duo have been building a bigger brewing system from scratch to allow greater distribution throughout the area.

Dragon's Gate Brewery, *Milton-Freewater, OR; DragonsGateBrewery.com*

One of the smallest breweries in the state, Dragon's Gate Brewery brews in 20-gallon batches. You can find the beers in bottles in the Milton-Freewater area as well as across the river in Walla Walla, Washington.

Humble Brewing, *Portland, OR; HumbleBrewing.com*

If you look at the Oregon Liquor Control Commission's monthly list of barrels of beer produced each month, you'll notice Humble Brewing consistently toward the bottom. This is known as Portland's smallest brewery. If you find the beer around town, consider yourself lucky and order it.

Short Snout Brewing, *Milwaukie, OR; ShortSnoutBrewing.com*

Located in the Portland suburb of Milwaukie, this small 1.5-barrel nano-brewery got its start with help from the crowd-funding website Kickstarter. You can find Short Snout beers on draft throughout the Portland area from time to time.

Solstice Brewing Company, *Prineville, OR; SolsticeBrewing.com*

With a start as a brewpub offering delicious pub food and a wide selection of beers, Solstice started brewing small batches of beer in 2012 using a 5-barrel system once used by Terminal Gravity Brewing. Solstice is a must-stop destination for beer lovers who find themselves in Prineville.

Santiam Brewing, *Salem, OR; SantiamBrewing.com*

Opened in 2012, Santiam Brewing is quickly making a name for itself. Despite its size, the hardworking brewery generally has 10 of its own beers on draft in the tasting room. Make sure to check the website for taproom hours, as hours are limited, but definitely seek the place out in Salem.

Seaside Brewing Company, *Seaside, OR; SeasideBrewery.com*

Arguably one of the most interesting locations in the state for a brewery, Seaside Brewing Company is located in the old city jail that also spent time as a firehouse and city hall. The old drunk tank was converted into a cooler with 15 taps. While most contain delicious beers from around the area, you can find a small selection of house-brewed beers in the pub.

Beer Bars

BROKEN TOP BOTTLE SHOP & ALE CAFE

1740 NW Pence Ln., Ste. 1, Bend, OR 97701; (541) 728-0703; BTBSBend.com;
@BTBSbend
Draft Beers: 12 **Bottled/Canned Beers:** 700

Finding good beer when you're in Bend isn't too difficult with all of the breweries the city has to offer. What are beer lovers to do, though, if they want to try beers from outside the city, or they just want to drink beers from multiple breweries? One good option is to head over to Broken Top Bottle Shop & Ale Cafe. The pub and bottle shop opened in 2012 and has quickly become a great destination for beer aficionados. With 12 rotating taps of carefully selected beers, a huge bottle selection expanding from all over the world, and a small selection of wine, there isn't a shortage of drinks. The bottles are broken down by state and city, while the international selection is categorized by country, with Belgium leading the way. You can usually expect to find a great selection on tap, flowing from local, West Coast, and international breweries.

The atmosphere has a warm feel that gives you a sense of belonging. With beautifully painted walls and beer posters hanging about, the design gives the cafe a touch of class while keeping a touch of fun. Next to the cafe is the bottle shop that features over 700 bottles and cans. Buy some to take home with you or drink it on site. No corking fee is charged, so find the perfect bottle to pair with your meal. While the beer selection is pretty extensive, the food menu is fairly healthy, yet well crafted. The huge selection of vegetarian, vegan, and gluten-free options is definitely a highlight. Choose from multiple options with sandwiches, smoked meats, soups, salads, and appetizers. All of the desserts are gluten free. The Cherry Chocolate Rain is a delicious option. It's a porter chocolate cheesecake with raw chocolate and house-made Bing cherry sauce. Live music is offered at times, so grab some friends and go get some great beer, food, and music.

PLATYPUS PUB

1203 NE 3rd St., Bend, OR 97701; (541) 323-3282; PlatypusPubBend.com;
@platypuspubbend
Draft Beers: 15 **Bottled/Canned Beers:** Over 550 in the bottle shop

If you're a beer lover, it's always great to find a place that is as excited about your favorite beverage as you are. It's also great to find a gigantic house of beer serving

everyone from the homebrewer to the occasional drinker. The Platypus Pub is just the place to visit if you're taking a break from visiting all of the local breweries in Bend. In this old Nazarene church building, you feel as if you're in a church of beer upon entering. The top floor is run as a separate business by the same owners called the Brew Shop. It's a nice space filled with a mix of homebrewing supplies, with a long row of beer fridges housing over 600 bottles of beer arranged by state and country. Once you get tired from shopping for your brewing supplies or bottled beer, head on down the stairs. You'll pass by a shrine of sorts dedicated to local Oregon sports. Apparently the name Platypus comes from a mix of the Oregon Ducks and Oregon State Beavers. Put them together and you get a platypus.

The pub is lined with wood paneling and a concrete floor. With dim lights, it feels a bit cold. There are 60 seats ready to be filled by patrons seeking out some great beers. At the other end of the bar sit a few dartboards and another exit if you want to leave without being tempted by all the beers up in the Brew Shop. The bar offers 15 rotating taps of a mix of local beers, beers from throughout the country, and a handful of ciders. Many of the beers are fairly rare or hard to find, so the tap list is always solid. The pub offers a menu consisting of pizza, burgers, sandwiches, soups, salads (which are pretty large), and a few select entrees such as mac and cheese, and fish and chips. Here's a tip, however: Stick with the salads and soups; they are your best bet.

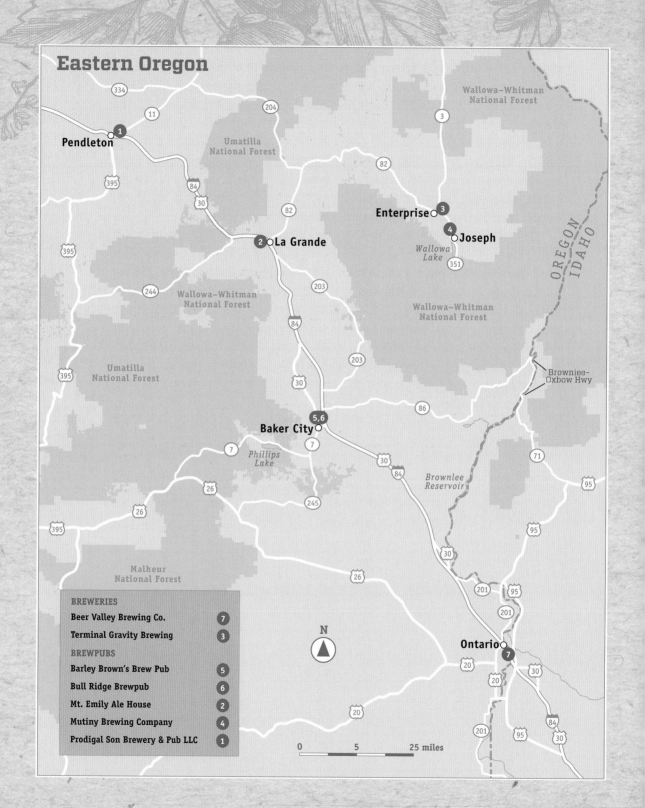

Eastern Oregon

Wallowa–Whitman National Forest

Umatilla National Forest

Pendleton 1

La Grande 2

Enterprise 3
Joseph 4
Wallowa Lake

Wallowa–Whitman National Forest

Umatilla National Forest

Baker City 5,6

Phillips Lake

Brownlee Reservoir

Brownlee-Oxbow Hwy

OREGON IDAHO

Malheur National Forest

BREWERIES
| Beer Valley Brewing Co. | 7 |
| Terminal Gravity Brewing | 3 |

BREWPUBS
Barley Brown's Brew Pub	5
Bull Ridge Brewpub	6
Mt. Emily Ale House	2
Mutiny Brewing Company	4
Prodigal Son Brewery & Pub LLC	1

Ontario 7

N

0   5   25 miles

Eastern Oregon

Historically, eastern Oregon hasn't been much of a draw for beer fans. While the region isn't as populated as many others in the state, the craft beer scene is slowly growing. Since the mid '90s Terminal Gravity Brewing has been producing one of the state's best IPAs while over in Ontario, Beer Valley Brewing is brewing up some incredible beers with plenty of alcohol. Scattered throughout the region you'll also find some great brewpubs, such as the award-winning Barley Brown's Brewpub in Baker City and the Prodigal Son Brewery & Pub in Pendleton. The area is still very rural, so you won't find a lot of the high-quality beer found in other parts of the state in many restaurants and bars, but you can find some great local spots producing some solid brews.

Breweries

BEER VALLEY BREWING COMPANY

937 SE 12th Ave., Ontario, OR 97914; (541) 881-9088; BeerValleyBrewing.com;
@beer_valley

Founded: 2007 **Founder:** Pete Ricks **Brewer:** Pete Ricks **Flagship Beer:** Black Flag
Year-round Beers: Black Flag Imperial Stout, Leafer Madness Imperial Pale Ale, Delta 9
IPA, Pigskin Pale Ale, Owyhee Amber Ale **Seasonals/Special Releases:** Highway to Ale
Barley Wine, Gone Fishin Mild Ale, Oregonberry Wheat Ale, Jackalope Imperial Pumpkin
Porter, Rosebud IPA **Tours:** First Sat of every month at 1 p.m. **Taproom:** Yes

The small town of Ontario, Oregon, lies on the Idaho border just next to the
Snake River. Known as the city where Oregon begins, it is also home to Beer

Beer Lover's Pick

Leafer Madness Imperial Pale Ale
Style: Imperial Pale Ale
ABV: 9 percent
Availability: Year-round
Beer Valley's owners say they created
this beer during the great hop shortage of 2008, yet that doesn't add up
with this bad boy. There is definitely
no shortage of hops in Leafer Madness
Imperial Pale. Hazy straw yellow–
orange in color, Leafer Madness has
an aroma packed with citrusy hops,
tropical fruits, caramel, and pine. The
hoppiness follows the nose in the flavor with lots of citrus, pine, and caramel, and a nice bitter yet sweet taste.
While it does pack a lot of hops,
it's balanced enough to avoid being
overly hoppy. If you can get it fresh
and on draft, it's even better.

Valley Brewing Company and the great beer produced within. Being located so far from craft beer hubs such as Portland or Bend doesn't stop Beer Valley from making brews that are packed with flavor. The beers are a bit extreme and might not cater to everyone's tastes, yet the brewery is doing just fine. Specializing in strong ales, the beer lineup is unique enough to make any beer lover get excited and start doing a hop dance. During hop harvest, brewer Pete Ricks seeks out a variety of fresh hops to make a handful of fresh-hopped special releases of some of the year-round beers, such as **Leafer Madness Imperial Pale Ale** and **Black Flag Imperial Stout,** giving those beers a unique and fresh twist.

One of the most interesting beers is the flagship Black Flag Imperial Stout. At a whopping 11 percent ABV and over 100 IBUs, this fairly black stout is packed with 8 different malts and 4 hop varieties. It is an extremely bitter stout, with the many flavors and aromas from the hops and malts creating an experience in a glass that is definitely worth seeking out if you can handle it. If you can get it in the hop harvest edition with fresh hops, it's even better.

With distribution in Oregon, Washington, Idaho, California, Nevada, Arizona, New Mexico, and Pennsylvania, Beer Valley is rapidly growing and gaining national recognition. If you're in the Ontario area, you can stop by the brewery to fill up a growler or buy some bottles or Beer Valley merchandise. However, there's no beer to drink in the tasting room. Stop by for a tour of the brewery on the first Saturday of every month at 1 p.m.

TERMINAL GRAVITY BREWING

803 SE School St., Enterprise, OR 97828; (541) 426-0158; TerminalGravityBrewing.com; @GravityFan

Founded: 1996 **Founders:** Steve Carper, Debra Duquette, Dean Duquette, and Rosa Duquette **Brewer:** Steve Carper **Flagship Beer:** IPA **Year-round Beers:** IPA, ESG (Extra Special Golden), Breakfast Porter, Pale Ale, Bar X Stout **Seasonals/Special Releases:** Tripel, Festivale, Bucolic Plague Barleywine, Pale Ale **Tours:** No **Taproom:** Yes

Most people have probably never been to Enterprise, Oregon, or even heard of it. Enterprise is a small (1.5 square miles) town in northeastern Oregon's Wallowa County, home to around 2,000 residents. It is also an unlikely place to find a brewery that produces one of Oregon's most beloved IPAs. Set with a beautiful view of the Wallowa Mountains, Terminal Gravity has a small-town vibe yet is growing at a pace that is starting to put Enterprise on the map. Started as a brewery and pub in a house, the brewery side of the business has taken off, allowing Terminal Gravity to expand and bring in more equipment to meet the demand.

Each beer is well crafted and brewed with a solid recipe. The **IPA** is an Oregon classic that is a great definition of a Northwest-style IPA. Along with the IPA Terminal Gravity brews a **Pale Ale** packed with a lot of flavor. The hops are a bit subdued, but the caramel and toffee flavors along with a semi-bitter and creamy finish give it character. In the winter they brew **Festivale,** a strong ale that is worth looking for. Complex malt and hop flavors come together to make a dry and hearty beer that is a favorite of many during the colder months.

If you happen to find yourself in Enterprise, make sure to stop by the public house and try the beer on draft. It's situated in an old Victorian home surrounded by aspen trees, a stream, outdoor tables, and, of course, the brewery. Besides a few beers that you can't get in bottles, they offer a selection of appetizers, salads, sandwiches, and entrees. If you're passing through to Wallowa Lake, stop to eat lunch or dinner. You can also relax and play foosball or darts, or watch a game on the big screen. Outside of Enterprise, the beer is available all over Oregon as well as in parts of Washington and Idaho.

Beer Lover's Pick

Terminal Gravity IPA
Style: IPA
ABV: 6.9 percent
Availability: Year-round
Terminal Gravity's flagship IPA is what the brewery is most known for, and for good reason: It's good. It seems that most Oregon breweries produce an IPA, yet the Terminal Gravity IPA has become one of the state standards. Using a specific yeast not found in the public domain, the beer has a unique flavor. It has beautiful balance of complex malts and citrusy grapefruit-like hops that leaves a somewhat piney taste at the end. If you want a decent representation of a West Coast–style IPA that doesn't blow your face off with bitterness, this is what you're looking for.

Brewpubs

BARLEY BROWN'S BREWPUB

2190 Main St., Baker City, OR 97814; (541) 523-4266; BarleyBrowns.com; @barleybrowns
Founded: 1998 **Founder:** Tyler Brown **Brewer:** Marks Lanham **Flagship Beer:** Turmoil **Year-round Beers:** Tumble Off Pale Ale, Shredder's Wheat, Hot Blonde, Tank Slapper DIPA, Turmoil, Pallet Jack, Jubilee Golden Ale, Coyote Peak Wheat, Two Smoke, DisOrder Stout, Twisted Whisker Scotch Ale **Seasonals/Special Releases:** Whiskey Malt, WFO IPA, Head Shake, Chaos, Sled Wreck Winter Ale, Espresso Stout, Hassle Brown, Barley Brown's 13

Eastern Oregon hasn't been a well-known area for brewing good beer. Over the past few years, more and more breweries have started to pop up, but until recently, few even existed. One of the first brewpubs in the area is the often-overlooked Barley Brown's Brewpub in Baker City. The small brewpub has been producing great beer since 1998, although the rest of the state might not have noticed. With multiple medals from both the North American Beer Awards and the Great American Beer Festival, Barley Brown's knows what they are doing when it comes to making quality beer. Confined to a small 4-barrel system, the bulk of their beer goes to keeping up with demand in the brewpub. This location is currently a brewpub only, but the owners are expanding into a new 20-barrel brewhouse that will allow them to distribute more beer outside the Baker City area.

The pub is in an old brick building with a few tables on the sidewalk out front. Inside there are multiple windows toward the ceiling that let in light, giving the space a bright and inviting feel. Through a large window in the restaurant, you can see the brew system, which is always interesting to watch. On one wall hang all of the medals they've won for the beer, giving you a glimpse of what you might expect when you order a pint. Choose pretty much any beer and you are in for a treat. The **Turmoil Black IPA** is a beautiful black masterpiece with lots of bitterness up front and a roasted malt back end. The grassy hops jump out and make you fall in love. If you go for food, there are pub favorites along with pastas, steak, ribs, grilled salmon, and multiple salads.

BULL RIDGE BREW PUB

1934 Broadway, Baker City, OR 97814; (541) 523-5833; BullRidgeBrewpub.com;
@bullridgebrew

Founded: 2011 **Founders:** Micah and Julie Blank **Brewer:** Walter Bourque **Flagship Beer:** None **Year-round Beers:** Reddy McTeddy Irish Red Ale, The Rambler Rye Amber Ale, The Merkin Returns Stout, Cream Ale, Blue Mountain Brown, CascaAle Chili Pepper Stout **Seasonals/Special Releases:** Rutt Mudd Stout, S & S Ale, Rye Swirly DIPA, Cool Runnings Bitter Rye, Dallas 2 Baker IPA, Belgian Triple, Brown Ale

Bull Ridge Brew Pub opened in September 2011 as Baker City's second brewery. Although the owners didn't start brewing their own beer right away, the place quickly became a destination for beer lovers. With a selection of beers from around the state and a great menu at the pub, the anticipation grew for the time Bull Ridge would be brewing its own beer. Once the licenses finally were approved, the brewery started out small. Generally there was one beer on tap at a time up until the 7-barrel brewhouse was installed in 2012.

The owners are still getting their feet wet with beer, but they aren't afraid to experiment. The draft list changes frequently with beers made with quite a few regional ingredients. Along with a constantly rotating beer menu, the food menu tends to get changed up based on customer feedback. You can find a wide range of pub-style food such as burgers, steak, pastas, and salads as well as a selection of items for kids.

MT. EMILY ALE HOUSE

1202 Adams Ave., La Grande, OR 97850; (541) 962-7711; MtEmilyAleHouse.com;
@mtemilyalehouse

Founded: 2009 **Founders:** Jerry Grant and Bob Kidney **Brewer:** Jerry Grant **Flagship Beer:** The Big **Year-round Beers:** Heifer-weizen, Northwest Porter, Hells Canyon IPA, Double IPA, The Big, Oregon Blonde Ale, Wildfire Red **Seasonals/Special Releases:** Pear Sour, Lemon Whiskey Sour, Hop Sour, Barley Wine, Ragin' Cajun

Mt. Emily Ale House is located in the historic downtown of La Grande on the corner of Adams and 4th. The building itself is a pretty unique setup for a brewpub, as it's in an old renovated bank. With high ceilings and tall windows, the space feels open and free. There is plenty of seating with great views of the brewery, which can be seen through windows. Richly painted walls give it a simple warmth, perfect for relaxing with a cold pint. There's a TV in the bar for watching games while original paintings fill the rest of the walls.

Most of the time you'll be able to find 9 house beers filling the tap lines, with at least 2 of those seasonals. All of the beers are made with organic ingredients and tend to be English-style ales. The house beer is called **The Big.** It's like a mix of an

IPA and an English ale, with its focal point being a strong malt profile. Hints of nuts, pine, and caramel all play into the unique but somewhat light beer. The **Northwest Porter** is a light-bodied porter with nice flavors of coffee and chocolate that are taken over by dark roasted malts. Both kegs and growlers can be filled on site. You can also order some of their tasty house-made root beer.

Periodically you can head down to Mt. Emily's for a wide range of live music, so make sure to get on the mailing list to stay informed about upcoming shows. Along with the music, order some of the delicious pizzas anytime they're open. You'll have good luck with any of the specialty pizzas on the menu.

MUTINY BREWING COMPANY

600 N. Main St., Joseph, OR 97846; (541) 432-5274; MutinyBrewing.com; @mutinybrewing
Founded: 2009 **Founder:** Kari Gjerdingen **Brewer:** Kari Gjerdingen **Flagship Beer:** None **Year-round Beers:** SssWheat, Pi Porter, Pale, Superpale, Sadler's Brown, Bittersweet **Seasonals/Special Releases:** None

The city of Joseph is one of the smallest in the state where you'll find a brewery. With the city limits only 0.9 square miles and a population of around 1,000 residents, it is an unlikely place to find a brewpub. Located on Main Street, Mutiny Brewing Company has been serving up beer and food to residents and travelers visiting Wallowa Lake since 2009. Outside, the building doesn't look like much, but step inside and you'll find a quaint wood-covered dining room. The booths have seat backs of carved wood, each featuring a different animal scene. The place has a small-town feel, fitting nicely with the surroundings. There are tables spread around outside nestled between flowers, as well as a raised deck with even more tables with views of the Wallowa Mountains. The mountain views are absolutely breathtaking, making it one of the best places in the state to sit and have a beer.

Head brewer and owner Kari Gjerdingen got her start at Terminal Gravity Brewing before venturing out and starting her own brewpub. With the 4-barrel brew system, the batches are small, leading to few beers on tap. Generally there are 2 or 3 house beers as well as a selection of bottles from other breweries. The first beer released was the **SssWheat,** a wheat beer brewed with chamomile, coriander, and orange peel. The **Pi Porter** is one of the hidden gems of this place. The Baltic-style porter has a great balance of roasted malts and a touch of hops, making it an easy-drinking beverage.

The food is a mix of Asian-inspired cuisine and pub food. A healthy dose of the menu is vegetarian along with fish tacos, rice bowls, noodles, salads, and soups. Along with beer and food, they also occasionally offer live music, so make sure to check Mutiny's Facebook page before heading out.

THE PRODIGAL SON BREWERY & PUB

230 SE Court Ave., Pendleton, OR 97801; (541) 276-6090; ProdigalSonBrewery.com; @prodigalsonbrew

Founded: 2010 **Founders:** Tim and Jennifer Guenther **Brewer:** Geoff Engel **Flagship Beer:** None **Year-round Beers:** A Beer Named Sue Golden Ale, Wheatstock Hefeweizen, Ella India Pale Ale, Bruce/Lee Porter, Max Power IIPA **Seasonals/Special Releases:** Sundown Saison, Cowboy Common, Splendor in the Glass, Christmas Carol(e), Fatted Calf Sacrificial Stout, Velocirapture, Little Magic Pale Ale, Solidarity Alt, East Brown & Down, and many more

Most known for its professional bull-riding event, the Round Up Rodeo, and its mysterious underground past, Pendleton is the perfect location to start a brewery. Founded in 2010 by husband-and-wife team Tim and Jennifer Guenther, the Prodigal Son Brewery & Pub has become a spring of great beer in downtown Pendleton. Located in the historic 1915 Haw Building, in an old Packard dealership, the pub has an Old West vibe to it. Old artifacts cover the walls and a mix of furniture gives it an almost Portland-like vibe. The pub is pretty massive with multiple small areas to explore. Large windows in the front let a lot of light in, but as you move toward the back bar area, you can hunker down and drink your sorrows away in the dim light.

The brewery has a 10-barrel system that keeps 7 or so house beers on tap. They don't mind bending the rules in their brewing, and prefer to explore beer without boundaries of style. One of the best beers on the menu is the **Bruce/Lee Porter.** It's like biting into a silky bar of milk chocolate with some subtle roasted malts and hints of dark chocolate. At 7.8 percent ABV, it isn't considered a session beer, but it would be easy to drink more than a couple in one sitting.

The food consists of burgers and other pub favorites such as sandwiches, chicken wings, salads, mac and cheese, and bratwurst. It's one of the better places to eat in Pendleton, so it does fill up on the weekends. If you visit, make sure to bring a growler and fill it up to take home.

Beer Festivals

If you love beer, very few things are more enjoyable than spending a day or weekend at a beer festival. Depending on the festival, you get to try beers rarely tasted or not available in your area. You also get to try new styles and beers from breweries just down the road to breweries on the other side of world, all while having a ton of fun.

It's pretty unbelievable that one state can host so many quality beer festivals throughout the year. From the massive Oregon Brewers Festival in Portland to the much smaller Brewers Memorial Ale Festival in Newport, you have a lot of festivals to choose from. Below you will find a handful of some of the biggest, best, or most interesting the state has to offer. Each of the events is organized by month, but the dates are subject to change. Make sure to check out the event website for the most up-to-date information on these fun festivals.

March

SPRING BEER & WINE FEST
Oregon Convention Center, 777 NE MLK Jr. Blvd., Portland, OR 97232; SpringBeerFest.com; @beerwinefestguy

The Spring Beer & Wine Fest is much more than the name suggests. Held each year in the spring at the Oregon Convention Center, the 2-day event attracts much more than just beer lovers. Don't worry, lots of breweries show up. While a majority of them come from Oregon and the West Coast, you'll also find a handful from across the country as well as across the globe. You'll want to bring your wine- and spirit-loving friends as well. Over 20 wineries readily serve samples along with multiple distilleries handing out sample tastes and cocktails. If that isn't enough, local cheese producers and chocolatiers are there to give you a treat along with a host of food booths to keep you from going hungry. The Chef's Stage will school you in the art of cooking with beer, wine, and spirits with demonstrations from some of the area's top chefs. Continue your learning by checking out multiple seminars that will help you pair beverages and an array of foods. Throughout the festival multiple musicians play on the stage, so grab a mug of your beverage of choice and relax to some tunes. It's only $5 to get in, but you'll need to pay for sampling tokens. Check the website for package discounts.

April

OREGON GARDEN BREW FEST
The Oregon Garden, 879 W. Main St., Silverton, OR 97381; OregonGarden.org

The Oregon Garden is a beautiful location in Silverton to have a brewing festival. With the over 20 specialty gardens and features, you'll have plenty of beauty to take in while visiting. Unlike a lot of festivals that feature an abundance of one-off beers that you can't find in the store, this one features many beers and ciders that are fairly easy to find around the state when you go back home. It's a great way to sample a lot of the local beers all in one location. You will find multiple out-of-state breweries; however, they generally distribute in Oregon. Along with great beers, the entertainment schedule often includes some fairly big-name acts as well as beer-tasting lessons and trivia. Homebrewers can enter their beers in the annual home-brew competition, and the winners are announced at the festival. You won't want to miss the brewer's tasting dinner. For $40 you get a 6-course meal, with each course paired with a beer from a different Oregon-based brewery. The brewers come to talk about each of their beers and are available for questions. Tickets to the event start at $15 for a 1-day tasting package and go up to $25 for a 2-day pass.

May

BREWERS MEMORIAL ALE FESTIVAL
Rogue Ales Brewery, 2320 OSU Dr., Newport, OR 97365; BrewersAlefest.com

Brewers Memorial Ale Festival is a celebration of both beer and dogs. The dog-friendly festival was started at the Rogue brewery in honor of Rogue brewmaster

Zwickelmania

During the beginning of the year, the Oregon Brewers Guild (oregonbeer.org/zwickelmania) organizes this statewide event that allows beer fans to get an inside look at their favorite breweries. Most of the breweries in Oregon participate in the 1-day free event, where they open up the brewery for tours, samples, "meet the brewer" events, and often food. It's a great way to get a tour of multiple breweries and meet the great people who make the beer you love to drink.

John Maier's faithful companion named Brewer. Although the festival is held at Rogue, over 50 breweries come out to the 3-day event, bringing a wide range of beers. It's one of the few beer festivals where dogs are encouraged, and hundreds of dogs get together to enjoy the time with their owners. Events such as doggy musical chairs, dog dancing, a dog fashion show, and celebrity dog look-alike contests provide quite a bit of entertainment for those who love K9s. Live music throughout the weekend and plenty of beer make for a great weekend no matter your preference for dogs. Tickets cost $10 to get in and get you started with four taster tickets. Proceeds of the event go to supporting multiple dog charities throughout the area. While it is open only to those who are 21 and over, dogs won't be checked for ID.

SASQUATCH BREW FEST
Eugene Hilton, 66 E. 6th Ave., Eugene, OR 97401; NorthwestLegendsFoundation.org

The Sasquatch Brew Fest was created to honor the memory of well-known area brewer Glen Falconer. Sasquatch, which was Glen's nickname, is a 1-day event held annually in the Eugene Hilton that showcases Northwest breweries and homebrewers. Each of the beers at the event is chosen by its respective brewery's head brewer, with most of them unique creations that you typically won't find in stores. To keep you drinking, they offer local food and music throughout the day. Homebrewers can enter a contest and get a chance to win multiple ribbons. In the evening you can buy tickets to the brewers' dinner, which consists of a multiple-course meal and an ocean of beer. There is also a silent auction that raises money along with the rest of the festival for the Glen Hay Falconer Foundation, a nonprofit organization started by Glen's family that supports craft brewing by giving away brewing scholarships each year. Tickets into the festival are just $10 and include a glass and two taste tickets.

June

NORTH AMERICAN ORGANIC BREWERS FESTIVAL
Overlook Park, Portland, OR; NAOBF.org;
@naobf

Sustainability and beer come together each year in Portland's Overlook Park at the North American Organic Brewers Festival. For three days in a row, visitors can try a range of organic beers and ciders from around the world, eat organic foods, visit booths of sustainability-oriented vendors, and enjoy live music. The beers range from many breweries' year-round offerings to special beers that are brewed just for the festival in a whole range of styles. With the festival's focus on organic beer, you'll find some very interesting beverages. The festival is held each year during the last week in June. Everything about the festival takes into consideration sustainable living. All of the glasses are made with 100 percent compostable cornstarch made from domestically grown corn. Food vendors are also required to provide compostable cutlery and plates, and plenty of recycling stations are provided throughout the festival. The volunteers even wear organic clothing. If you live within riding distance, they offer free bike parking where volunteers will watch over your bike while you enjoy the festival. Admission is free, although you'll need to buy tokens to sample the over 50 beers at the festival. Kids are welcome to come and play in the children's area.

July

OREGON BREWERS FESTIVAL
Tom McCall Waterfront Park, Portland, OR; OregonBrewFest.com; @oregonbrewfest

Held every year on the last full weekend in July, the Oregon Brewers Festival is one of the longest-running and largest craft beer festivals in the nation. The 4-day event features 80 breweries from all over the US, each of which can enter only one beer each year. A mix of styles ranging from fruit beers to stouts and everything in between are poured from trailers lining the park. On the first day of the event, you can be a part of the opening-day parade as it winds through the city, delivers the first keg of the festival, and starts the event with an opening ceremony. Throughout the weekend multiple events such as live music, homebrewing demonstrations, and special keg tappings take place to keep beer lovers entertained. Multiple food vendors are on site to feed the masses. With free admission and a long history, the festival draws over 80,000 attendees a year. At times kegs run out and long lines form, especially on Friday and Saturday night. If you want to make sure you can try all the beers you want, make sure to get there earlier in the day. You'll still have to wait in small lines, but it's worth it to beat the crowds that are there strictly to get drunk.

Beer Week Celebrations

Beer weeks are a growing trend around Oregon. During these weeks, breweries, restaurants, and bars host events, tastings, classes, and all kinds of fun to celebrate the different regions' beer. Below are a handful of celebrations you can find and enjoy throughout the state.

Central Oregon Beer Week, *CentralOregonBeerWeek.com*
As one of the best areas in the state for beer lovers, central Oregon offers a weeklong celebration in Bend and the surrounding area. Beer lovers can find tastings, "meet the brewer" events, beer dinners, tours, and a ton of other events.

Corvallis Beer Week, *CorvallisBeerWeek.com*
In the state, Corvallis is quickly becoming a great beer city. To celebrate its beer culture, Corvallis Beer Week was started offering beer tastings, brewery tours, entertainment, "meet the brewer" events, and a ton of fun events packed into the week designed just for beer lovers.

Eugene Beer Week, *EugeneBeerWeek.org*
During Eugene's beer week, you can easily keep yourself busy with beer-related events all week taking place at breweries, restaurants, and bottle shops. It's more of a celebration of beer culture that embraces not just Eugene-based beers, but beers from around the state as well.

Medford Beer Week, *MedfordBeerWeek.com*
Medford's beer week is a celebration of the city's beer culture. With a mix of local and regional beer events as well as plenty of events at area restaurants that show an appreciation for good craft beer, you have plenty of options to choose from to entertain yourself throughout the week.

Portland Beer Week, *PDXBeerWeek.com*
To celebrate the great beer culture the city has to offer, PDX Beer Week offers a selection of beer-related seminars, special beer releases, small festivals, and lots of beer. Helping make it one of the greatest weeks of the year, the organizers decided to add a few extra days, making it a 10-day week of beer festivities.

PORTLAND INTERNATIONAL BEER FESTIVAL

Pearl District North Blocks, Portland, OR; Portland-Beerfest.com; @PDXBeerfest

Where do you go if you want to try beer from all over the world but don't want to pay the travel costs? The Portland International Beer Festival, of course. The 3-day event located in the north park blocks of the Pearl District in Portland offers over 160 beers hailing from at least 15 countries. You'll find many rare, extreme, and just plain odd styles of beer. While a lot of the beers do come from the US, quite a few show up from Belgium, Germany, England, New Zealand, Japan, Scotland, Canada, and Denmark, among others. Whether you're looking for a beer with over 18 percent ABV that will knock you on your face or a light fruit beer to sip on while you enjoy the festival, you'll be able to find it. The festival includes many rare beers, so make sure to show up early if you want to try them, as they tend to go fast. Kids aren't allowed into the festival, but you can bring along your dogs. In fact, the event is a benefit for local animal charities. Tickets start at $30 to get in, which gives you entry, a glass, and beer tickets to get you started. Buy your tickets online in advance and you'll save $5.

August

BEND BREW FEST

Les Schwab Amphitheater, 344 SW Shevlin-Hixon Dr., Bend, OR 97701; BendBrewfest.com; @bendbrewfest

The beer culture in Bend is growing fast, and this is one of the best places in the country to be if you love beer. If you plan on visiting in the summer, August is a great time during the annual Bend Brewfest. With over 125 drinks from 50 or more breweries and cider companies, it's a great event to get a taste for what's available in the state. Each of the breweries brings two beers to the event, with most either off their year-round lineup or regular seasonal brews you can find around the state. A majority of the breweries come from Oregon, though breweries from around the country show up to pour beers that are locally distributed. They offer plenty of food and entertainment options, and you can even bring the kids until 7 p.m. each day. Entrance is free and you can get started drinking for just $10, which includes a souvenir mug and tasting tokens. The event benefits the Big Brothers Big Sisters of Central Oregon organization. If you're looking for an excuse to visit Bend, plan a trip during this 3-day brew fest and sample all that the area has to offer.

September

HOOD RIVER HOPS FEST
Downtown Hood River, OR; hoodriver.org/events-festivals/chamber-events/hops-fest

Every year toward the end of September in one of the most scenic areas of Oregon, masses of hop lovers gather for the harvest of freshly picked hops. To celebrate fresh hops, Hood River's chamber of commerce puts together a 1-day festival that features over 20 beers brewed from Oregon breweries. Each beer uses hops that have been picked and put into the brew kettle or fermenter within a day or so of their harvest instead of as pellets or dried hops. This gives each beer a unique flavor that can be enjoyed only once a year during the harvest. The festival features lots of Northwest-brewed hoppy beers, live music, and plenty of local food to keep your hunger from getting the best of you. The event is open to those over 21, although pets aren't allowed. One thing to note is that it can get packed quickly, so make sure to show up early.

November–December

HOLIDAY ALE FESTIVAL
Pioneer Courthouse Square, Portland, OR; HolidayAle.com; @holidayale

What better way to celebrate the holidays than with a winter ale festival? Portland's Holiday Ale Festival is held in the heart of the city at the Pioneer Courthouse Square during the winter. Fortunately, they put up huge tents with cozy heaters so you can drink your huge winter beers without getting rained on. The 5-day event features big winter-style beers such as stouts, barleywines, sours, and beers that will keep you warm over the holidays. With over 50 beers all packing in a lot of alcohol content, the event is spread out, making it convenient to visit multiple nights so you can try everything you want without getting so drunk you pass out. The beers come from many breweries in Oregon and the West Coast, with a few others showing up from out of the country. To enter the festival you need to buy an entrance pack that's $25, but it allows you reentry throughout the event. If you have to drive to this festival, do so only if you have a designated driver, as the beer is big. A designated-driver pass costs only $5 and drivers can drink all the soda they want. The location is in a spot with a ton of hotels around, so make a weekend of it and take in the city while you're there.

BYOB: Brew Your Own Beer

Homebrew Shops

There really isn't a better hobby in the world than brewing your own beer. From coming up with your own recipe and spending a day enjoying friends and brewing, to the day you take that first sip of your own creation, brewing is just plain fun. Luckily Oregon is home to multiple homebrew supply shops that cater to the needs of people brand-new to the hobby, as well as to those who have been brewing for years. Most offer an assortment of ingredients and equipment needed to brew beer, along with supplies to craft your own wine, meads, ciders, and even vinegar and cheeses.

Below you will find just a handful of the many shops available in the state to get you started. There are many shops around, so seek one out if the following aren't found near you.

THE BREW SHOP
1203 NE 3rd St., Bend, OR 97701; (541) 323-2318; TheBrewShopBend.com

If you're in central Oregon, the Brew Shop offers you the best selection of beer-related items. In the basement of the shop is the Platypus Pub, which offers a wide array of beer on draft and quite a bit of food. Stop by there afterward, as you might be tired from all the shopping upstairs. The shop has a pretty decent selection of homebrewing equipment and ingredients for all skill levels. If you need help picking out a recipe, there are quite a few for you to choose from, both all-grain and extract brewing. On the back wall is a row of coolers with over 600 different bottles of beer. Think of it as a homebrew and bottle shop in one. Make sure to bring your growlers, as there are taps in the shop of some amazing beers.

F. H. STEINBART CO.
234 SE 12th Ave., Portland, OR 97214; (503) 232-8793; FHSteinbart.com

As the state's oldest homebrewing shop, F. H. Steinbart Co. has become one of the most recognized shops in Oregon. Founded in 1918 in southeast Portland, what once served as a supply shop for the area's many commercial breweries turned into a homebrewing supply shop during Prohibition. Today F. H. Steinbart Co. serves both brewers and winemakers with a variety of products and services for every skill level. The extensive selection of ingredients, brewing equipment, and brewing books makes this one of the best places in Portland for those looking at making their own beer. The draft equipment selection is huge and is a perfect place to visit if you're looking to set up a home kegerator or need a commercial system for a restaurant or bar. They also offer a big selection of grains and hops from all over the world.

For those just starting out in the hobby of brewing beer, there's a great selection of classes taught by a staff with quite a bit of brewing experience. You can find everything from starter kits to mash tuns and grain mills, depending on your needs. If you're in the Portland area and brew beer, make sure to pay a visit to F. H. Steinbart Co.

FALLING SKY FERMENTATION SUPPLY SHOP
30 E. 13th Ave., Eugene, OR 97401; (541) 484-3322; BrewABeer.com

Started as Valley Vintner & Brewing in Eugene, this small homebrewing shop got a name change once owner Jason Carriere started up Falling Sky Brewing. Located next door, Falling Sky Fermentation Supply Shop carries everything you need to brew some really great beers. From grains and hops to brewing equipment and cleaning supplies, you'll find what you're looking for or else they'll help you get it. One of the qualities that define Falling Sky is their extensive brewing knowledge. From beginner to advanced questions, you can ask them anything and chances are they'll be able to help you out. You can also find a selection of winemaking supplies to help you get started crafting your own wines. Make sure to contact them about classes for beginners, as they do offer them periodically.

PORTLAND U-BREW & PUB
6237 SE Milwaukie Ave., Portland, OR 97202; (503) 943-2727; PortlandUBrewAndPub.com

No matter whether you're a homebrewer or not, Portland U-Brew & Pub needs to be on your list of places to visit in Portland. On one side is a full homebrew supply shop that offers a range of ingredients and brewing equipment for all levels of brewers. Those newer to brewing or needing space to brew can head downstairs and brew a beer of their choice on the system. Throughout the process of your brewing, the staff offers help so you don't feel lost. Once your beer is brewed, you leave it there to ferment and come back when it's ready to bottle. It's a great experience for all levels of homebrewers, as this is a fantastic system to brew on.

After your brewing and shopping are done, head over to the on-site pub. They serve 8 taps from multiple breweries including their own selection of beers brewed on site. With a rotating tap list, a small food selection, and a great atmosphere to watch games or throw some darts, it's a great stop in Portland for homebrewers and those who just love beer.

Clone Beer Recipes

DESCHUTES BLACK BUTTE PORTER

As one of the most recognized beers out of Oregon, Deschutes Black Butte Porter is a complex yet easy-drinking beer. A touch of bitterness gives way to a chocolate and roasted finish that can be enjoyed pretty much any time of the year. Give it a try with barbecue for a perfect pairing.

OG 1.056

FG 1.014

IBU 31.7

SRM 30.2

7 pounds Light LME
1.5 pounds wheat malt
1 pound chocolate malt
.75 pound crystal 80L malt
.5 pounds carapils (dextrin) malt
.75 ounce Galena hops 12.5 percent AA (60-minute addition)
.5 ounce Cascade hops 7.1 percent AA (30-minute addition)
.5 ounce Tettnang hops 4.5 percent AA (5-minute addition)
Wyeast 1098 British ale yeast
1 Whirlfloc tablet or 1 teaspoon Irish moss

Steep grains at 152 degrees in a steeping bag for 30 minutes in 3.5 gallons of water. Remove grains and bring to a boil. Once boiling remove from heat and add 7 pounds of Light LME. Stir in thoroughly, return to heat, bring back to boil, and add .75 ounce of Galena hops. At 30 minutes add .5 ounce of Cascade hops. At 15 minutes add Whirlfloc tablet or 1 teaspoon of Irish moss. At 5 minutes add .5 ounce of Tettnang hops.

Chill to 70 degrees, top up fermenter to 5 gallons with cold water, then add yeast.

Ferment at 68 degrees.

When primary fermentation is complete (7 days or so), rack to secondary. After 3 weeks, rack to bottling bucket and add 4.0 ounces of dextrose that has been boiled for 10 minutes in 2 cups of water. Bottle and let sit at room temp to carbonate for 2 weeks. Chill and enjoy after that.

COURTESY OF DUKE GEREN OF F. H. STEINBART CO. (P. 208)

DOUBLE MOUNTAIN VAPORIZER

If you're looking to brew an amazing pale ale, try this clone of Double Mountain's Vaporizer. Using 100 percent Gambrinus Pilsner malt and Magnum and Challenger hops, it's a pretty easy beer to brew. Make sure to add the Challenger dry-hop addition to really give it the hoppy aroma it deserves.

OG 1.060

FG 1.014

IBU 50

SRM 5.1

8 pounds Pilsner LME
2 pounds Gambrinus Pilsner malt
1 ounce Magnum hops 15.5 percent AA (60-minute addition)
1.25 ounce Challenger hops 7.1 percent AA (5-minute addition)
1.5 ounce Challenger hops 7.1 percent AA (dry hop)
1 package Wyeast Belgian Abbey II (1763)
1 Whirlfloc tablet or 1 teaspoon of Irish moss

Steep grains at 152 degrees in a steeping bag for 30 minutes in 3.5 gallons of water. Remove grains and bring to a boil. Once boiling remove from heat and add 8 pounds of Pilsner LME. Stir in thoroughly, return to heat, bring back to boil, and add 1 ounce of Magnum hops; 45 minutes later add Whirlfloc tablet or 1 teaspoon of Irish moss; 10 minutes later add 1.25 ounce of Challenger hops.

Chill to 70 degrees, top up fermenter to 5 gallons with cold water, then add yeast.

When primary fermentation is complete (7 days or so), rack to secondary, add remaining 1.5 ounce of Challenger hops to dry hop the beer. After 1 week, rack to bottling bucket and add 4.5 ounces of dextrose that has been boiled for 10 minutes in 2 cups of water. Bottle and let sit at room temp to carbonate for 2 weeks. Chill and enjoy after that.

COURTESY OF DUKE GEREN OF F. H. STEINBART CO. (P. 208)

PORTLAND-STYLE HEFEWEIZEN (WIDMER HEFEWEIZEN CLONE)

Widmer made the Hefeweizen style popular in the Northwest, but it's not your typical German-style Hefeweizen. The popular Northwest-style Hefe has been the gateway beer for thousands of people who had never tried craft beer. Packed with wheat and yeasty flavors, it's an enjoyable beer that even non–beer lovers tend to enjoy.

OG 1.052

FG 1.012

IBU 31.2

SRM 9.6

7 pounds wheat LME
.75 pounds Munich malt
.5 pounds crystal 40L malt
.5 ounce Nugget hops 13.0 percent AA (60-minute addition)
.5 ounce Cascade hops 7.1 percent AA (20-minute addition)
.5 ounce Cascade hops 7.1 percent AA (10-minute addition)
.5 ounce Willamette hops 5.5 percent AA (5-minute addition)
Wyeast 1007 German ale
1 Whirlfloc tablet or 1 teaspoon Irish moss

Steep grains at 152 degrees in a steeping bag for 30 minutes in 3.5 gallons of water. Remove grains and bring to a boil. Once boiling remove from heat and add 7 pounds of wheat LME. Stir in thoroughly, return to heat, bring back to boil, and add .5 ounce of Nugget hops. At 20 minutes add .5 ounce of Cascade hops. At 15 minutes add Whirlfloc tablet or 1 teaspoon of Irish moss. At 10 minutes add .5 ounce of Cascade hops. At 5 minutes add .5 ounce of Willamette hops.

Chill to 70 degrees, top up fermenter to 5 gallons with cold water, then add yeast.

Try to ferment as cool as possible, preferably between 62 and 66 degrees.

When primary fermentation is complete (7 days or so), rack to secondary. After 1 week, rack to bottling bucket and add 4.0 ounces of dextrose that has been boiled for 10 minutes in 2 cups of water. Bottle and let sit at room temp to carbonate for 2 weeks. Chill and enjoy after that.

COURTESY OF DUKE GEREN OF F. H. STEINBART CO. (P. 208)

ROGUE DEAD GUY ALE

Dead Guy Ale from Rogue is a German maibock that can be found on store shelves all over the state. It's a malty brew with just a touch of bitterness coming from the Perle and Saaz hops. Try pairing your homebrew with pork chops for a delicious combination.

OG 1.063

FG 1.016

IBU 38.8

SRM 13.2

8 pounds light LME
1 pound Munich 20L
1 pound Cara-Munich 60L
.5 pound crystal 40L
1.25 ounce Perle hops 8.0 percent AA (60-minute addition)
1 ounce Perle hops 8.0 percent AA (30-minute addition)
.5 ounce Perle hops 8.0 percent AA (5-minute addition)
.5 ounce Saaz hops 4.5 percent AA (5-minute addition)
1 Whirlfloc tablet or 1 teaspoon Irish moss
Wyeast Pacman yeast (Rogue house yeast)

Steep grains at 154 degrees in a steeping bag for 30 minutes in 3.5 gallons of water. Remove grains and bring to a boil. Once boiling remove from heat and add 8 pounds of Light LME. Stir in thoroughly, return to heat, bring back to boil, and add 1.25 ounce of Perle hops. At 30 minutes add 1 ounce of Perle Hops. At 15 minutes add Whirlfloc tablet or 1 teaspoon of Irish moss. At 5 minutes add .5 ounce of Perle hops and .5 ounce of Saaz Hops.

Chill to 70 degrees, top up fermenter to 5 gallons with cold water, then add yeast.

Ferment at 68 degrees.

When primary fermentation is complete (7 days or so), rack to secondary. After 2 weeks, rack to bottling bucket and add 4.0 ounces of dextrose that has been boiled for 10 minutes in 2 cups of water. Bottle and let sit at room temp to carbonate for 2 weeks. Chill and enjoy after that.

COURTESY OF DUKE GEREN OF F. H. STEINBART CO. (P. 208)

FULL SAIL AMBER

As one of Oregon's oldest craft beers, Full Sail Amber was the first commercially brewed amber in the state back in 1989. It was also the first craft beer to be bottled and has been the brewery's flagship beer ever since. It has some nice malt sweetness with a spicy floral hop finish.

OG 1.055

FG 1.014

IBU 30

SRM 24

ABV 5.3 percent

9.5 pounds 2-row pale malt
1 pound, 14 ounce (1.875 pounds) crystal malt 60L
4.2 ounce chocolate malt
2.6 AAU Halltertauer hops 45 minutes
3.3 AAU Cascade 45 minutes
1 ounce Halltertauer 10 minutes
1 teaspoon Irish moss 15 minutes
Wyeast 1028 London ale, or Wyeast 1318 London ale III, or White Labs WLP013
    London ale, or WLP023 Burton ale

Mash grains for at least 45 minutes at 150. Boil wort for 60 minutes.

Boil hops and Irish moss for times indicated. Chill wort, aerate, and pitch yeast. Ferment at 68 degrees.

COURTESY OF JAMES EMMERSON, EXECUTIVE BREWMASTER OF FULL SAIL BREWING (P. 100)

In the Kitchen

While pairing food with beer can be a whole lot of fun, cooking with beer can be downright delicious. In this chapter you'll find recipes from some fantastic brewpubs in Oregon that use beer in their recipes. Below is an 8-pack of appetizers, entrees, and desserts you can create on your own using some popular local beers. If you want to compare, make sure to visit each brewpub and taste how well yours turned out compared to the original.

Food Recipes

APRICOT JUBELALE SCONES

Beer and scones don't ordinarily go in the same sentence; however, pastry chef Jill Ramseier of Portland's Deschutes Brew Pub has created a delicious winter treat combining the two along with apricots. Deschutes Jubelale comes out each winter and is a fine addition to these scones that work as either a breakfast or dessert.

MAKES 12 SCONES & 1 CUP ICING

> 5 cups all-purpose flour
> 2 tablespoons baking powder
> 1$^{1}/_{2}$ teaspoons salt
> ½ cup sugar
> ½ cup diced dried apricots (or your favorite dried fruit)
> 2 cups heavy cream
> 12-ounce bottle Deschutes Jubelale beer or similar strong ale
> 2 cups powdered sugar
> 1 teaspoon vanilla extract

Preheat oven to 375°F.

In a mixing bowl, mix the flour, baking powder, salt, sugar, and apricots. Add cream and 1 cup Jubelale.

Stir with a wooden spoon until combined (do not overmix or scones will be tough).

Drop in large spoonfuls onto a cookie sheet lined with parchment paper.

Bake for 20 minutes until golden brown.

While they are baking, make icing:

Sift powdered sugar. Add vanilla and 4 tablespoons Jubelale; stir vigorously until smooth with no clumps. When scones have cooled for 10 minutes (it's okay if they are still slightly warm), drizzle with Jubelale icing.

COURTESY OF JILL RAMSEIER, PASTRY/SOUS CHEF OF DESCHUTES BREWERY PORTLAND PUBLIC HOUSE (P. 173)

CHILI BEER CHILI

Calapooia Brewing Co. knows a thing or two about making an excellent chile beer. They also have created an amazing chili recipe that uses their award-winning beer. You can find their Chili Beer in 22-ounce bottles throughout Oregon to add to this delicious chili with a kick.

6 10-OUNCE PORTIONS

1½ pounds ground chuck (we use beef fattened on spent brewery grain from Oregon Natural Meats)
1 cup sweet onion, diced
4 garlic cloves, minced
2 cups stewed tomatoes, diced (reserve juice for looser chili)
1 cup roasted Anaheim or poblano peppers, peeled, seeded, and diced
2 cups kidney or pinto beans (we use kidney)
1¾ cups tomato sauce
2 tablespoons dark chili powder
1 tablespoon ground cumin
2 teaspoons Mexican oregano
1 teaspoon white pepper
1 (22-ounce) bottle Calapooia Brewing Co. Chili Beer
Your favorite tortilla chips
Sea salt
1 lime
Shredded cheddar, queso fresco, or Cotija
1 bunch scallions (green onions)

In a medium to large stewpot, brown the beef. Remove beef and strain out the fat.

Pour a little of the fat back into the pot to cook the onions at medium-high heat until they begin to brown around the edges. Add the garlic and return the beef and stir it all together. Add the diced tomatoes, roasted peppers, beans, tomato sauce, and spices, and fully incorporate.

Pour in half of the Chili Beer, reserving the rest for drinking while cooking.

Bring to a simmer, stirring often, and then crush 2 handfuls of your favorite tortilla chips into the chili to thicken.

Add sea salt in pinches until it's to your specific saltiness. Remember that the chips will bring salt of their own.

Allow to simmer for at least 2 hours, stirring occasionally to prevent sticking/burning.

Squeeze and stir in the lime before serving and place in bowls topped with shredded cheese, queso fresco, or Cojita and a sprinkling of scallions.

COURTESY OF CALAPOOIA BREWING CO. (P. 117)

INDIA PELICAN ALE GAZPACHO

Gazpacho is a tomato-based soup that often scares people away because it's served cold. Pelican Pub & Brewery has taken its version of the soup and cranked it up a notch with the addition of its IPA, India Pelican Ale. The addition of jalapeños gives it a slight kick perfect for enjoying on warm summer days. The recipe is simple to follow and mighty delicious.

> 1¼ pound fresh tomato, diced
> 1 cucumber, peeled, seeded, and diced
> 1 red onion, diced
> .5 jalapeño, seeded and chopped (gloves recommended)
> 4 cloves garlic, chopped
> 6 cups tomato juice
> ¼ cup sherry vinegar
> 1½ cups India Pelican Ale
> Salt and pepper
> ¼ cup extra-virgin olive oil
> Croutons

Garnish
> 2 cucumbers, small dice
> 4 tomatoes, small dice

Use a food processor to puree the tomato, cucumber, red onion, jalapeño, and garlic until smooth.

In a large bowl add the tomato juice, vinegar, and India Pelican Ale. Season with salt and pepper.

Stir in the cucumber and tomato garnish and refrigerate for 2 hours before serving. Serve with extra-virgin olive oil and croutons.

COURTESY OF EXECUTIVE CHEF GED AYDELOTT OF PELICAN PUB & BREWERY (P. 86)

YELLOW BELLY BURGER

Deschutes Brewery's Yellow Belly Burger is one of the best burgers you'll find in Oregon. The burger even won the *Portland Monthly* magazine's Best Burger at their brew and burger event in 2011. Created with the robust Obsidian Stout, it's a succulent and memorable feast.

Obsidian Stout Braised Pork Belly

Slice some cured, smoked pork belly to ½-inch thick (¾-inch if you want to get really wild!), place it in a shallow roasting pan, and barely cover with Deschutes Obsidian Stout beer. Cover pan with foil and roast at 325 degrees for 3 hours. Gently remove from liquid with a slotted spoon and use immediately, or you can cool if making it ahead, in which case reserve some of the braising liquid for reheating.

Spicy Jalapeño Pesto

> 1 cup jalapeño peppers, sliced (remove stem, seeds, and pith unless you want really hot pesto—gloves recommended)
>
> 2 cups cilantro
>
> ¼ cup Parmesan cheese
>
> ¼ cup pine nuts
>
> 2 tablespoons mild olive oil
>
> 2 tablespoons garlic cloves
>
> 1 teaspoon kosher salt (you may need to add more depending on your taste preference)
>
> Juice of 1 lime

Puree all ingredients in a food processor.

Candied Yellow Pear Tomatoes

Mix yellow pear tomatoes with some slivered yellow onions to your preferred taste, lightly coat with a touch of olive oil, sprinkle liberally with kosher salt and fresh ground pepper, and spread onto a sheet tray. Roast in a 400-degree oven for 20 minutes or until they just begin to brown and split open. Cool.

The above components are combined with beef patties and served on toasted ciabatta or hamburger buns.

COURTESY OF JILL RAMSEIER, PASTRY/SOUS CHEF OF DESCHUTES BREWERY PORTLAND PUBLIC HOUSE (P. 173)

MOULES DE BLONDE

One of the specialties served at Bazi Bierbrasserie is the Moules de Blonde they serve alongside french fries. The seafood dish is a beautiful combination of mussels, Belgian-style Wit beer, and a handful of other ingredients that results in one incredible meal. Feel free to try different Wit beers in the recipe based on your preference or availability.

1 tablespoon olive oil
2 ounces or roughly $1/3$ cup fennel, chopped
2 ounces or roughly $1/3$ cup celery, chopped
1 tablespoon shallots, chopped
1 tablespoon fresh garlic, chopped
2–3 ounces Wit beer (such as those by The Commons, Upright, and Pfriem
    to name a few)
9 large cleaned mussels
4 tablespoons butter
¼ teaspoon salt
¼ teaspoon ground pepper
1 cup heavy whipping cream
Additional salt and pepper to taste

Heat olive oil in a sauté pan; add fennel and celery, tossing occasionally. Once the aromatics brown very slightly, add the shallots and garlic. Sweat the shallots and garlic lightly and then pour in the beer. Reduce the beer by half and then add the mussels, butter, salt, and pepper. Toss lightly and then add the cream and cover with a lid. Check the contents every few seconds until all the mussels have steamed open, and remove any dead or unopened mussels. Reduce the sauce by half or so until sauce is thick, but not too thick (somewhere between runny and Alfredo). Taste the sauce and season accordingly.

To serve:

Simply dump contents into large bowl and make sure all ingredients are evenly distributed. Adorn with 2 slices of baguette sticking up from the center, wipe any smudges on the rim, and serve with a small bowl for shells.

COURTESY OF HILDA STEVENS, MANAGER OF BAZI BIERBRASSERIE (P. 49)

CHOCOLATE UNDERTOW CUPCAKES

Adding beer to chocolate is usually a wise choice, especially with stouts. Calapooia Brewing Co. owner Laura Bryngelson created this succulent cupcake recipe using the brewery's Undertow Imperial Stout. While it currently isn't bottled, you can get growlers of it filled at the brewery to help make these awesome treats.

12 REGULAR-SIZE CUPCAKES

Cupcakes

¾ cup unsweetened cocoa

1⅔ cup sugar

2 cups flour

1 teaspoon baking soda

⅛ teaspoon salt

16 ounces Undertow Imperial Stout

1 stick butter, room temperature

1 tablespoon vanilla extract

3 eggs, room temperature

¾ cup sour cream

Frosting

8 ounces cream cheese, room temperature

¼ cup butter, softened to room temperature

2½ cups powdered sugar

1 tablespoon Undertow Imperial Stout

1 teaspoon vanilla extract

1 teaspoon cinnamon

Preheat oven to 350°F.

In a large mixing bowl, whisk together the cocoa, sugar, flour, baking soda, and salt.

In another medium mixing bowl, combine the stout, softened butter, and vanilla. Beat in eggs, 1 at time. Mix in sour cream until thoroughly combined and smooth. Gradually mix the dry ingredients into the wet mixture.

Lightly grease 24 mini-muffin tins. Divide the batter equally between muffin tins, filling each ¾ full.

Bake for about 6 minutes and then rotate the pans. Bake another 6 minutes until risen, nicely domed, and set in the middle but still soft and tender. Cool before turning out. If using full-size muffin tins, cook for 10 minutes for each rotation.

To make the icing:

In a medium bowl with a hand mixer, beat the cream cheese and butter on medium speed until light and fluffy. Gradually beat in the powdered sugar until incorporated and smooth. Add stout, vanilla, and cinnamon and beat.

Top each cupcake with a heap of frosting and dust with cocoa.

COURTESY OF CALAPOOIA BREWING CO. (P. 117)

DORYMAN'S DARK ALE APPLE AND RAISIN BREAD PUDDING

Pelican Pub & Brewery's Doryman's Dark Ale is a brown ale perfect for adding to a number of dishes. Chef Ged Aydelott and his team know what they're doing when it comes to creating amazing food recipes with their award-winning beers. Their bread pudding is no exception. Serve it by itself or along with a scoop of ice cream and drizzle it with the caramel sauce for a tasty dessert.

¼ cup golden raisins
¼ cup Doryman's Dark Ale
½ loaf wheat bread, cubed and dried overnight
1 Granny Smith apple
1 teaspoon ground cinnamon
1 tablespoon sugar

Custard

1½ cups heavy cream
¼ cup Doryman's Dark Ale
½ cup sugar
5 egg yolks
1 teaspoon vanilla extract

Doryman's Caramel Sauce

1 cup sugar
¼ cup water
½ cup heavy cream
½ cup Doryman's Dark Ale
6 tablespoons unsalted butter
½ teaspoon vanilla extract
¼ teaspoon salt

Soak the raisins in the beer for 4–8 hours or microwave them for 5 minutes. They can be used warm or cooled.

For the custard:

Heat the cream, beer, and sugar together in a medium-size pan on medium high until it is almost boiling. Temper into the egg yolks. Pour into an ice bath (i.e., put in a container that is surrounded by ice and water) and add vanilla. Cool.

For the caramel sauce:

In a deep pot place the sugar and water. Heat on medium-high until dark brown. Carefully add cream and beer. It will steam. If the caramel seizes, take a wooden spoon and stir until smooth. Add butter, vanilla extract, and salt. Stir until incorporated.

Right before preparing the bread pudding, peel and dice the apple into small cubes. Toss them in sugar and cinnamon.

Butter a medium-size baking dish and coat with sugar. Tap off excess.

In a large bowl place bread, raisin mixture, and apple mixture and toss together. Pour custard over bread and let soak. Place everything in the prepared dish and gently press it down to help custard incorporate into bread. Cover with tinfoil and poke 6 holes around the edge. Preheat the oven to 350°F. Place in oven for 30 minutes. After 30 minutes remove the foil, sprinkle the top with sugar, and place in oven for another 30 minutes. Remove and let set for 10 minutes. Cut and drizzle with Doryman's caramel sauce. It is really good with ice cream on top as well.

COURTESY OF EXECUTIVE CHEF GED AYDELOTT OF PELICAN PUB & BREWERY (P. 86)

JEANNEKE BEER COCKTAIL

As craft beer has grown, a new trend of using beer as an ingredient in cocktails has been picking up as well. One of the best places in Portland not only to find a selection of great beers but to order some great beer cocktails is Bazi Bierbrasserie. One of their best cocktails is the Jeanneke Beer Cocktail made with a Belgian-style Wit.

    $1^1/_2$ ounce vodka
    $1^1/_2$ ounce Wit beer (such as those by The Commons, Upright, and Pfriem,
        to name a few)
    $^1/_2$ ounce lemon juice
    1 bar spoon honey coriander syrup (recipe below)
    $^3/_4$ ounce Aperol

Pour ingredients into a shaker. Ice and shake. Serve on the rocks with orange zest.

Honey coriander syrup
    2 cups honey
    1 cup hot water
    30 coriander seeds
    5 whole cloves

Mix honey with hot water. Lightly toast coriander seeds and cloves in dry pan. Add to honey syrup while still hot, and let sit for 20 minutes. Filter into a squeeze bottle for easy use.

COURTESY OF HILDA STEVENS, MANAGER OF BAZI BIERBRASSERIE (P. 49)

Pub Crawls

One of the best parts about being in a state that loves its beer is the sheer volume of great places you can visit and drink very well. You can go to an area and visit breweries, restaurants, and beer bars all while sampling what each has to offer. A pub crawl is a great way to see multiple places in one day and allows you to do so safely as long as you walk, take a cab, or find someone willing to be your designated driver.

In this chapter we highlight a few itineraries of pub crawls throughout the state. While each city is packed with great places to visit, look at this as a starting point for your next pub crawl adventure.

Portland: Northeast

The northeast section of Portland is home to some great breweries and bars, yet it is fairly spread out. This pub crawl takes you into the growing neighborhood of Boise, also known as the Historic Mississippi District.

Bridgetown Beerhouse, 915 N. Shaver St., Portland, OR 97227; (503) 477-8763; BridgetownBeerhouse.com. Is there a better way to start a pub crawl than with a beer? Bridgetown Beerhouse is just the place to get the crawl started. They offer 5 well-selected rotating beer taps and over 500 bottles. You might find Pliny the Elder on tap, along with a number of other awesome beers. They don't have food, but you'll find some great food carts nearby. Have a pint or two before heading on to the next location.

Head east on N. Shaver Street and take the first right onto Mississippi until you reach Beech Street. You'll see Amnesia Brewing on the corner with a sea of wooden tables outside.

Amnesia Brewing, 832 N. Beech St., Portland, OR 97227; (503) 281-7708. Head on inside and order some beers and bring them out to the front patio. They don't offer a lot of food, so split a sausage with a friend if you're hungry. Otherwise eat a quick snack on your walk from Bridgetown. Amnesia's beers have a very Northwest feel to them. Choose what sounds good to you and you'll most likely be happy with what you get. Copacetic IPA is one of the best in the city.

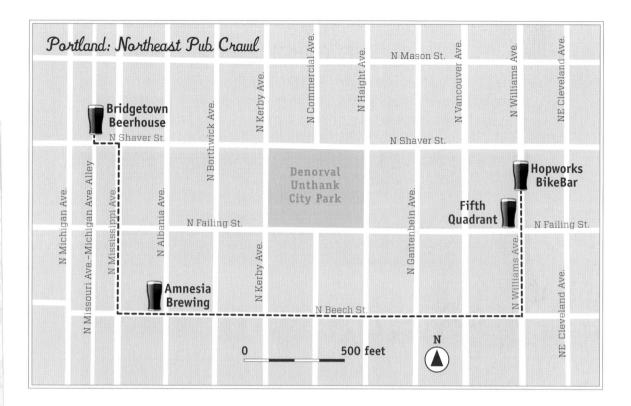

You're probably hungry by now, so head east on N. Beech Street for about 0.4 mile and take a left on N. Williams Avenue. Head a block north and you'll see Lompoc's Fifth Quadrant.

Lompoc's Fifth Quadrant, 3901 N. Williams Ave., Portland, OR 97227; (503) 288-3996; LompocBrewing.com. Either sit inside or outside at the covered patio and ask for a dinner menu. All this beer drinking has probably got you ready to chow down on some good food. Luckily the Fifth Quadrant has you covered. Choose from options such as crab mac and cheese, bangers and mash, steelhead, salads, burgers, and sandwiches. Their beer selection is always interesting and you never know when a winter beer might show up in summer. One suggestion is to try not to overdo it on the big hoppy beers; they are coming up at your last stop.

If you're feeling pretty relaxed by now, don't worry, you're only going next door. Just walk north on N. Williams and you'll see Hopworks BikeBar.

Hopworks BikeBar, 3947 N. Williams Ave., Portland, OR 97227; (503) 287-6258; HopworksBeer.com. You have reached the land of hoppy beers. If you're into biking, take in the beauty of bike frames hanging all over and the lineup of old beer cans. They usually have 10 beers on draft and 1 on cask. If you order the sampler, it will come on a tray that looks like a bike wheel and includes 10 beers. Try the Survival Stout brownie, fresh-baked pie, or chocolate chip cookie if you're looking for something sweet. Happy hour starts at 9 p.m. and includes some great deals to help you end your evening.

Portland: Northwest/Southwest

Northwest and southwest Portland definitely have some great places for beer fans to visit. With the close proximity of everything, this pub crawl packs in four locations offering a few hundred different options of beer, so you might want to start early.

Pints Brewing, 412 NW 5th Ave., Portland, OR 97209; (503) 564-2739; PintsBrewing .com. Located in Oldtown/Chinatown, Pints Brewing is one of Portland's newest breweries. During the morning it's a coffee shop before it turns into a taproom. You're going to want to pace yourself today and Pints has some great beers with lower alcohol content. Try the Tavern Ale, Legalize Wit, or Red Brick Rye and a quick snack before heading out.

Head to NW Flanders Street and head west. Turn left on NW Broadway and walk about 5 blocks to Bailey's Taproom.

Bailey's Taproom, 213 SW Broadway, Portland, OR 97205; (503) 295-1004; BaileysTaproom.com. Bailey's Taproom is the best place downtown to find a big selection of beers from multiple breweries. With 20 rotating taps and an extensive bottle selection, it's a great place to stop for a drink or two. They have sampler trays if interested, or just order a pint. They don't offer food, just liquid nourishment.

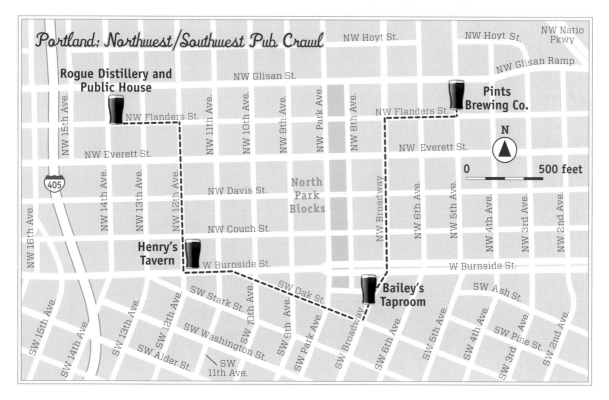

Hop On the Bus . . . The Beer Bus

While visiting breweries is a lot of fun, it's always important to make sure you have a designated driver to haul you around to keep you and others safe. Though persuading a friend to be your designated driver for the day while touring multiple breweries isn't a bad way to go, you can get a lot more out of your experience if you invite the friend along to drink with you and let someone else drive you around. Throughout Oregon multiple companies offer beer buses, guided tours that pack in a lot of extra value than just visiting breweries yourself. While each offers a slightly different experience, you'll learn a lot of history, get to meet brewers, sample a ton of beers, and have a blast hanging out with other beer-loving patrons while you get whisked around the cities you're touring. You can either make it a party and fill up the bus with your closest friends, or sign up for one of the public tours.

If you're looking for a beer bus in Portland, you have a couple of options. The first is the oldest tour, known as **The Portland BrewBus** (brewbus.com). You pack into either a yellow school bus or a small charter bus and hear a lot about the city's great beer history. Each tour stops at different breweries, so you can take the tour without getting bored. Along the way you'll try a ton of beers, eat some great food, and learn a lot about the Portland beer scene. Another touring company that offers multiple options in the Portland area is **Brewvana** (experiencebrewvana.com). They offer a wide range of tours covering Portland, Corvallis, Hood River, and more. Get behind the scenes with brewers, sample beers, plus receive your own personal beer journal and pretzel necklace. The tours are a lot of fun and allow you to meet fellow beer lovers on the public tours.

In Bend you can hop on the **Bend Brew Bus** (bendbrewbus.com). Much like the Portland tours, you'll visit a ton of breweries in Bend and get to sample a lot of beer. If you're visiting, they'll even pick you up right from your hotel so you don't need to worry about driving at all. They also offer wine and spirits tours so you can experience how multiple drinks are crafted. If you find yourself in southern Oregon you can board **The Magic Brew Bus** (Ashland-tours .com/BrewTours.php) weekly. They take you on a 4-hour tour of multiple breweries and pubs such as Standing Stone Brewing, Wild River, Southern Oregon Brewing, and Caldera. You'll get to experience the growing beer scene of southern Oregon and learn a lot about what goes into their beer.

Once your thirst is quenched for the time being, lace up your shoes and start heading south on SW Broadway. Take a right onto SW Oak Street and walk until it merges with W. Burnside Street. Walk a block (it's a one-way street, so you need to walk using these directions) and turn right on 12th and you'll see the sign for Henry's.

Henry's Tavern, 10 NW 12th Ave., Portland, OR 97209; (503) 227-5320; HenrysTavern .com. At this point it's your choice. Head to the left and you're in the bar or wait for a table and get some dinner. They have an extensive dinner menu that can be ordered in any part of the restaurant along with more than 100 beers on draft. Make sure to allow enough time to read the novel of a beer list. They offer everything from local beers to imports; you'll have a hard time choosing. For dinner choose from a huge menu of salads, sandwiches, sausages, burgers, Asian cuisine, steak, and mouthwatering desserts. Try not to stuff yourself too much, though; you still have more beer to drink.

Don't spend too much time at any one place today. It's time to head north on 12th before taking a left on NW Flanders Street in 4 blocks. Walk 2 blocks and end up at Rogue Ales Public House on the right side of the street.

Rogue Distillery & Public House, 1339 NW Flanders, Portland, OR 97209; (503) 222-5910; Rogue.com. It's wouldn't be right to have a pub crawl without visiting Rogue in the Pearl District. Hopefully you're a good decision maker because there are 38 beers on draft from both Rogue and affiliate breweries, such as Buckman, Eugene City Brewery, and the Issaquah Brewery. They also have some pretty delicious pizzas that make a great late-night snack or dinner.

Portland: Southeast

Southeast Portland is packed with breweries, restaurants, and just all-around great beer culture. Technically the boundaries of southeast Portland consist of Burnside Street to the north and the Willamette River to the east. This pub crawl starts off at the world-famous Hair of the Dog.

Hair of the Dog Brewing Company, 61 SE Yamhill St., Portland, OR 97214; (503) 232-6585; HairoftheDog.com. If you want to start your crawl off right, visit one of the best breweries in the city. Their tasting room is closed Sunday and Monday, so keep that in mind. You're also in for some big beers, so don't be afraid to buy a few bottles to take home. To ease into the day, start with a Ruth or Lila before moving up to stronger beers. Or for the best experience just jump in and try the sampler. Make sure to get an appetizer or snack while there, as you'll have a little bit of a walk to the next destination.

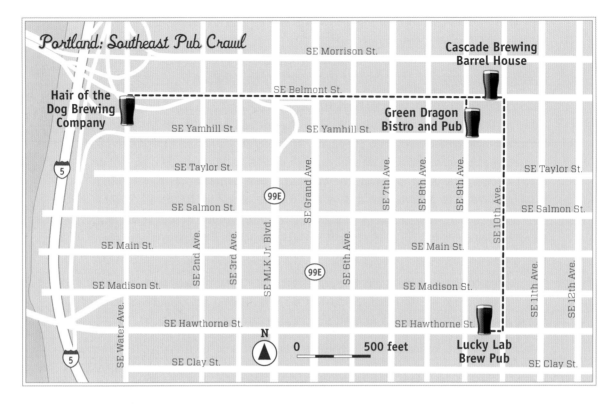

Portland: Southeast Pub Crawl

SE Morrison St.

Cascade Brewing
Barrel House

SE Belmont St.

Hair of the
Dog Brewing
Company

SE Yamhill St.   SE Yamhill St.   Green Dragon
Bistro and Pub

SE Taylor St.   SE Taylor St.

SE Salmon St.   SE Salmon St.

SE Main St.   SE Main St.

SE Madison St.   SE Madison St.

SE Hawthorne St.   SE Hawthorne St.

N   0   500 feet   Lucky Lab
Brew Pub

SE Clay St.   SE Clay St.

Once you're satisfied, head north on SE Water Avenue and take the first right on SE Belmont Street. Walk 9 blocks until you arrive at the Green Dragon on 9th Avenue.

Green Dragon, 928 SE 9th Ave., Portland, OR 97214; (503) 517-0660; PDXGreenDragon .com. The Green Dragon is a beer lover's paradise. Walk in and take notice of the 50 beers on tap: 30 at the back bar and 20 at the front. You could spend the rest of the night here and not even get through very many beers. The Green Dragon is also home to Buckman Brewery, so take a peek through the window in the back and see if anyone's working. Because you're there, make sure to try a Buckman beer as well; they make some interesting tea-like beers. You'll probably want to eat some dinner here, as they have some great burgers and Belgian-style fries.

Your next location is just a stone's throw away. Walk north on 9th and take a right on SE Belmont Street. You'll see Cascade Brewing Barrel House on the left.

Cascade Brewing Barrel House, 939 SE Belmont St., Portland, OR 97214; (503) 265-8603; CascadeBrewingBarrelHouse.com. If you're a sour-beer fan, you're in for a treat. You'll find some of the best sour beers in the country pouring at this small

pub. When it's warm outside, the front patio gets packed. Choose any of the 16 beers on draft or 2 on cask. If you're not a sour fan, their IPA and Portland Pale are both great beers to try. They also have an interesting food menu of snacks to pair with your beers.

If you're still thirsty or want to bypass the sour beers, head south on 10th Avenue and take a right on SE Hawthorne Boulevard and you'll see Lucky Lab Brew Pub.

Lucky Lab Brew Pub, 915 SE Hawthorne Blvd., Portland, OR 97214; (503) 236-3555; LuckyLab.com. One of Portland's most recognized neighborhood pubs, the Lucky Lab has delicious beer and a lively atmosphere to end your evening. They usually have a beer on cask and one on nitro along with their usual lineup. If their black stout is on nitro, it would be a perfectly smooth beer to finish off your pub crawl.

Bend

With the amount of breweries in Bend, there are many excellent options for pub crawls. If you want to try to visit all of the breweries, make sure to check out the famous Bend Ale Trail. If, however, you have limited time and want a great experience, follow this pub crawl downtown.

Bend Brewing Company, 1019 NW Brooks St., Bend, OR 97701; (541) 383-1599; BendBrewingCo.com. What better way to start a pub crawl than at a brewery that has won a ton of awards for their beers? Either sit on the patio if it's summer or belly up to the bar and look up into the brewery. They have some really good beer with high alcohol, but you might want to take it easy to start. If they have Ching

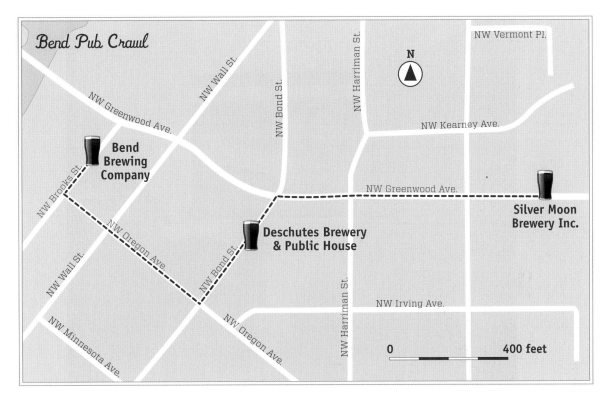

Ching on tap, try that. The always tasty Elk Lake IPA or Pinnacle Porter is also a great option. If you're getting hungry, get some hummus dip or calamari to tide you over until the next stop.

When you're ready to move on, head southwest on NW Brooks Street, take a left onto NW Oregon Avenue, and another left in 2 blocks onto NW Bond Street. On the right you'll spot Deschutes Brewery & Public House.

Deschutes Brewery & Public House, 1044 NW Bond St., Bend, OR 97701; (541) 382-9242; DeschutesBrewery.com. As a beer lover you'll love Deschutes Public House. While there tends to be a long wait at times, it's definitely worth it. There is always a great selection of pub-exclusive beers you won't be able to find anywhere else along with the regular lineup of Deschutes beers. You're going to have a tough time deciding what to order, so just get the sampler and try a lot of great beer. Come hungry, as they have a great selection of burgers and entrees that pair well with your beer. You'd also better end dinner with dessert here, as the next stop doesn't have many options in the sweets department, and Deschutes knows how to create some amazing treats. Check out their mouthwatering peanut butter pie, made with

a malted Oreo crust, topped with chocolate ganache, and drizzled with homemade pale ale caramel.

If you can still move after dinner, head northeast on NW Bond Street and turn right on NW Greenwood Avenue. Walk about 0.2 mile on the north sidewalk and end up at Silver Moon Brewing Company.

Silver Moon Brewing Company, 24 NW Greenwood Ave., Bend, OR 97701; (541) 388-8331; SilverMoonBrewing.com. End your evening at Silver Moon drinking great beer and having a lot of fun. Despite how real the painting looks of the brewhouse on the back wall, it's just a painting. The real brewhouse can't be seen from inside. If you enjoy live music, make sure to coordinate your visit with their live-show schedule found on their website. The place can fill up quickly and there is a cover charge when live music is playing. They have a great selection of beers to choose from including Snake Bite Porter, HOPpopatamus, Hoptagon, and multiple pub-only creations. They're open until midnight every day except Sunday, so settle in and enjoy your stay.

The Bend Ale Trail

If you're visiting Bend on vacation, the Bend Ale Trail (bendaletrail.com) is a must-do activity that can be experienced any time of the year. With 14 breweries and counting in the city, Bend has more breweries per capita than any other city in Oregon. To explore them, the Bend Visitor Center has put together a passport that you can print out and get stamped each time you visit one of the nine participating breweries in Bend. Get extra credit for visiting Three Creeks Brewing in nearby Sisters. Once it's completed, take your passport to the Bend Visitor Center for a prize.

Eugene

Eugene is home to multiple breweries, brewpubs, bars, and bottle shops, all making it a great city for a pub crawl. It's a bit spread out if you want to hit Ninkasi and Oakshire, so hit those up with a designated driver or if you want a good walk. If you're in the mood to walk around, here's a pub crawl that is all about great beer selections.

The Bier Stein, 345 E. 11th Ave., Eugene, OR 97401; (541) 485-2437; TheBierStein .com. Start the crawl off right by visiting the city's best bottle shop that also doubles as a pub. Their tap list is stellar and usually includes a decent selection of international beers. You can choose from 10 beers on draft and over 1,000 bottles that can also be consumed on site. Make sure to get some food in your belly before you start your crawl. They offer some pretty decent appetizers, such as chips and salsa, artichoke dip, German sausage, and an antipasto plate. If you have a place to drop things off, make sure to pick up a few bottles to take home before heading out.

While you could spend a lot of time at the Bier Stein, it's time to move on to your next destination. Head west on 11th Avenue and take a left onto Oak Alley. Walk about 0.2 mile and you'll arrive at Falling Sky Brewing.

Falling Sky Brewing, 1334 Oak Alley, Eugene, OR 97401; (541) 505-7096; FallingSkyBrewing.com. Falling Sky Brewing is a great stop for dinner. If the brewers are still working, you can watch them work behind the glass windows. Otherwise you can just marvel at their beautiful copper tanks while taking in some of their great beers. Because this is the only brewery on the pub crawl, you should definitely opt

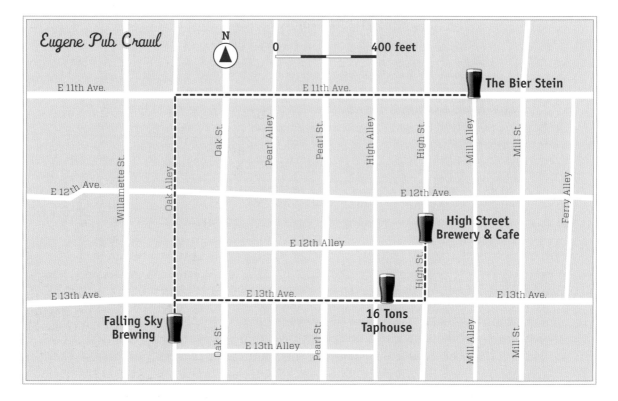

Eugene Pub Crawl

N

0   400 feet

E 11th Ave.   E 11th Ave.

The Bier Stein

Willamette St.

Oak St.

Oak Alley

Pearl Alley

Pearl St.

High Alley

High St.

Mill Alley

Mill St.

Ferry Alley

E 12th Ave.   E 12th Ave.

High Street
Brewery & Cafe

E 12th Alley

High St.

16 Tons
Taphouse

E 13th Ave.   E 13th Ave.   E 13th Ave.

Falling Sky
Brewing

Oak St.

E 13th Alley

Pearl St.

Mill Alley

Mill St.

for the sampler. The flight comes in a cloud-shaped tray with six of their beers, all of which are available only at the pub. Hopefully you're hungry, because they have some pretty tasty dinner options. Their menu changes based on the season and does a great job of pairing with their seasonal brews.

Once you're full of food and beer, head north on Oak Alley and turn right on E. 13th Avenue. Walk just 0.2 mile and 16 Tons Taphouse will be on your left.

16 Tons Taphouse, 265 E. 13th Ave., Eugene, OR 97401; SixteenTons.biz. Okay, so 16 Tons Taphouse isn't your typical late-night joint. However, they have arguably the best tap list in the city, with 18 awesome brews on draft. They're also a bottle shop, so you can crack open any of the 600-plus bottled beers on site. Unfortunately, they don't offer food, so if you're still hungry, make sure to pick up some food on your way. While the atmosphere isn't party central, it's a great destination for true beer lovers.

If you're still hungry or just want to experience more beer, you're already really close to your final destination. Just head east on E. 13th Ave and take the first left onto High St. Walk about a block and you'll see McMenamins High Street Brewery on the right.

Mid-Valley Brewfest

Sometimes beer festivals focus on just one thing and do it really well. At the Mid-Valley Brewfest at McMenamins High Street Brewery & Cafe, the beer is the attraction. Sure, there's food, but that's about it. It's a celebration of beer from multiple McMenamins breweries as well as other Eugene-area breweries. They don't do any competitions like some of the other McMenamins festivals have, yet they provide a great and entertaining time.

McMenamins High Street Brewery & Cafe, 1243 High Street, Eugene, OR 97401; Mcmenamins.com/261-high-street-brewery-café-home. It's open most nights of the week until 1 a.m., so come get a pint of McMenamins regular lineup, or a seasonal selection found only at their High Street location. They specialize in a rotation of strong ales that are sure to keep you warm on those cool Eugene nights. During warmer months the backyard beer garden is quite the relaxing place to enjoy a brew and pub style food.

Hood River

The beer scene in Hood River gets better and better every year. With new breweries, pubs, and restaurants dedicated to serving great beer and the easy navigation of the city, it makes for a great place for a pub crawl.

Full Sail Brewing, 506 Columbia St., Hood River, OR 97031; (541) 386-2247; FullSailBrewing.com. Start off your crawl with a tour of Full Sail Brewing. They offer free tours at 1, 2, 3, and 4 p.m. daily, each lasting about 30 minutes. Their brewery is massive and is one of the largest manually run brewing operations around. The tour provides a great start to your crawl, as you'll get to taste multiple malts, smell hops, and watch as beer is being brewed. After the tour stop by Full Sail's tasting room for an appetizer and a beer or two. Try one of their Brewer's Share beers that are exclusive to the pub. If it's a nice day, sit outside on the patio, which overlooks the Columbia River.

After leaving Full Sail, walk across Columbia Street and head toward 4th Street. In less than 2 minutes you'll be at Double Mountain Brewery.

Double Mountain Brewery, 8 4th St., Hood River, OR 97031; (541) 387-0042; DoubleMountainBrewery.com. While at Double Mountain you can't go wrong with pretty much any of their beers. Look for their Molten Lava Imperial IPA if you like big hoppy beers and it's available. Their India Red Ale is a hopped-up red ale that is perfect to pair with their pizza. Speaking of pizza, skip over everything else on the menu and order one. Sure, their other food is good, but the pizza is amazing. The Truffle Shuffle or the Jersey Pie will get your taste buds zinging. Split a salad if you're feeling hungry or order the truffle bruschetta. Make sure to sample some

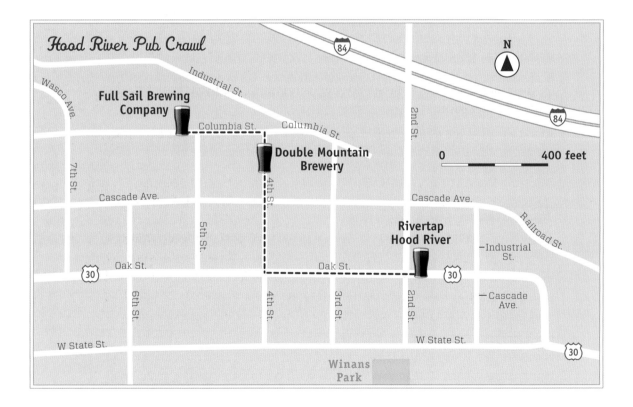

of their sour beers, such as Devil's Kriek or Rainier Kriek, after your meal if you like tart and fruity beers.

Head south on 4th Street and turn left onto Oak Street and walk 2 blocks until you reach Rivertap.

Rivertap Hood River, 112A Oak St., Hood River, OR 97031; (541) 386-9900; River Tap.com. If you're looking for a fun place to end your evening, Rivertap has you covered. With 11 taps of mostly Oregon beers, you'll be drinking well. If for some reason you're still hungry, check out their bratwurst sliders or Hell Burger. Wings are always a great evening choice and they offer 10 different sauces. Stay late and play some pool or visit on the weekends for a dance party. If at the end of your crawl, they still have a few beers you want to try, but know it's time to stop drinking, just bring a growler. You can take beer home with you from some of Oregon's best breweries.

Appendix

Paul's Porter, Long Brewing, Robust Porter, 129

Phat Matt's Kölsch, Phat Matt's Brewing Company, Kölsch, 178

Pils, Heater Allen Brewing, Czech Pilsner, 126

Pitch Black IPA, Widmer Brothers Brewing, Cascadian Dark Ale, 33

Rainier Kriek, Double Mountain Brewery, American Wild Ale, 100

Razz Wheat, Vertigo Brewing, American Wheat Ale, 75

Sahalie, The Ale Apothecary, Wild Ale, 162

Sang Noir, Cascade Brewing, Wild Ale, 9

Scotch Ale, Two Kilts Brewing Company, Scotch Ale, 72

Scottish Ale, Fearless Brewing Company, Scottish Ale, 70

Seizoen Bretta, Logsdon Farmhouse Ales, Saison, 103

Snake Bite Porter, Silver Moon Brewing, Robust Porter, 179

Steam Fired Stout, Fire Mountain Brew House, American Stout, 120

Terminal Gravity IPA, Terminal Gravity Brewing, IPA, 196

Tricerahops Double IPA, Ninkasi Brewing Company, Double IPA, 131

Two Cats Kölsch, Captured by Porches Brewing Company, Kölsch, 68

Urban Farmhouse Ale, The Commons Brewery, Saison, 14

Vanilla Porter, Klamath Basin Brewing Company, American Porter, 151

Vortex IPA, Fort George Brewery, IPA, 86

Wakonda Beachcomber Creme Ale, Wakonda Brewing Company, Cream Ale, 90

Wandelpad, Block 15 Restaurant & Brewery, Belgian Pale Ale, 117

Workhorse IPA, Laurelwood Brewing Company, IPA, 22

Index

MAY **1 3** 2013

Chicago Tribune

WON
FOR THE AGES

HOW THE CHICAGO CUBS BECAME THE
2016 WORLD SERIES CHAMPIONS

Chris Sweda/Chicago Tribune

Chicago Tribune

R. Bruce Dole, Publisher & Editor-in-Chief
Peter Kendall, Managing Editor
Colin McMahon, Associate Editor
George Papajohn, Investigations Editor
Margaret Holt, Standards Editor
John P. McCormick, Editorial Page Editor
Marie C. Dillon, Deputy Editorial Page Editor
Marcia Lythcott, Associate Editor, Commentary

Associate Managing Editors:
  Amy Carr, Features
  Robin Daughtridge, Photography
  Mark Jacob, Metro
  Cristi Kempf, Editing & Presentation
  Joe Knowles, Sports
  Mary Ellen Podmolik, Business

WON
FOR THE AGES

This book is book is available in quantity
at special discounts for your group or
organization.

For further information, contact:

Triumph Books LLC
814 North Franklin Street
Chicago, Illinois 60610
Phone: (312) 337-0747
www.triumphbooks.com

Printed in U.S.A.
ISBN: 978-1-62937-290-7

Content packaged by Mojo Media, Inc.
Joe Funk: Editor
Jason Hinman: Creative Director

Front and Back Cover Photos by
Brian Cassella/Chicago Tribune

Erin Hooley/Chicago Tribune

CONTENTS

FINALLY!

A season so special you didn't want to see it end

By PAUL SULLIVAN

This is not a dream. The Cubs did it. It was real, and it was spectacular. The most epic drought in sports history is over, and the Cubs are world champions. The Cubs won the 2016 World Series with an 8-7, 10-inning Game 7 victory over the Indians at Progressive Field. The triumph completed their climb back from a 3-1 Series deficit to claim their first championship since 1908.

Tears flowed across Cubs Nation after the final out, and fans responded with the world's biggest group hug, remembering all the loved ones who could only imagine what it would be like to experience this moment of pure bliss. The 1969 Cubs, the team that defined the word "collapse," were off the hook. So were their predecessors in '84 and 2003, who also came close only to suffer painful endings that scarred two generations of Cubs fans and kept the drought alive. The billy goat is gone, and the black cat too. And what was the name of the foul-ball dude? No matter. It was never really his fault, and now he's just a footnote in Cubs history.

The catchphrase Cubs fans uttered over the last century and change has been "just one before I die," a plea that fell on deaf ears decade after decade. Well, you can die in peace now, thanks to Joe Maddon's resilient club.

The road trips to cemeteries can now commence, where caps, balls, pennants and news clippings will be placed on markers of loved ones, letting them know they did it. The Cubs did it. It may look like the final scene of "Field of Dreams,"

a caravan of cars on a mission of closure.

The funny thing about waiting since 1908 for a championship was that when it finally happened, you didn't want the season to end. It was that much fun, from Kyle Schwarber's smashing of a windshield outside the outfield wall with a spring training home run to Wednesday night. This was a team in the truest sense of the word. These Cubs worked together and partied together, and some of them prayed together. The moments were so delicious you could watch them on an endless loop. Dexter Fowler's surprise return in Arizona. Anthony Rizzo hopping on top of the brick wall. Javier Baez's backhand swipe to pick off Conor Gillaspie at first in the National League Division Series. Kris Bryant's home run off the top of a cartoon car at AT&T Park. David Ross' final regular-season game at Wrigley. Aroldis Chapman's marathon outing to save the season in Game 5 of the Series.

It was one thing after another, and you loved every second.

When it came down to the final do-or-done game – as it surely had to – it was one for the ages, with more twists and turns than a San Francisco street.

They had it, they blew it, and then came a 17-minute rain delay.

After waiting 108 years, what was another 17 minutes?

It took a while, and it wasn't the way they'd drawn it up.

But they did it.

The Cubs did it. ●

Ben Zobrist celebrates his RBI double in the top of the 10th inning in Game 7. Zobrist was named the World Series MVP. (Brian Cassella/Chicago Tribune)

AT LAST!

Comeback of the century a fitting ending for Cubs and their fans

By PAUL SULLIVAN

PAUL SULLIVAN

It had to end like this, after a 108-year drought that consumed Cubs fans and vexed the experts for decade after decade.

It had to end with the Cubs beating the Indians 8-7 in ten innings in Game 7 of the World Series, in a ballpark occupied by thousands of road-tripping Cubs fans, on a summer-like night in November, in a season where everything fell into place from start to glorious finish.

And it had to end with a Cubbie Occurrence, a Grandpa goodbye, an eighth-inning collapse and a night more nerve-wracking than a presidential election.

The Cubs blew a four-run lead before coming back in extra innings before 38,104 shell-shocked fans at Progressive Field, culminating a comeback from a 3-1 Series deficit and kick-starting a party in Chicago that may not end until the last snowbank melts next spring.

After Aroldis Chapman gave up a game-tying, two-run homer to Rajai Davis in the eighth, Ben Zobrist's RBI double put the Cubs on top on the tenth, and Miguel Montero added a pinch-RBI single for insurance.

After the Indians closed to within one on Davis' RBI single off Carl Edwards Jr., Mike Montgomery induced a grounder to Kris Bryant, ending one of the craziest Game 7s in World Series annals.

Manager Joe Maddon's team lived up to its "we never quit" mantra, finishing off the Series with three straight wins to keep the Indians' 68-year drought alive while ending their own.

Zobrist was named Series MVP, finishing with a .357 average and the game-winning double.

Raise a glass, Cubs fans, for the ones who weren't here, and take a bow for keeping the faith when logic told you to give up.

You wouldn't want it any other way, would you?

This was going to be a classic all along. David Ross, playing in the final game of his career, figured that out during the Game 6 victory.

"I started thinking about it a lot more, just saying, 'Wow, my career is going to end in a Game 7 World Series, how lucky and fortunate am I to be with these guys?'" Ross said. "I kept watching them play and thinking, 'Man, I'm part of something special here. And I'm very, very lucky to be on this team.'"

Ross was involved in the Cubbie Occurrence – a wild pitch by Jon Lester in the fifth that ricocheted off Ross' mask to the backstop, allowing two runs to score and allowing the Indians to creep to within two runs. The worst fears of Cubs fans crept into the back of your mind, if only for a moment.

"Grandpa" Ross alleviated those fears a few minutes later, cranking a 402-foot home run off uber-reliever Andrew Miller, making him the oldest player to homer in a Series.

The sea of blue-and-white jerseys in the stands two hours before the first pitch made it apparent this was not going to be just another road game. The Cubs received a raucous ovation as they walked off the field at the end of batting practice.

But no one could've imagined just how huge the contingent was until Dexter Fowler led off the game with a 406-foot solo home run to center off Corey Kluber.

The ballpark erupted. Occupation Cleveland was underway.

Cubs manager Joe Maddon celebrates after the Cubs' World Series win. (Nuccio DiNuzzo/Chicago Tribune)

Kluber was mocked by fans in his own park in the first inning, and when the Indians put a graphic on the video board exhorting their fans to cheer, Cubs fans out-shouted them with a "Let's go, Cubs" chant.

Kyle Hendricks started and pitched well into the fifth, and the Cubs grabbed a 3-1 lead with a two-run fourth that starred Davis.

Third-base coach Gary Jones sent Bryant home on a pop to shallow center by Russell, and when Davis' throw to the plate was high, Bryant slid between the legs of catcher Roberto Perez to retake the lead. Davis got a bad jump on Willson Contreras' fly to deep center, resulting in an RBI double that made it 3-1.

Baez made up for two errors with a solo homer in the fifth, knocking out Kluber, and Bryant scored all the way from first on Rizzo's single later in the inning to make it 5-1.

Lester, Jake Arrieta and John Lackey had slowly marched out to the bullpen along with Ross in the second, looking like a scene from an old black-and-white war movie, with Lester playing John Wayne.

Maddon said before the game he didn't want to bring Lester in in a "dirty inning" but did just that with two outs and a man on in the fifth. Ross made a throwing error to put runners on second and third, and Lester bounced a wild pitch that went to the fence and allowed both runs to score, awakening the crowd.

Lester stiffened and got the Cubs into the eighth, when Maddon summoned Chapman, who proved his rubber arm wasn't made of rubber after all. Maddon took a beating on the internet for over-taxing Chapman, but the Cubs saved him from being the designated goat.

The blown save was only a prelude to an ending that will live on forever, on a night Chicago waited 108 years to witness. ●

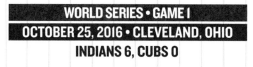

SWINGIN' AMISS

Kluber, 2 relievers strike out 15 Cubs in opener

By Mark Gonzales and David Haugh

The slow retreats to the dugout and Jon Lester's stares at plate umpire Larry Vanover seemed as tedious as the 71-year wait since the Cubs' last World Series.

There was no equalizer for the Cubs on a night when Kyle Schwarber made a personally triumphant return from injury and Jason Heyward was left on the bench.

The biggest reason for the Cubs' failure was the precision of Corey Kluber, who made the Indians' return to the World Series for the first time since 1997 a joyful event.

Kluber pitched with remote-control sharpness as he struck out nine in six-plus innings of a 6-0 victory in Game 1 of the World Series at Progressive Field.

The Cubs, embarking on the final lap of their mission to win the franchise's first World Series since 1908, couldn't solve the darting pitches of Kluber to both sides of the plate. Five of Kluber's first six strikeouts were on called third strikes as the 2014 American League Cy Young Award winner established a Series record with eight strikeouts in the first three innings.

"That's the first time I've seen him, and he was pretty nasty," Javy Baez said.

Adding to the Cubs' misery was that the Indians scored two runs in the first on Jose Ramirez's 45-foot single and Lester hitting Brandon Guyer with a pitch with the bases loaded.

That immediately took some of the hoopla out of the Cubs' optimism following their 103-victory season and postseason triumphs over the Giants and Dodgers.

Indians catcher Roberto Perez put the game out of reach with his second home run -- a three-run shot off Hector Rondon in the eighth.

Schwarber, who didn't believe that returning from two torn ligaments in his left knee was possible until six days ago, wore a brace that didn't seem to harness him too much while handling the designated hitter duties.

But Cubs president Theo Epstein stopped short of declaring him ready to play the field, so the Cubs will have him available only for pinch hitting when the series shifts to Wrigley Field.

"If it's appropriate, we can always go back to the doctors and take a fresh look at it," Epstein said. "But for right now, it's not a consideration."

The Cubs mounted threats in the seventh and eighth innings against formidable Indians reliever Andrew Miller but came away empty. Miller struck out Addison Russell and David Ross to get out of a bases-loaded jam in the seventh and struck out Schwarber with two runners on to end the eighth.

Cleveland starting pitcher Corey Kluber throws the first pitch to Dexter Fowler in Game 1 of the World Series. Kluber pitched six innings and struck out nine Cubs in the Indians' 6-0 win. (Nuccio DiNuzzo/Chicago Tribune)

Miller was forced to throw a season-high 46 pitches in his two innings.

Lester, who entered the game with a 3-0 record and 0.43 ERA in World Series play and had allowed only two runs in 21 postseason innings this month, disagreed with Vanover on several pitches that led to two-out walks to Mike Napoli and Carlos Santana to load the bases and set up the Indians' first two runs.

Nobody told Kluber that October supposedly belonged to his more experienced counterpart.

Instead, Kluber played the role of poised veteran – and the Indians indirectly can thank Cubs general manager Jed Hoyer. Hoyer was the Padres general manager in 2010 when he traded Kluber, a Double-A prospect projected as a reliever, in a three-way deal with the Cardinals and Indians that brought outfielder Ryan Ludwick to San Diego. Never has that move paid off bigger for the Indians.

"I don't think anybody is hanging his head in here," Anthony Rizzo said in the Cubs clubhouse. "Give (Kluber) credit. He hit his spots. ●

LEAVIN' EVEN

Batmen return as Cubs square Series and head home

By MARK GONZALES

Jake Arrieta's dominating performance was just what the doctor ordered after the Cubs had dropped the World Series opener.

Now if they can compensate for the potential full-time loss of Kyle Schwarber without a designated hitter for Games 3, 4 and 5 of the World Series at Wrigley Field their championship prospects may swell.

In an effort reminiscent of some of his starts during his 2015 National League Cy Young Award season, Arrieta didn't allow a hit until he gave up two in the sixth inning. And left-hander Mike Montgomery provided timely support in relief for the Cubs to beat the Indians 5-1 at chilly Progressive Field to even the best-of-seven series at one game apiece.

Schwarber continued his amazing recovery from left knee surgery with two RBI singles while serving as the DH for the second consecutive game.

"You feel like he has been here all year," Dexter Fowler said.

Schwarber hadn't played since April 7 after tearing two ligaments and was believed to be sidelined until spring training.

The Cubs knocked out nine hits and patiently drew eight walks. But in the next three games

Schwarber likely will be limited to pinch hitting with no DH in the National League park.

Manager Joe Maddon has been encouraged by Schwarber's sharp eye as well as his mobility, adding that Schwarber could practice in the outfield between games if medically cleared.

"There's nothing about watching him that tells me he's inhibited right now," Maddon said.

For his part, Arrieta seemed immune to the blustery conditions Wednesday night as he declined to wear a long-sleeved shirt under his jersey and rode a stationary bike between innings as he dominated the Indians after issuing two walks with two outs in the first. Jason Kipnis got the Indians' first hit, legging out a one-out double in the sixth.

"I kind of had my foot on the gas a little too much at the start, trying to do more than I needed to," Arrieta said. "Then I got back to executing good pitches toward the bottom of the zone."

Montgomery again showed his value as he induced Jose Ramirez to ground back to the mound to get Arrieta out of a jam in the sixth after a second hit. In the seventh, Montgomery struck out three -- capped when he whiffed Carlos Santana on a breaking pitch with runners at first and second.

Jake Arrieta was solid in Game 2 of the World Series, tossing 5⅔ innings, striking out six and picking up the win for the Cubs. (Nuccio DiNuzzo/Chicago Tribune)

After being blanked in Game 1, Maddon opted for a lineup that featured right-handed batters Jorge Soler and rookie Willson Contreras against Trevor Bauer.

Four Cubs starters 25 or younger -- Kris Bryant, Javier Baez, Schwarber and Addison Russell -- collected hits.

"They're scratching the surface of how good they can be," Maddon said.

The Cubs worked Bauer for several deep counts, while the Indians committed a few untimely miscues.

Anthony Rizzo smacked a double down the right-field line in the first, and Bryant scored easily from first when right fielder Lonnie Chisenhall threw to second base instead of toward home.

Ben Zobrist fouled off six consecutive pitches during a 10-pitch at-bat in the first. Rizzo helped give Arrieta a larger cushion when he fouled off five consecutive pitches before working reliever Zach McAllister for a walk with one out in the fifth.

"We wore them down," Fowler said. "If it's not one guy, it's another guy. Rizz was that guy."

Since Rizzo broke out of his slump with a home run using Matt Szczur's bat in the fifth inning of Game 4 of the NLCS, he hasn't looked back. In his last five games, he's 8-for-21 with three doubles, two home runs, five runs and six RBIs.

"I'm going to ride this out with Szczur's bat all the way," Rizzo said. "Hail, Szczur." ●

Kyle Schwarber continued to make his impact felt in his return to the lineup, getting two hits and two RBIs in the Game 2 victory. (Brian Cassella/Chicago Tribune)

WORLD SERIES • GAME 3
OCTOBER 28, 2016 • CHICAGO, ILLINOIS
INDIANS 1, CUBS 0

NOTHING IN RETURN

Tomlin and bullpen shut door on Cubs in Wrigley's first World Series game since 1945

By PAUL SULLIVAN

From Billy Williams' ceremonial first pitch to a last-gasp rally in the bottom of the ninth, fans savored every morsel of Wrigley Field's first World Series game in 71 years.

But good karma was not in the cards for the Cubs, and a crowd of 41,703 could not will them to win on a historic night just because it felt right.

The Indians pulled out a 1-0 win and went ahead 2-1 in the Series, assuring Chicago will not have a Cubs clincher at Wrigley.

Even as the Cubs offense wheezed and coughed against Josh Tomlin and three relievers, the idea of a not-so-secret weapon was in the back of everyone's minds.

As the zeros mounted up on the ancient center-field scoreboard, it seemed as though the entire city was simply waiting for Kyle Schwarber to come off the bench and save the day, just as it was written in the Gospel of Maddon.

But when Schwarber finally appeared in the eighth and received his expected Wrigley roar of approval, the result was not what the script doctor ordered. Indians reliever Bryan Shaw turned Schwarber's bat into a bunch of toothpicks, inducing him to hit a soft pop to short.

Miracle whipped.

"I wasn't trying to hit the ball out of the ballpark," Schwarber said. "I just wanted to hit the ball hard. ... If it gets in the air it's probably gone, but that's not in my mind."

The Cubs threatened in the ninth on a leadoff single by Anthony Rizzo and a two-out error by Mike Napoli on Jason Heyward's grounder. But with the tying and winning runs in scoring position, Cody Allen struck out Javier Baez to end the night with a whisper.

"That's the way it is," Rizzo said. "We knew it was not going to be easy. We've been in this situation before, being down in a series. We've just got to come back and do what we do."

The Cubs had several chances, but a lack of hustle may have spoiled one.

After a rousing seventh-inning stretch performance by Bill Murray, who reminded fans it was last call for beer, Lonnie Chisenhall misplayed Jorge Soler's fly to the right-field corner, turning it into a triple.

Soler seemed to forget he was playing in a World Series, watching the ball before jogging down the line until Chisenhall missed it, only then turning on the burners.

Soler thought it was a foul ball and said he "didn't think so" when asked if he could've scored had he run hard.

Would he have liked to have found out?

Javier Baez strikes out to end Game 3, a 1-0 loss for the Cubs. It was a frustrating night for Baez, who went hitless in four at-bats. (Brian Cassella/Chicago Tribune)

"Of course I would," he said. "But I don't think I would have gone any farther if I did (run hard)."

Shaw fell behind Baez 2-0 before getting Baez to ground out to short, stranding Soler on third and ending the threat.

After all the pregame hype, the Game 3 loss was tough to swallow. It was apparent this would be a day unlike any in recent memory for Cubs fans, a day most of them had been waiting a lifetime to witness.

The Cubs were actually playing in a World Series game at the corner of Clark and Addison.

"People are so happy and in such a great mood," President Theo Epstein said before the game. "Families are connecting with one another, generations. ... It's so many things on so many levels."

Epstein was told there was no way out now. The Cubs had to win this thing.

"Can't screw it up," he said with a grin. "We better win now.

"Wouldn't want to taint the memory for anyone."

A memorable night, yes, but the result was one they'd all rather forget. ●

WORLD SERIES • GAME 4
OCTOBER 29, 2016 • CHICAGO, ILLINOIS
INDIANS 7, CUBS 2

PARTY CRASHERS

For second straight game, Indians stifle Cubs bats

By DAVID HAUGH

The disaster ended fittingly at Wrigley Field, with Javy Baez hitting a feeble grounder to the pitcher's mound for the final out of an ugly 7-2 loss to the Indians.

There were no loud boos, a few jeers, but mostly stunned silence from the crowd of 41,706. Anxiety seldom shouts down anybody.

What just happened? Will the real Chicago Cubs please stand up? Anybody seen Kris Bryant?

Save the slogans and forget the mantras. Not even Cubs manager Joe Maddon can talk his team out of this mess, a 3-1 World Series deficit after a devastating defeat in Game 4. The Cubs will have to hit again before anybody takes their hopes for an epic comeback seriously. Baseball history says it can happen but the Cubs have no business looking further into the future than nine innings. They have lost the right to look ahead, not to mention their confidence at the plate. They have starters Jon Lester, Jake Arrieta and Kyle Hendricks prepared to pitch three consecutive gems but it won't matter if the Cubs can't score runs to support them.

"We made mistakes but we have to do more offensively to give us a chance," Maddon said.

On a night actor Vince Vaughn sang during the seventh-inning stretch, the Indians reprised their role as party crashers. The Cubs still haven't won a World Series game at Wrigley Field since Oct. 8, 1945.

Maddon can avoid visiting what he calls "Negative Town," but welcome to reality: The Indians need only need one more victory with two of the next three games scheduled for Progressive Field – and the unhittable Corey Kluber looming if Game 7 is necessary. If the Cubs can pull off this unlikely feat, it will be the best history they have made yet.

The Cubs can insist they remain the best team in baseball but the Indians arrived the hottest. Unseasonable temperatures for late October made it 59 degrees at game time but Cubs bats stayed as cold as January. While the Indians successfully swung for contact, the Cubs too often tried to hit the ball into Evanston. Maybe the Cubs' talented group of twentysomethings suddenly realized how big the stage was and froze or maybe they have tried too hard not to suck. Whatever, they now stand one loss away from having all offseason to ponder the reasons why. This is indisputable: For the second straight postseason, the Cubs picked the worst possible time to slump.

Pitching on three days' rest, Kluber looked more efficient than overpowering, giving up just one run in six innings. Kluber struck out six, despite his fastball and breaking pitches lacking the sharpness seen in Game 1. He now has given up three earned runs in 30 $\frac{1}{3}$ postseason innings. Only Cleveland sports immortality awaits.

Willson Contreras goes down swinging in Game 4, one of three strikeouts for Contreras on the night. The offense struggled for the Cubs once again, as they were limited to two runs and seven hits in the loss. (Brian Cassella/Chicago Tribune)

Cubs counterpart John Lackey struggled with command and composure, unraveling in second inning. Throughout October, they consistently have viewed Lackey through the prism of the past decade rather than the past six weeks or months.

Lackey gave up the 381-foot home run to Carlos Santana that erased an early 1-0 Cubs lead. He failed to strike out Kluber and gave up Kluber's swinging bunt single that scored the go-ahead run. He lacked the Lackey-like performance on which the Cubs had counted.

The Indians chased history by preparing their ace to take the mound three times in the World Series and the Cubs stubbornly stuck to the rotation they set last December.

Before the first pitch, actor Jeff Garlin took the microphone at home plate and shouted: "Last night, it was too quiet. Tonight, we make noise!"

Cubs bats, however, stayed far too silent, again. ●

WORLD SERIES • GAME 5
OCTOBER 30, 2016 • CHICAGO, ILLINOIS
CUBS 3, INDIANS 2

NOW IT'S 2 OR DIE

Lester, Chapman hold off Indians, force Game 6

By Paul Sullivan and Colleen Kane

The Cubs could not do this the easy way, of course. One-hundred and eight years of waiting would not allow that to happen.

Riding the arms of Jon Lester and Aroldis Chapman, the Cubs hung on for a tense 3-2 victory over the Indians in Game 5 of the World Series to keep hope alive and send the Series back to Cleveland for Game 6.

The Cubs are attempting to become the first team to escape a 3-1 Series deficit since the 1985 Royals.

After 57 postgame parties at Wrigley during the regular season and four more in the division series and league championship series, the Cubs left their special party room unused during the first two home games of the World Series.

Making matters worse, the Indians threatened to throw their own clinching party on Sunday night at Wrigley, prolonging the Cubs' championship drought and ending their own.

"A lot of people in Chicago had not seen a World Series win in 71 years," Anthony Rizzo said. "I'm sure it was emotional. It was emotional for us. Seeing (David Ross) each at-bat ... talking to him before the game just trying to hold it all in. This could be his last

start. That last at-bat ... we love each other."

A three-run fourth inning highlighted by Kris Bryant's leadoff home run saved the season, while Chapman escaped a self-induced jam in the eighth to avoid permanent goat status in Chicago sports history.

"Whatever it takes," Rizzo said. "Chappy going out there for six innings, or whatever it was. Lester grinding his way through. It was big for us."

Chapman's appearance marked the first time since May 17, 2012 that he entered a game as early as the seventh.

Manager Joe Maddon had asked Chapman before the game if he could turn in an old-school save that flashed back to the Goose Gossage era.

"I told him I'm ready," Chapman said. "I mentally prepared myself and physically prepared myself to come in as early as possible. I was ready to come in at a moment's notice."

With a runner on second with one out in the seventh after a single and passed ball by Willson Contreras, Maddon called on Chapman to clock in early, stealing a page from the Terry Francona "Miller Time" playbook.

After getting out of the seventh, Chapman took

Aroldis Chapman is hugged by Willson Contreras after the series-saving Game 5 win. Chapman was superb in relief, going 2⅔ innings to close out the game. (Brian Cassella/Chicago Tribune)

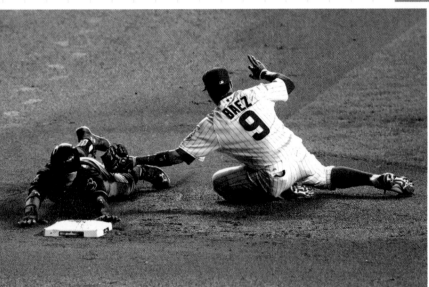

a nap in the eighth and allowed Rajai Davis to reach by neglecting to cover first on a grounder that Rizzo snagged. Davis wound up stealing second and third with ease before Chapman caught Lindor looking to end the inning.

When Chapman struck out Ramirez on a 101-mph fastball for the final out, the ballpark exploded one last time.

"That's what you do when you get the lead and have a closer like that," Indians shortstop Francisco Lindor said. "You get the lead, put him in the game and let him ride.

"We wanted to finish it here, but it's part of the game. We know they have a good team. We knew it wasn't going to be easy."

Considering how much these two franchises have been through, easy was never going to be an option. ●

Above: Javier Baez tags Francisco Lindor, preventing the Cleveland shortstop from stealing second base in the 6th inning of Game 5. (Chris Sweda/Chicago Tribune) Opposite: Jason Heyward swipes third base in the eighth inning of Game 5, one of two stolen bases for Heyward in the inning. (Brian Cassella/Chicago Tribune)

WORLD SERIES • GAME 6
NOVEMBER 1, 2016 • CLEVELAND, OHIO
CUBS 9, INDIANS 3

CARRY THAT WAIT

Early rally takes air out of Indians, sets up grand finale

By David Haugh

In a play that symbolized the Cubs' state of mind, mild-mannered Ben Zobrist pummeled Indians catcher Roberto Perez at the plate with the kind of violent hit on a defenseless receiver that usually draws a flag in the NFL.

Zobrist delivered a forearm shiver to Perez's chest, knocking his helmet off and bowling him over with a full head of steam built while scoring from first on a fly ball the Indians botched.

Talk about crashing a party.

The first-inning sequence in a 9-3 victory at Progressive Field stunned a nervous crowd of 38,116 into silence and announced, loudly, that the Cubs had come ready to rise to the occasion. Facing a win-or-go-home scenario, the Cubs arrived with an intensity the Indians failed to match. Zobrist smacking Anthony Rizzo's hand with more emotion than he has shown all season only underscored the impact of the collision. Passion is contagious too.

By the time Addison Russell hit the first Series grand slam in Cubs history in the third, Cubs fans knew. Everybody knew. From Zobrist's zealous reaction to Russell's expressive response rounding the bases, the Cubs made clear from the get-go they had no intention of going home. One of the biggest

innings of the season occurred in the first, when the Cubs scored three runs and locked-in starter Jake Arrieta struck out two of his first three hitters, as if to say, "I've got this."

Arrieta had better stuff than command, keeping the Indians hitless until Jason Kipnis led off the fourth with a double and gutting through 5 $\frac{2}{3}$ innings. Before the game, manager Joe Maddon compared Arrieta to an artist, and while the pitcher's effort wasn't necessarily aesthetically pleasing, the Cubs always will consider it something to admire.

"He was outstanding," Maddon said.

Improving to 2-0 on the road in the Series, Arrieta struck out nine and gave up two runs and three hits. A 96 mph fastball on his first strikeout showed how strong he felt, a reminder of how the Cubs started planning for this start in March. There were summer games when Arrieta objected to coming out before he was ready, but nobody's complaining in November – not after he helped force a Game 7 that the Cubs enter with a renewed sense of confidence.

Maddon oddly called on closer Aroldis Chapman again in the seventh with two out and a 7-2 lead, a decision that stretched the meaning of unorthodox.

Kris Bryant watches his solo home run off of Indians starter Josh Tomlin in the first inning of Game 6. (Chris Sweda/Chicago Tribune)

The word "unnecessary" first came to mind. Only 48 hours earlier, Chapman threw 42 pitches, yet here he was again in what could qualify as mop-up duty.

"I thought the game could have been lost right there if we did not take care of it properly," Maddon said.

A World Series Game 7 between the Cubs and Indians sounds less like an agenda than a movie script, the perfect Hollywood plot with an ending nobody believes but everybody deserves. The only certainty is that destiny will play a starring role. As even casual fans know by now, the Indians have gone since 1948 without a World Series title. The Cubs call that a good start, having not celebrated a championship since 1908.

"It's just correct and apt that we'd go seven games," Maddon said correctly.

Thank you, baseball gods. ●

Above: Jake Arrieta struck out nine batters in 5⅔ innings in Game 6. (John J. Kim/Chicago Tribune) Opposite: Addison Russell is greeted at home plate after hitting a grand slam in the third inning to give the Cubs a 7-0 lead. (Brian Cassella/Chicago Tribune)

WORLD SERIES • GAME 7
NOVEMBER 2, 2016 • CLEVELAND, OHIO
CUBS 8, INDIANS 7 (10 INNINGS)

LET IT REIGN

Unforgettable Game 7 ends a 108-year wait

By David Haugh

Standing at second base after his 10th-inning double drove in the go-ahead run in Game 7 of the World Series, Ben Zobrist pumped his fist as the Cubs dugout went crazy.

Bedlam also ensued on the field as players celebrated an 8-7 victory over the Indians, ending the 108-year wait, at last.

For generations of fans, those will be the enduring images of Chicago sports for years to come. None of us will live long enough to see anything better, any moment packed with more meaning than the Cubs celebrating their first World Series since 1908. This is the view from the top of the sports world, the center of baseball utopia, a place where doubt and dread and devastation no longer reside, a place where the World Series-winning Cubs and their loyal fans now occupy.

Just before midnight at Progressive Field, 108 years of suffering ended, officially marking the greatest moment in Chicago sports history. Holy cow, they did it, Harry. Hey, hey, Jack, the Cubs are world champions. Click your heels together in heaven, Ronnie. The wait is over, Ernie, after all those seasons you believed when nobody else did.

The last great American sports story has an ending now, the happiest one ever, pleasing baseball romantics and fulfilling the lives of so many Cubs fans. Many of the longest-suffering ones will say they can die happy now, no exaggeration. The younger fans who consider Ryne Sandberg old will expect more championships to follow, and they will. The rest of us can celebrate the death of redundancy when discussing the Cubs because this forever changes their tradition.

It seems impossible to write yet even harder to fathom. The Cubs have won the World Series. That is no longer a punch line or part of a movie pitch. The Cubs have won the World Series without pigs flying or Hell freezing over. That might not sink in for Cubs fans until they stop smiling maybe sometime next summer. Or maybe never.

Nothing came easily. The Cubs waited out a 17-minute rain delay before the 10th. They paid for Joe Maddon's unnecessary use of closer Aroldis Chapman, who threw 20 pitches 24 hours earlier with a five-run lead. Chapman came on in the eighth with the Cubs four outs from history and his weary left arm gave up three runs   a double to Brandon Guyer and a home run to Rajai Davis   to send the game into extra innings. Every jaw back in Chicago hit the floor and every blood pressure rose. This felt like a cruel joke to Cubs fans.

Third baseman Kris Bryant cheers after throwing out Michael Martinez for the final out of Game 7.
(Nuccio DiNuzzo/Chicago Tribune)

But Zobrist, the Series' most valuable player, bailed his manager out.

The wait is over, at last. Has any sports league ever crowned a champion whose fan base deserved a title more than the Cubs'? Has Major League Baseball ever played a more significant World Series game than this one?

This is the championship the sports world has been waiting for longer than any other, the one that establishes Chicago's richest local legacy.

The Cubs close generation gaps, connect neighborhoods and clear racial or ethnic barriers, all with a capital C. Their reach extends beyond baseball, across countries and continents, and into the hearts of millions worldwide who were overjoyed the lovable losers finally won it all.

Next year was here. It really did happen. ●

Above: Javier Baez homers in the fifth inning of Game 7 to give the Cubs a 4-1 lead. (Nuccio DiNuzzo/Chicago Tribune) Opposite: Kris Bryant scores on an Addison Russell sacrifice fly in the fourth. (Brian Cassella/Chicago Tribune)

2016 SEASON

SWEET 16 FROM '16

16 memorable victories that paved road to playoffs

By MARK GONZALES

April 7: After Kyle Schwarber's season-ending knee injury in the second inning, the Cubs storm back from a 4-2 deficit to score 12 runs and roll to a 14-6 win over the Diamondbacks.

April 21: (Right) Kris Bryant hits two home runs and drives in six runs, but he's upstaged as Jake Arrieta throws the second no-hitter of his career in a 16-0 pounding of the Reds.

May 8: (Page 36) The Cubs frustrate the Nationals by walking Bryce Harper six times, and Javier Baez homers in the bottom of the 13th for a 4-3 win that caps a four-game sweep.

May 20: Jason Heyward scampers nearly 90 feet to make an over-the-shoulder catch of Denard Span's drive before crashing into the fence in right-center and suffering a deep bruise near his right ribs and hip. Heyward's catch in the first sparks an 8-1 win in San Francisco.

May 25: Arrieta allows four earned runs for the first time in 30 starts, but Bryant hits a three-run homer in the sixth and Hector Rondon retires Jedd Gyorko with the tying and winning runs on base to preserve a 9-8 win over the Cardinals.

June 19: Willson Contreras homers on his first major-league swing as the Cubs slug five home runs en route to a 10-5 win over the Pirates, completing a three-game sweep and extending their lead in the NL Central to 12 1/2 games.

June 28: In what became known as the "Left Field Game," relievers Travis Wood, Spencer Patton and Pedro Strop each play left in the late stages of a 7-2, 15-inning victory over the Reds.

July 10: In the closest thing to a "must-win" game, the Cubs snap a five-game losing streak with a 6-5 win in Pittsburgh and end the first half with a seven-game lead.

July 27: Aroldis Chapman makes his Cubs debut, hitting triple digits on the radar gun and striking out two in the 9th inning of an 8-1 win over the White Sox at Wrigley Field.

July 31: Pitcher Jon Lester comes off the bench to execute a squeeze bunt in the bottom of the 12th for a 7-6 win over the Mariners after trailing 6-0 through three innings.

Aug. 16: (Page 38 bottom left) First baseman Anthony Rizzo steps on the wall along the right-field line at Wrigley Field, reaches into the stands to snare a foul ball and manages to retain his balance in a gold-medal-worthy performance as the Cubs coast to a 4-1 win over the Brewers.

Aug. 18: (Page 38 top left) Bryant fortifies his MVP credentials with a 5-for-5, two-homer, five-RBI performance in a 9-6 win over the Brewers.

Aug. 26: Bryant fuels a 6-4 comeback win with a homer in the eighth and a two-r un shot in the 10th to earn chants of "MVP, MVP" at Dodger Stadium.

Aug. 29: Trailing the Pirates by one entering the bottom of the 13th, the Cubs avoid their first three-game losing streak of the second half by rallying on RBI singles by Rizzo and Miguel Montero for an 8-7 win.

Sept. 12: Kyle Hendricks pitches eight no-hit innings before allowing a home run to the Cardinals' Jeremy Hazelbaker, while manager Joe Maddon adds some spice to the Cubs' 4-1 win by cussing out umpire Joe West after getting ejected.

Sept. 16: (Page 39) The NL Central title was clinched about 16 hours earlier with a late-night Cardinals loss to the Giants, and Montero puts everyone in a festive mood at Wrigley by homering in the 10th for a 5-4 victory over the Brewers.

Nancy Stone/Chicago Tribune

Antonio Perez/Chicago Tribune

Nuccio DiNuzzo/Chicago Tribune

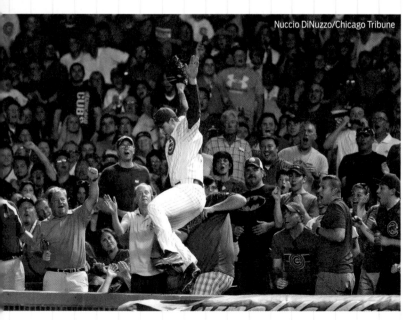

Chris Sweda/Chicago Tribune

Flame-throwing closer Aroldis Chapman was exactly what the Cubs needed to fortify the back end of the bullpen. (Chris Sweda/Staff)

ALL THE RIGHT MOVES

Dec. 8, 2015: The Cubs announce the signing of two veteran free agents, pitcher John Lackey and infielder/ outfielder Ben Zobrist. Lackey adds depth and experience to the starting rotation and Zobrist's versatility provides manager Joe Maddon's with a multitude of lineup options.

Dec. 15, 2015: Outfielder Jason Heyward, one of the premier free agents on the market, signs an eight-year, $184 million contract with the Cubs.

Dec. 18, 2015: Starlin Castro, one of the last holdovers from the previous regime, is traded to the Yankees for pitcher Adam Warren. The deal opens up playing time for budding star Javier Baez.

Feb. 25, 2016: Despite reports that he had already agreed to join the Baltimore Orioles, center fielder and leadoff man Dexter Fowler signs a free-agent deal to return to the Cubs.

June 7, 2016: Albert Almora Jr., the first draft pick of the Theo Epstein era, makes his major-league debut with the Cubs. In two stints with the big club, Almora bats .277 in 47 games and shines defensively in the outfield.

June 17, 2016: With David Ross hampered by the after-effects of a concussion, the Cubs recall catcher Willson Contreras from the minors. Two days later, Contreras hits a home run in his first major-league at-bat.

July 20, 2016: The Cubs acquire veteran left-handed pitcher Mike Montgomery from the Seattle Mariners. Montgomery becomes a valuable part of the pitching staff, making five spot starts in the second half.

July 25, 2016: The Cubs trade four prospects to the Yankees in exchange for flame-throwing left-handed closer Aroldis Chapman. The deal is controversial due to Chapman's off-the-field issues, but he goes on to save 16 games and post a 1.01 ERA for the Cubs in the final months of the season.

THEO EPSTEIN

Best-Laid Plans

Former boy wonder Epstein finds perspective as he puts team in position to make history

By TED GREGORY

The day before the Chicago Cubs announced Theo Epstein's five-year contract extension, he sat in a vacant Wrigley Field and considered how he has changed since 2002. That year the Boston Red Sox made him the youngest general manager in baseball history.

"I think I believed a lot more of my own bull... back then than I do now," the Cubs' president of baseball operations said, laughing. "The world is gray and I used to love making it black or white."

Back then, he was the Yale grad and fervent Red Sox fan from Brookline, Mass., who was the team's third choice to be general manager. Then he led the Red Sox to their first World Series championship in 86 years. Three years later, they won it again.

But glee deteriorated in Boston, and Epstein came to Chicago in 2011. Today, he is a 42-year-old husband and father who plays rock guitar for charity and leads the Cubs on an odyssey that might carry more angst and euphoria than the Red Sox championship run of 2004.

The Cubs, who have not won a World Series since 1908, are favorites to win it all this year -- champs instead of chumps. Giddy anticipation is at epic levels among a global fan base that deserves a lifetime achievement award for optimism and perseverance.

While all that swirls, the man who with two lieutenants assembled the team is trying to maintain perspective, something he said he has gained over the years while he nurtured his empathetic side. He also has come to terms with his internal struggle over focusing his extraordinary mind and work ethic on a game; at least that's what he says.

"That's definitely something that I've felt and thought about and articulated to my friends," Epstein told the Tribune in a 90-minute conversation at Wrigley.

"They always have really good answers for me," Epstein added, laughing again, "which is that in the right situation, you could impact a lot of people in a lot of positive ways by rebuilding a team that faces adversity and triumphs in the end."

Watching from the bleachers disguised in a fake mustache, Theo Epstein (bottom right) stands for the seventh inning stretch during the Cubs' September 16 game against the Milwaukee Brewers. (Brian Cassella/Chicago Tribune)

His connection to baseball

Epstein, of course, views baseball as much more than a kid's game, although it resonated deeply in him as a very small child, before he can remember. His parents tell him stories.

His father and passionate Red Sox fan, Leslie Epstein, remembers 4-year-old Theo routinely hitting balls out of the Upper West Side park they visited when the family lived in New York, where Theo Epstein was born.

After the Epsteins moved in 1978 to Brookline, where they would walk to Fenway Park, young Theo learned to keep score at Red Sox games.

His Little League coach came to the family apartment after a season to thank him for his strategy help. Once, Leslie Epstein recalled, he and 8-year-old Theo were watching a Red Sox game on TV and the boy pointed out that the center fielder should move to the left three steps.

The next pitch was hit barely out of reach to the center fielder's left.

Baseball, Theo Epstein said, has an "intrinsic connection" to him on many levels.

"Not to get too flowery about it," Epstein said, "it exists in its own, little alternative world, kind of like in a way that language does or math does, where it makes sense in its own universe."

He said he loves the symmetry, the action, the timelessness, even "the unknown" of baseball. He loves how it reflects the real world's adversity and provides escape.

"You're allowed into it when you're playing, or watching or working in it," he said, "and it's really fulfilling ... you can gain these little insights and sort of chip away at the unknown in ways that are really rewarding, well, useful to my job now. But also just rewarding to help you see the game in maybe a slightly different way than you saw it the day before."

Successful family

Epstein is a twin, one of three sets in his lineage. His mother, Ilene, has run a high-end women's boutique in Brookline for nearly 40 years with her twin sister and a friend. His grandfather, Philip Epstein, wrote the Oscar-winning screenplay for "Casablanca" with his twin brother, Julius.

Epstein's father is a Boston University English professor, Rhodes scholar and author of 11 works of fiction. Epstein's sister, Anya, is a television writer and producer whose projects include "Homicide: Life on the Street."

His brother, Paul, whom Theo and Leslie call "the saint of the family," is a social worker at Brookline High School who raised millions of dollars to build a teen center there before starting a foundation with Theo.

Epstein and his wife, Marie Whitney, have two young sons. She runs a women's jacket boutique that donates a school uniform to a girl in need in Africa for every jacket sold. The family lives a few blocks from Wrigley, allowing Epstein to walk between home and the ballpark.

In conversation after conversation, those who know Epstein talk about his intelligence.

While working full time with the San Diego Padres, Epstein earned a law degree at the University of San Diego but rarely attended classes. Instead, he traded Padres tickets for class notes.

Epstein loves to play guitar, and in fact, his jamming as part of Hot Stove Cool Music events in Chicago and Boston has helped raise $8 million for the Foundation To Be Named Later, the nonprofit he and his brother created in 2005 to help urban youth and families.

Theo Epstein orchestrated a surprise moment when Dexter Fowler re-signed with the Cubs and arrived unannounced at the Cubs' spring training camp. (Armando L. Sanchez/Chicago Tribune)

Though his passion is baseball, he may have been a better soccer player and enjoys kicking field goals on the football field.

His wit is sharp and he does hilarious, spot-on impersonations of friends and relatives, occasionally veering into obnoxious, frat-boy humor. One of the most repeated Theo Epstein anecdotes centers on those times when he and his management group would launch golf balls after hours in the Boston Red Sox offices.

In 2004, he showed up at a card game in a San Diego pitcher's hotel suite while the team was playing in Boston. The pitcher, David Wells, was a wine connoisseur.

After Wells gave an eloquent discourse on a particular wine worth several hundred dollars, Epstein grabbed the bottle and tipped it in his mouth while pretending to crank a handle near his left ear. After a few moments, he spit the wine into a bucket.

"Yeah," Epstein said, laughing, "that's one of my go-to moves after a few drinks when I want to make fun of people who drink expensive wine. You had to be there, though."

Sam Kennedy, who played third base while Epstein played second and pitched on their high school baseball team, now is president of the Red Sox. He dismisses Epstein's contention that he is an introvert who occasionally engages in extroversion.

"This whole introvert thing has evolved with his celebrity," Kennedy said in an email. "He gave as much (crap) out as he took, if not more."

Unraveling in Boston

As a freshman at Yale, Epstein landed a summer internship with the Baltimore Orioles, where he worked for the next three summers and made his mark by proposing an All-Star Game tribute in 1993 to the Negro League, a subject that had intrigued Epstein since childhood.

He attracted the attention of Orioles CEO Larry Lucchino, who took the same job with the San Diego Padres in 1995 and brought Epstein there that year.

Epstein worked in the entertainment and public relations departments and started hanging around general manager Kevin Towers' office, expressing an interest in baseball operations.

The general manager gave the kid different projects. Epstein excelled at all of them. Towers recommended Epstein get a law degree and made him baseball operations director.

In 2002, Lucchino became president and CEO of the Red Sox. Again, he brought Epstein with him. As assistant general manager, Epstein led the search for a new general manager, "which I completely screwed up because the two guys I recommended turned the job down," he said.

The position fell to Epstein, who recalled feeling ready to take on "the baseball part" of the job.

"But, on the personal side," he said, "my emotional intelligence wasn't what it needed to be. I was still kind of holding on to the college thing," and, yes, was an introvert. He called those early years "almost a fraternity or a boiler room" where the group attacked their jobs and their fun relentlessly.

In that "really playful culture, really informal culture, self-deprecating culture," Epstein developed a hybrid approach that blended thorough statistical analysis and deep personal research on ballplayers. He even created a video game that tests how quickly a player's mind adjusts to a pitch.

The result was two World Series championships in four years. After the first, Epstein gave his World

Series ring to his father.

But the unraveling began then, too, when the notion of bringing a championship to the Cubs "really called out to me," Epstein said. "In some ways, I started thinking about the Cubs the day after the '04 World Series."

Then, in 2011, the Red Sox suffered a heinous collapse in the last month of the season. Epstein wrote in the *Boston Globe* that fall that a change after nearly a decade would be best for the organization and himself and that the Cubs were "the one team I could imagine working for after such a fulfilling Red Sox experience."

Building the Cubs

The vision of a Cubs-Red Sox World Series is perhaps Major League Baseball's dream. It would in some ways be Theo vs. Theo – he brought onboard 11 Red Sox and Cubs players who competed in the 2016 All-Star game.

The teams were built in slightly different ways. When he arrived in Chicago and soon brought longtime friends Jed Hoyer and Jason McLeod to create his cabinet, they knew the Cubs lacked a nucleus of championship-quality players.

The only move, he said, "was to build from the ground."

They started with an organizational meeting of 150 scouts, minor league personnel and major league coaches for four days in a Mesa, Ariz., hotel, and composed a vision of the Cubs Way: from pitching and hitting philosophy to how they would teach defense to the personality makeup of players.

For the next three years, Epstein, Hoyer and McLeod focused on obtaining young talent by trading aging players for prospects.

And, the spirit created at those meetings began to percolate on the fields where minor league and instructional league players were learning the game, Epstein said. Players started shouting, "That's Cub" as a compliment when one of them made a great play or demonstrated another core value.

"Meanwhile, our big league club is losing 100 games and when someone says, 'That's Cub,' it has the complete opposite implication," Epstein said. "We were living this dichotomy, suffering through these big league seasons but so enthused about everything that was happening in the minor leagues."

Then came 2015, when key players reached the major league team, which got to the National League Championship Series.

Midwest kindness

For all the talk of him being the merry prankster, Epstein regularly performs thoughtful gestures under the radar.

He flew a friend fighting breast cancer to Chicago for a concert. He delayed the sale of his home in Boston so an associate who was between houses and whose child was experiencing a medical crisis could live in Epstein's place.

In mid-September, his brother told him about a former student who'd become homeless with his wife and child and was living out of town. The family needed to get back to Boston. Epstein immediately wired money.

Epstein said he has matured as anyone would from 28 to 42 years old, although he still gets accused of being an absolutist. His family said he's more at ease with himself, more genial with fans and not devoured by the job. They say Midwestern kindness has helped ratchet down his stress.

"Being a father and being married now, and having been through a lot of ups and some downs in Boston," Epstein said, "I think I just have a better appreciation for how ... there are a lot of different ways to do things and maybe ... understanding where people are coming from and how they fit into the big picture."

It is incredibly difficult to be a model father and husband while running a baseball team, he said. If you try, "you're probably going to fry yourself" and not be very effective in any of those roles.

"I think the key is to maintain that passion and enthusiasm that you might find in an absolutist," Epstein said, "but mix it with the sort of understanding you might find from a pragmatist. Hopefully, that's where I'm at. I mean, I try to. I still make plenty of mistakes."

Next challenge

A guy who starts thinking about the next challenge seven years before he takes it on, as Epstein did in Boston, might be thinking about the next challenge even when he signs a five-year contract extension that reportedly pays him $10 million a year.

"I don't know that I'm going to do this forever," Epstein said. In front of him, a steady flow of groups toured Wrigley Field, accompanied by organ music. A few hundred feet behind him, construction crews built the organization's new offices on what had been a parking lot. "I mean, I don't know what to say about that, except that I don't know."

He's been mentioned as baseball commissioner material, a team owner. His father joked that Epstein could run the United Nations or Ford Foundation.

"In a crazy way," Leslie Epstein said, "the Cubs don't need Theo anymore because he's set everything up."

Former San Diego Padres GM Towers, now in the Cincinnati Reds' front office, doubts Epstein is a baseball lifer. Kennedy says the exact opposite about his former high school teammate.

"He will talk about new challenges and pursuing other intellectually stimulating activities," Kennedy said, "but he's full of (crap). He will be in baseball forever."

When pressed, Epstein said he definitely wants to stay connected with the game in some way, but he's not thinking past winning a World Series with the Cubs. He'll have a better answer for the What's Next question after the team accomplishes that, Epstein said.

But maybe he already hears that answer calling. And maybe that's OK with Cubs fans, provided the one-time boy wonder with the wisdom of middle age and the gray-tinted beard stubble delivers a certain piece of hardware that's been missing on Chicago's North Side since 1908.

Theo Epstein talks on the phone during the Cubs' workout at Dodger Stadium during the NLCS.

27

ADDISON RUSSELL

Sudden Stardom

2016 a breakout season for well-rounded Russell

By PAUL SULLIVAN

Growing up playing baseball in Florida, Addison Russell knew where he would wind up.

"It was always my love to just get dirty," he said. "At shortstop, you get to move left and right, get to jump, show off your arm, so initially shortstop was a no-brainer."

In his first full season at the position for the Cubs, Russell has emerged as one of the best all-around shortstops in the game. At 22, he added power to his repertoire, became a solid run producer and continued to make spectacular plays in the field, which is likely to lead to his first Gold Glove Award.

Russell was voted to the National League All-Star team in July and no longer is considered just one of the many talented Cubs prospects. He has evolved into a star.

"It's definitely a blessing and humbling at the same time," Russell said. "I just go about my business the same way. The attention is nice and the opportunity is grand, always. And I'm very fortunate and lucky to have all of that. It's one of the many reasons I do what I do, so I can inspire people and touch some lives along the way.

"I know my family is happy with my success, and without my family I wouldn't be where I'm at today, without my wife, Melisa, doing what she does. It's just one big contributing factor."

Russell, who is half-Filipino and half-black, grew up in Pensacola, Fla., the oldest of four siblings. His parents were young when he was born, so he spent a lot of time helping raise his younger siblings and admitted in a 2014 Tribune interview that he didn't even watch much major-league baseball.

"I was just busy trying to be a kid," he said. "I played a lot of baseball and football and babysat my (siblings) when I wasn't playing sports. That's where the time went."

Russell was talented in both sports but was skilled enough in baseball to merit the A's making him the No. 11 pick of the 2012 draft, and he seemingly was put on a fast path to the major leagues. But the A's were in contention in 2014 with one of the best teams in baseball, and GM Billy Beane sent Russell

Addison Russell watches as his home run leaves the park during an August 2016 game against the Cardinals. Russell made his first All-Star team in 2016. (Anthony Souffle/Chicago Tribune)

to the Cubs in a multiplayer deal for pitchers Jeff Samardzija and Jason Hammel.

It's funny now to recall some criticized President Theo Epstein for acquiring Russell when the Cubs already had a young major-league shortstop in Starlin Castro and another on the way in top prospect Javier Baez. Epstein didn't care about stockpiling shortstops and knew it would all work out eventually.

"We're not smart enough to know how all the pieces fit together," he said shortly after the deal. "But it's easy to be excited about a lot of the different permutations."

Russell started out at second base with the Cubs but replaced Castro at short in the second half of 2015, allowing Epstein to deal Castro to the Yankees in the offseason and make Baez a valuable utility player.

No one is questioning the move now.

After spending most of his rookie season in the No. 9 hole, Russell moved to the middle of the lineup this season and showed he could deliver in the clutch. He had 19 go-ahead RBIs and 11 game-winning RBIs, and his total of 95 RBIs was the second-highest among shortstops and highest for a Cubs player at 22 or younger since at least 1913.

"My goals this year as far as offense were more mental, more being in tune to what the pitcher is trying to do to me, and that's what I focused on," he said. "If you look at my season, I came (up) in some pretty good spots, so I know my focus was in the right spot.

"That's the main thing I wanted to get through. Next year is probably going to be a different story as far as me developing, but I had to develop the mental side first."

Russell's defense was never in question, but his offensive production has been somewhat of a surprise.

"It's nice," first baseman Anthony Rizzo said. "He has gotten a lot of (RBI) opportunities and has taken off. It's fun to watch, fun to see his spirit, how he's getting more into that comfort level."

Russell said he was "impressed" with his season but isn't letting it go to his head. He ranked fifth in

the majors in defensive WAR (2.7), according to BaseballReference.com, which could lead to gold.

"I'm not thinking Gold Glove at all," he said. "I'll let whoever decides that decide that. If I just keep that out of my head, it should be a little easier to perform."

Russell has been healthy all year after missing the NL Championship Series last year with a hamstring injury he suffered in Game 3 of the division series against the Cardinals. He conceded it was "pretty tough" to sit and watch the Cubs lose in four games to

In his first full season as the Cubs' starting shortstop, Addison Russell hit 21 home runs to go along with 95 RBIs. (Brian Cassella/Chicago Tribune)

the Mets, but he knew they would get another chance.

"You live and learn, man," he said. "That's the big thing about this year. I listened to my body and made sure I was healthy, starting with offseason training and in spring training.

"It all comes down to this, right now. The body is in great shape and I feel it should hold up for the whole playoffs. Everything is a go."

He and Melisa have two young children at home, so Russell has his hands full on and off the field. But

he said it has helped him become a better man and a better player, and he knows he has more to learn.

"Just coming into the league, making a splash last year, becoming a father of two and handling all this stuff has been a whirlwind," he said. "But I knew it was going to happen someday. I'm enjoying the process now, and I'm young and I'm still learning. (I) just can't wait to see where I'm going to be at in five years."

He's not alone.

28

KYLE HENDRICKS

Low-Key, Big Results

Hendricks took unconventional path to become Cubs' unlikely ace

By DAVID HAUGH

On the campus of Dartmouth College, bookish pitcher Kyle Hendricks fit in so well with the rest of the Ivy Leaguers in his freshman class that baseball coach Bob Whalen caught himself making a mistake he often sees others make.

"People make assumptions about Ivy League schools that, because they're elite academic institutions, they don't take their sports that seriously," Whalen recalled over the phone. "And one of the first times I met Kyle, I asked him one question: 'How important is baseball to you?'"

It seemed like a fair question at the time.

North Siders have come to know Hendricks as baseball's Everyman pitching like nobody expected for the Cubs this unforgettable season, confusing hitters with a crafty changeup and insinuating himself into the debate over who is the ace of the best team in the majors.

But Whalen can be forgiven for initially wondering about baseball's role in Hendricks'

future back when he majored in economics at Dartmouth after achieving a 4.0 grade-point average at Capistrano Valley High School in Mission Viejo, Calif. Math always came easier than baseball for Hendricks, a studious natural athlete who learned well enough from his father, John, a golf pro, to stay stroke for stroke at an event with pro golfer Rory Sabbatini as a teenager.

Showing maturity impossible to measure with sabermetrics, Hendricks safely chose the collegiate route in 2008 over the circuitous path offered by the Angels when they drafted him in the 39th round. Tall and lean with dark hair parted perfectly to the side, Hendricks the matriculating Dartmouth freshman looked more like Joe College than anybody's image of a future Cy Young Award candidate -- looks that can be deceiving.

"He answered my question by looking me right in the eyes, in a relaxed way, but he had that look and said, 'Coach, baseball is the most important thing to me,' " Whalen said. "You could tell he meant it.

Kyle Hendricks began the 2016 season as the Cubs' fifth starter. By October, the 26-year-old was a 16-game winner and the second starter in the team's playoff rotation. (Nuccio DiNuzzo/Chicago Tribune)

There was no false bravado, trying to make me think it was more important than it was. He comes across a humble, understated young man -- and he is.

"But make no mistake, Kyle's confident and competitive. And after he answered, I remember saying to myself, 'I think we have a keeper here.' "

Nine months later, Hendricks proved Whalen right. Dartmouth stood one win from its first Ivy League championship in 22 years and called on Hendricks, who threw seven shutout innings in a 10-0 victory. Whalen, the son of longtime Pirates scout Chick Whalen, always told recruits major-league teams will find talent no matter where they attended school. Hendricks, whose childhood dream of attending Stanford died when the Cardinal recruited a staff of power arms, offered Whalen evidence immediately by outthinking hitters more than overpowering them for the Big Green.

"Baseball always has been what I wanted to try to do with my life, and going to Dartmouth was part of that decision," Hendricks, 26, said in the Cubs dugout. "All Coach Whalen said was, 'You don't have a spot and you'll have to work like everybody else.' I always respected that."

When Hendricks found out last October he was pitching Game 2 in St. Louis in the National League Division Series, he invited Whalen.

Hours after Hendricks' one-hit performance against the Cardinals on Monday, his finest major-league start, he texted his college coach to arrange a conversation.

You might say Hendricks knows how to finish pitches.

"One of the most loyal kids I've ever had," Whalen said. "He's comfortable with who he is. I don't think he has a chip on his shoulder about his lack of velocity. Everybody talks about the lack of

velocity, but all I know is every time I see him pitch, the ball is not put on the barrel."

'He won't throw that here'

Clyde Wright warned Rod Carew, the Hall of Fame hitter, what was coming. Wright, an Angels pitcher from 1966 to '73 who runs a pitching school in Southern California, and Carew, a family friend who once gave Kyle bunting tips, were regulars at high school games Hendricks pitched.

"One day, Kyle had a kid 3-2 with the bases loaded and I said, 'Rod, watch him throw this curveball,' " Wright, 75, recalled over the phone.

"Rod said, 'He won't throw that here.' I knew he would because I had told Kyle not to be afraid to throw any pitch in any situation. And he just froze the kid at the plate. Rod was like, 'Wow.' "

Hendricks began working with Wright – and wowing him -- when he was 11. The longer Wright sat on a bucket catching Hendricks' pitches, the more he sensed something special about this particular Little Leaguer.

"He had extremely big hands and fingers and good mechanics already," Wright said. "I told him: 'You know what you're doing. Listen to me and we might make something ... and if you don't listen, I'm going to kick your ass.' He just looked at me like, what in the world is that old man doing?"

Reminded of that encounter, Hendricks laughed. The two used to spend so much time together that Wright's wife kidded him he paid more attention to Hendricks than his own son, Jaret, a former Indians pitcher. Hendricks cherishes the memories.

"He's a big character, and every pitch I'd throw he'd be yelling something back at me in that Tennessee accent," Hendricks said. "I was a quiet kid. It was me and him ... and he'd tell me what to do. He opened me up and we became pretty close. The biggest thing was he taught me how to throw a curveball, so when I was at the right age I'd know how to throw a healthy one."

As a high school pitcher under Wright's direction, Hendricks added a changeup.

His repertoire made him more of a pitcher than a thrower, making Wright wary whether pro scouts eventually would see what he saw in the right-hander.

"I thought he had the capability to pitch in the big leagues, but the big thing against him was he didn't throw that hard, so we were just hoping somebody would give him a chance," Wright said.

"I think he's thrown the same speed the last six, seven years."

That Hendricks became one of baseball's top pitchers without a fastball that travels faster than 91 mph makes his ascent even more impressive. The further his career goes, the more his mind races back to where he first believed all of this was possible.

"I had decent mechanics, but (Wright) taught me all the basic checkpoints and the right sensations and feelings with body control," Hendricks said. "That's the foundation of where I became a pitcher."

'Be a jerk on the mound'

On that foundation Hendricks began to build a warehouse of information, gleaned from everybody he encountered on his way to becoming the unlikeliest of aces.

His dad, for example, taught him a changeup in the side yard one night after a rough high school outing. The array of strong influences ranges from Whalen and Wright to Brad Holman, Hendricks' pitching coach at Class A Myrtle Beach in the Rangers organization, and Cubs pitching coach Chris Bosio.

Then there was Scott Budner, a pitching coach whose input over a three-year period from 2009 to 2011 improved Hendricks' changeup and, just as significantly, altered his makeup.

"I taught him how to be a bastard on the mound and have an attitude," Budner said.

One night in 2009, Budner went to watch Hendricks pitch for Dartmouth. A well-traveled pitching coach for several organizations, Budner was evaluating pitchers for West Coast Sports Management in Pasadena, Calif., at the time. He liked everything he saw in Hendricks.

Well, almost everything.

"The game I saw, he never pitched inside or challenged hitters, so I told him bluntly that he was a nice kid but needed to push a different button out there to be effective and be a jerk on the mound," said Budner, now a coach with the Angels' Double-A affiliate in Little Rock, Ark. "I challenged his manhood, and his mama didn't like me much for that ... but she likes me now."

Besides advising Hendricks to sharpen an edge, Budner adjusted the grip on a changeup that eventually became Hendricks' most effective pitch. A four-seamer that cuts slightly and works best against right-handed hitters was born; the two-seamer that fades against lefties came later. They complement a curveball mixed in with the sneaky-fast fastball.

Remember when Cubs manager Joe Maddon said about the 6-foot-3, 190-pound mound magician: "Put the radar gun in your back pocket and look at what he's doing"? Budner echoed that advice for appreciating Hendricks.

"I hope everybody sees how Kyle does it," Budner said. "It's the beautiful essence of pitching. He repeats his pitches and stays within himself, not worried about all those (speed) guns. He makes it about the art of pitching.

"I hope someday kids growing up see it's not just about power and pitching 97 (mph). I'd never put anybody in Greg Maddux's class, but Kyle is pitching like that right now."

Budner paused to chuckle.

"Sorry," he said. "I still kind of giggle when I watch on TV and see him use that changeup and know I had a little to do with it."

'I'd like to have that one back'

Rest assured Rangers general manager Jon Daniels doesn't giggle watching Hendricks pitch. Gag maybe. But Daniels still can smile about the part he played in Hendricks' progress.

On July 31, 2012, hours before the trade deadline, Daniels included Hendricks as the secondary piece with third-base prospect Christian Villanueva in a deal with the Cubs for 35-year-old pitcher Ryan Dempster. Dempster disappointed the Rangers in 12 starts, and the trade remains among Daniels' worst. Hendricks, an eighth-round draft pick of the Rangers in 2011, looks like one of the smartest acquisitions of the Theo Epstein regime.

"He was a tough guy to put in the deal, and I'd like to have that one back," Daniels said in a phone interview. "Obviously I did not see this coming at this level or we wouldn't have traded Kyle.

"The thing that always stood out about Kyle was (he was) very intelligent, always had (an) ability to make pitches, got better at each level, was able to take instruction. Everybody's favorite. Credit to the Cubs for maximizing his ability."

Credit also goes to Hendricks, who focused more on the Cubs wanting him than the Rangers considering him expendable. His ego is even smaller than his earned-run average -- the lowest in major-league baseball at 2.03.

"I've always been pretty low-key and always known this is what I want to do with my life, but it's nothing too exquisite or special to me necessarily," Hendricks said. "I just feel very happy and fortunate to be in this situation, trust me."

Daniels has made enough good trades to know even the best GMs make bad ones. He recalled the relaxed side of Hendricks coming out while charting pitches as they sat next to each other at a Class A game in Myrtle Beach, S.C.

"He didn't have quite the same eye of the tiger, and that was a really relaxed conversation that stands out to me," said Daniels, who got to know Hendricks' parents, John and Ann Marie, described affectionately by her son as "a loud, Southern lady" from New Orleans.

"They're really fun people, really down-to-earth folks who love the game, and you can tell a lot about someone from their parents," Daniels said. "I genuinely root for the guy."

Baseball fans in Chicago can relate.

Kyle Hendricks throws during Game 2 of the NLCS against the Dodgers. In his second full season, Hendricks led the major leagues with a 2.13 earned run average in 2016. (Brian Cassella/Chicago Tribune)

SECOND BASEMAN

9

JAVIER BAEZ

Losses Form a Winner

Deaths of father, sister help inspire breakout star of playoffs

By PAUL SKRBINA

The cheers spilled onto Waveland Avenue and into the early morning after Javier Baez had turned a tense, scoreless game into a raucous Wrigleyville party. Earlier, the 23-year-old infielder had defied Mother Nature by smacking an eighth-inning home run into a stiff wind for the lone run in the Cubs' playoff-opening victory over the Giants.

It was a magical moment -- the ball was a home run by the barest of measures, landing in the protective basket on top of the left-field wall -- but only the first act in a performance that has made Baez the breakout star of the Cubs' 2016 postseason run.

Grown men and women, many of whom had given Baez a standing ovation inside Wrigley Field after the home run, pressed their faces against the cold, metal fence on Waveland, just outside the stadium, to steal a glimpse of Baez and his teammates as they exited.

"Javy! Javy! Javy!" they screamed. One onlooker proposed marriage.

But Baez had a few other tricks up his sleeve. His October magic show was just getting started.

A new beginning

Javier Baez had a BB gun. But there were no squirrels.

He had his glove and bat. But there was no year-round baseball.

There was no chance Baez was staying.

He had just moved from Puerto Rico to a small town in North Carolina. .Neither he nor his mother, Nelida; his older brother Gadiel nor his sister, Noely, spoke English.

The high school baseball season didn't begin until the following spring. It was the middle of summer in the middle of nowhere, and Baez was "going really crazy."

"I cried to go back to Puerto Rico," he said. "There was nothing to do. I didn't know anybody. Just sit in the house with no school, no baseball."

Nelida cried too. Every day.

Baez's father, Angel Luis Baez, was a landscaper. He had died a year earlier after falling and hitting his

Cubs infielder Javier Baez celebrates after scoring in the second inning of Game 2. (Brian Cassella/Chicago Tribune)

head. Noely, Javier's best friend, was in need of better health care to help with the birth defect spina bifida, or split spine.

Javier was 12 years old.

"We were lost," Gadiel said.

Two weeks after arriving in the United States, Javier begged his mother to let him move back to Puerto Rico to live with his other brother, Rolando.

Instead the Baezes left North Carolina in search of a better life.

In search of year-round baseball. In search of a good place for Noely, who wasn't supposed to live more than a few hours after she was born but instead lived 21 years before dying in early 2015.

That place turned out to be Jacksonville, Fla.

'Mi angel'

Baez grins when he thinks of Noely, who was 11 months his junior. He has a picture of her face tattooed on his right shoulder.

"Mi angel," it says in script.

My angel.

One of the biggest reasons he wanted to be a baseball player was so he could take care of her. He's grateful she saw him achieve his dream -- their dream, really -- when she watched in person as he made his major-league debut in Denver in 2014.

"I was prepared for her to go way before she did," Baez said. "Everything she wanted, she got. She could ride a jet ski, she got a motorcycle. The only thing she couldn't do was walk."

Baez would have fixed that, too, if he could have. When he was 7, his mother heard him tell his sister he wished he could switch legs with her so she would know what it felt like to walk.

"Everything I did in my life, it was because of her," Baez said. "My mom stopped living her life to live my sister's life. She was so big for my family. It was something incredible."

Inspiring tattoos

There's a tattoo of the Major League Baseball logo on Baez's nape, his first tattoo, that demonstrates his appetite for expectation. He got it when he was 16.

He and his brothers received identical tattoos after Javier spotted the logo while playing on a travel baseball team.

Baez also has his siblings' and parents' names tattooed on his body. His right arm is dedicated mostly to his native land.

The tributes help Baez cope with the losses he has experienced and remember the places he has been.

They inspire him to keep going forward.

Baez's favorite number is 9. He wears it on the back of his uniform for the Cubs, who picked him ninth overall in the 2011 draft.

Baez's other angel, his father, Angel Luis, died on 9-9-2004. His death hit Javier hard.

"I was really close with him too," Baez said. "I saw my father go away from my hands. It was something really strong for me."

And something he also memorialized on his body with these words: "I will take your place and I will provide for our family."

Stone's throw...

His Game 1 home run into the wind in the National League Division Series notwithstanding, Baez isn't undefeated against Mother Nature.

He can thank the mango tree in the front yard of his grandparents' house in Puerto Rico for that.

Gadiel and a cousin were throwing rocks there one day, trying to knock fruit from the tree, when Javier showed up "out of nowhere," Gadiel said.

"I was throwing, my cousin was throwing; we couldn't get any," Gadiel said. "So he gets a rock and throws it straight up. He was staring at it, waiting for the mango to come down."

But he made a rare error. He took his eyes off the tree, unaware of his fate or the rock's gravitational destination, and bent over to pick up another stone.

"When he gets ready to throw it, the rock came down and hit him straight in the forehead. He started bleeding," Gadiel said.

Javier played it cool. Reassured everyone he was OK.

Master glovework

Cubs catcher David Ross, playing his 15th and final major-league season, called Baez the best defensive player he has played with. Pitcher Kyle Hendricks said Baez has the best instincts he has seen.

Third baseman Kris Bryant and manager Joe Maddon suggested baseball create a Gold Glove Award for utility players in Baez's honor. He arguably is the team's best third baseman, shortstop and second baseman but has embraced being something of a defensive vagabond.

Maddon said Baez likely would find a permanent home at second base someday. He has manned every infield position, plus left field. He's the team's emergency catcher.

"He tops everyone with the amount of gloves he has," shortstop Addison Russell said. "Even the pitchers."

He recently pared the collection he carries with him to three or four.

He has used them well.

Baez played 62 games at third, 59 at second and 25 at short this season, making him the first player in baseball history to play at least 25 at each position in one season.

His 11 defensive runs saved at second base during the regular season tied him for second in the majors with the Mariners' Robinson Cano -- in almost 1,000 fewer innings than Cano played there.

He has made throws from angles that seem impossible to quantify -- from his back, from his side. In the Division Series, Baez fired a 72 mph, cross-body bouncer to first that so impressed the umpire, he called the Giants' Denard Span out before replay ruled otherwise.

He has developed a reputation around the big leagues for being the best tagger around.

"He has done some things on the field I haven't seen," Russell said. "The type of talent he has, not only with the glove but on the offensive side ... he's a heavy slugger."

But one who struck out at an alarming 41.5 percent rate when he was called up in 2014. The number dropped to 30 percent in 28 major-league games in 2015.

This year Baez is down to 24 percent. He batted .342 in the first two rounds of the postseason with a home run, seven RBI and two stolen bases. He hit .273 with 14 homers and 59 RBIs during the regular season.

None of this surprised Gadiel Baez.

"I knew he was going to be something big," he said. "I knew this moment would come. "He was just good at everything he would do. He wants to dunk, he can dunk. Super easy."

Still, he has had his share of learning moments, even amid the recent glory. Ross stared him down during the NLDS after Baez didn't hustle on the basepaths.

His teammates, like his family, have no problem humbling him.

And he has no problem taking it.

34

JON LESTER

Deal Lands an Ace

Giants offered more money, but Cubs got their man in Lester

By Paul Sullivan

Giants catcher Buster Posey showed up on Jon Lester's doorstep one fall morning in 2014 and made a modest proposal.

"I want to be your catcher," Posey said.

The wooing of Lester was in full swing, and the Giants had pulled out all the stops, sending Posey and manager Bruce Bochy along with team executives to recruit the top free-agent pitcher on the market. They had just won their third World Series in five years and were hungry for more.

Lester could join Madison Bumgarner as an unstoppable 1-2 punch at the top of the rotation, keeping the Giants dynasty going for years.

The Cubs low-keyed their pursuit, relatively speaking, sending Lester some camo Cubs caps for hunting and a bottle of wine and flowers for his wife, Farrah. They were still in the middle of their rebuild, having just hired manager Joe Maddon, who called but did not visit Lester at his home in Georgia.

Cubs President Theo Epstein could offer Lester only a ton of money, access to a private jet and a chance to own Chicago if he could help end the drought.

"It was driven home that the organization hasn't won in a century, and he could be part of something historic, something unique and something extraordinary," Lester's agent, Seth Levinson said.

The decision was easy.

Lester chose a chance at immortality, turning down more money from the Giants to sign a six-year, $155 million deal to pitch for the Cubs.

Nearly two years later, with that elusive championship seemingly theirs for the taking, the Cubs kick off their postseason Friday night at Wrigley Field in Game 1 of the National League Division Series, with Lester facing Posey and the Giants.

Maddon's choice to start Game 1 was a no-brainer, even though Kyle Hendricks won the major-league earned-run average title. With two Series championships under his belt with the Red Sox, Lester is time-tested in October, and he's coming off a Cy Young-caliber season that re-established him as the team's ace.

Jon Lester throws during his masterful Game 1 performance against the Giants, a team which also courted him before the 2015 season. (Brian Cassella/Chicago Tribune)

"Jon has been on a really significant roll since August," Maddon said. "There's almost a component of meritocracy involved, I think, the fact he has earned the right to be this guy."

Lester's 19 victories were second in the National League, and his ERA of 2.44 was second to Hendricks. All in all, he had the kind of season the Cubs were looking for when they brought him in.

"This one was pretty special on a personal level, just where everything's at at the finish," Lester said. "It'll probably go down as one of the better, if not the best, years of my career, and hopefully there is more to come.

"A lot of personal satisfaction there. You try to look at that, but at the same time, now we have the real business to get down to."

That real business included three strong starts from Lester in the playoffs -- all Cubs victories -- to help the team reach the World Series.

Lester was the first big free-agent signing of Epstein's plan, and their relationship from their days together in Boston figured prominently in the wooing. Epstein was there for Lester in 2006 when he was diagnosed with cancer of the lymph nodes. He was also there for the recovery and watched Lester coolly win the World Series-clinching game in their sweep of the Rockies in 2007.

And when the Red Sox collapsed down the stretch in 2011, leading to Epstein's departure, it was Lester who was fingered in the famous fried-chicken-and-beer controversy that painted the clubhouse as out of control. Lester, John Lackey and Josh Beckett were the main culprits, reportedly drinking and munching on Popeye's instead of supporting their teammates in the dugout.

"We probably ordered chicken from Popeye's like once a month," Lester told the Boston Globe. "But that's not the reason we lost. It was a ninth-inning-rally beer. ... Was it a bad habit? Yes, I should have been on the bench more than I was. But we just played bad baseball as a team in September. We stunk. To be honest, we were doing the same things all season when we had the best record in baseball."

Epstein and manager Terry Francona were gone, and the Red Sox crumbled to last place in 2012 only to bounce back in 2013 and win another World Series, with Lester taking Games 1 and 5 and Lackey winning Game 6.

After failing to sign Lester to an extension in 2014, the Red Sox dealt him to the A's before the trade deadline for Yoenis Cespedes.

The A's considered him their missing link and he started for them against the Royals in the American League wild-card game. But he helped blow a four-run lead in the eighth and watched the Royals win in extra innings. That sent Lester into free agency with the Cubs, Giants and Red Sox in pursuit.

That November, Lester arrived in Chicago for a recruiting visit during a polar vortex. When he visited Wrigley Field, the bleachers were still under construction and the ballpark looked like a wreck.

Chicago was a tough sell.

Epstein had former Cubs Ryan Dempster, Jeff Samardzija and Jason Hammel talk to Lester about how cool it was to be a Cub and play at Wrigley, but Lester still wasn't totally convinced.

"Are these guys close?" Lester asked Samardzija. "Are they there?"

Jon Lester, a 2016 All-Star, watches the Home Run Derby while holding his two sons. (Nuccio DiNuzzo/Chicago Tribune)

At that point, before Kris Bryant, Kyle Schwarber or Addison Russell had arrived in the majors, no one could be certain.

In the book "The Arm," Epstein told author Jeff Passan he wrote a series of notes to Lester during the free-agent process, trying to entice him to take the plunge. The Giants were offering more money, but Epstein knew money wouldn't be the deciding factor for Lester.

In his final message to Lester before baseball's winter meetings, Epstein wrote: "If you do decide to join us in Chicago, we look forward to taking care of your family, to great fun to be had together, and to the biggest celebration in the history of sports!"

The Hail Mary pitch worked. Lester agreed to sign with the Cubs, accelerating the Plan.

"The biggest thing that made me believe in the Cubs was (general manager Jed Hoyer) and Theo," Lester told Passan. "They made me believe in what they believe in."

Now Lester is on the doorstep of something special, something historic. Dozens of free agents have come to the Cubs believing they could make a difference and be on the team that ended the drought, from Andre Dawson to Greg Maddux to Alfonso Soriano.

Will Lester be the one finally to make it happen?

He knows how to pitch in October, knows how to attack hitters. In two previous World Series with the Red Sox, Lester went 3-0 with an 0.43 ERA.

"We'll have a game plan going in." he said. "I have strengths that have gotten me to this point in my career that I've relied upon, and we'll probably start there and make adjustments."

Having Lester on the mound for Game 1 of the World Series was a good place to start.

Jon Lester throws against the Milwaukee Brewers on Aug. 17, a game in which he recorded his 13th win and allowed just one run. (Chris Sweda/ Chicago Tribune)

44

ANTHONY RIZZO

A Leader, Born and Bred

Family's strong roots system sprouts a star

By Teddy Greenstein

This story begins on July 10, 2014. The 100-win Cubs of 2016 are 100 miles away, or so it seems. This group is 14 below .500, and the Reds are honing in on a five-game series sweep. A Homer Bailey pitch bruised Anthony Rizzo's right arm in the first, but the Cubs' connoisseur of black and blue only takes exception in the ninth after Aroldis Chapman fires pitches of 101 and 100 mph over the head of teammate Nate Schierholtz.

Rizzo trots to first, hears some squawking from the Reds and does something extraordinary: He drops his glove, removes his cap and marches directly toward the Reds dugout. He's ready to fight – 1 against 25.

"I loved that. Loved it," says Rizzo's father, John, a man whose sporting life began in New Jersey, where he played hockey with frozen rats. "It didn't surprise me one frickin' bit. Even when he was a little kid, he stuck up for his teammates."

One of those teammates now is Chapman.

"These things happen in the heat of battle," Chapman says through interpreter Mike Moreno. "It's

nothing where we should hold a grudge. I feel he's an awesome player and teammate. I'm very happy he's on my side."

Rizzo, it seems, is incapable of having an enemy -- especially in the Cubs clubhouse. He organizes group dinners on the road and makes it a point to welcome new teammates.

"He's one of the easiest people to get along with," Ben Zobrist says. "His personality is so infectious. You gotta like him."

Miguel Montero calls Rizzo "the face of the franchise," but that poster child is not above getting razzed. Montero was playing for the Diamondbacks in 2014 and remembers watching the Reds incident on TV. Montero's thought?

"He was looking for votes for the All-Star Game," the veteran catcher says. "It ended up getting him a lot of attention. He got the votes. Smart move."

Indeed, Rizzo received 8.8 million votes, enough to overtake the Rockies' Justin Morneau and snag the final spot on the National League team.

While hitting 32 home runs and driving in 109 runs, Anthony Rizzo had plenty to smile about during the 2016 season. (Nuccio DiNuzzo/Chicago Tribune)

Rizzo's brother, Johnny, also remembered thinking that Rizzo's Rambo moment could propel him to his first Midsummer Classic.

Is this why Rizzo did what he did?

"No," Johnny replies. "I think he saw 102 right at his teammate's head. Hey, you have to stand up for your teammates. That's one of my favorite moments."

'Help us win'

This story continues in the fall of 2012.

The Cubs have selected Albert Almora Jr. with the sixth pick in the draft. Rizzo, a fellow south Floridian, wants to meet the first selection of the Theo Epstein era.

"I'm an 18-year-old kid and Anthony Rizzo shows up at my house," Almora says. "I remember almost everything about it. I showed him my backyard, and he tried my climbing rope. We didn't even talk much about baseball, more about life. Since then, we get along great."

Rizzo is 23 years old. He's already a leader in the mold of Jonathan Toews, named the Blackhawks' captain at 20. Both are economical in their words. And both can be counted on to do the right thing.

The Cubs have established veteran leaders in left-hander Jon Lester and catcher David Ross, so Rizzo is free to be himself. That's plenty good enough for manager Joe Maddon.

"He's always upbeat, positive," Maddon says. "He plays every day, plays with enthusiasm, is definitely not afraid and is very supportive of the rest of the group. And what he does on defense, he's there to pick everyone up. He has a great outlook on the day."

He's a gamer, and that spirit comes from his father and big brother.

John is 62, does programming and service for Tyco Security and still speaks in a distinct Jersey accent. Anthony has suggested he retire, but John says: "It's a mental thing. I want to keep going, even though he makes more in one paycheck than I do in five years."

Johnny earned his keep at Florida Atlantic University, where he began as a walk-on and started nearly every game of his career, earning second-team all-Sun Belt honors at right guard.

His university-produced bio includes this entry for 2006: "(Has) reputation for playing hard-nosed football despite being banged up...was exemplified during preseason when he didn't miss a day despite extensive rib contusions among other conditions."

"If I was healthy enough to play, I was gonna play," Johnny says. "That's how I felt. Anthony only takes a day off if Joe makes him."

'He was a freak'

This story continues in the mid-'60s.

The Jersey-bred John Sr. pitches quarters and plays stickball, handball and rat hockey. He's not allowed to play ball in the house and promises himself that when he has kids, he'll practically require them to play ball inside.

Wife Laurie was working as a bartender and after she would leave in the late afternoon, John says he and his boys would play "everything -- handball off the wall, football, baseball. I started playing golf around the time we moved (from New Jersey to Florida). Anthony was 2 or 3. I was chipping golf balls one day and he comes out with a glove. He's a little kid, staggering and drooling, and says, 'Dad, hit me balls.'

"I thought: I'm gonna kill him. But he caught like 10 in a row. He even caught the ones I bladed."

John's goal was to spend as much time with his kids as possible. So he coached them in every sport. A college wrestler, he knew so little about soccer he had his team play catch at his first practice.

"There was a Brazilian guy there and he said,

Anthony Rizzo celebrates after scoring a run against the Milwaukee Brewers in April 2016. (Brian Cassella/Chicago Tribune)

'What do you have, 12 goalies?'"

Anthony excelled in every sport he tried, especially hockey and baseball.

"Once he got into T-ball, Little League, he was a freak," John says. "By end of the season, the kids were asking him to sign their ball. The parents were saying, 'He's gonna be in the pros.' "

John wasn't sure, but he knew this: His kids would stay straight, not give into whatever temptations were rampant in Parkland, Fla., west of Boca Raton. He would eyeball every one of Johnny and Anthony's friends and expel the troublemakers.

"I knew who could be selling weed, who could be a crack freak, who would try to talk them into going with some hookers somewhere," John says. "One time we had kids over and I see one of them with a pipe wrench. Someone tells me he's huffing (inhaling chemical vapors to get a high) and says, 'He's gonna take Freon from your air conditioning (unit).' I grabbed the kid by the neck, called his old man and said, 'I never want to see your kid with mine again.'

"We made sure the drugs and steroids stayed out."

'They have to win'

This story continues Aug. 17 of 2016.

Rizzo hustles to the seats off first base at Wrigley Field. He steps on the ledge of the brick wall, reaches in with a backhand and snares a popup against the Brewers, somehow managing to keep his balance and not fall into the lap of a guy wearing a Batman T-shirt.

John, watching from home in Florida, immediately texted his oldest son with a recollection from their ball-playing days in the house: Was that the over-the-shoulder, over-the-couch catch, or over-the-shoulder, over-the-stairs catch?

Says Johnny: "I was cracking up."

At the time, Anthony joked: "It's one of those plays where if you make it, you look great. If you don't make it, you're a fool. It's nice I made it."

Says Almora: "He goes balls to the wall. It's what you want in a teammate, someone who will go all out to win a ballgame."

Asked recently whether catches like that reflect his leadership, Anthony replies: "That's bonus stuff, in my opinion. It's more about running out the ground balls, running out the popups, taking the extra base first to third, doing the little things you can control. In this game you can hit the ball hard and do everything right and still fail. It's about what Joe says: 'Respect 90 (feet) all the time.' I feel like that pays off in the end."

The biggest payoff would come in late October or early November, if the World Series goes six or seven games.

Anthony refers to a Cubs title as a "when," not an "if," telling Sports Illustrated: "When it happens, it's going to be epic."

He's not the only one with faith.

Johnny, an investment banker and financial adviser who handles Anthony's money, says of his plans to watch the playoffs: "We'll be up (in Chicago) a lot. Definitely weekend games -- and all the World Series games."

Whoa, that's confidence.

"Oh, yeah," Johnny says. "They have to win. They're gonna win. The young guys play fearless. They know they're good."

This story concludes with how no Cubs story has ended since 1908.

There's the father who would not let his son stray, the older brother who set the right example, the mother who runs the family foundation meticulously and the youngest son, the face of the franchise, delivering a title.

He's right: It will be epic.

Anthony Rizzo, who hit a career-high .292 during the 2016 regular season, rounds the bases during an April victory. (Chris Sweda/Chicago Tribune)

THIRD BASEMAN

17

KRIS BRYANT

Two Good to be True

In just his second year, Bryant is 'something special'

By **K.C. JOHNSON**

Kris Bryant pushed his champagne-soaked protective eyewear atop his forehead and took a break from sticking fistfuls of ice cubes down teammates' backs to ponder the scene – and question – in front of him. What would it mean for the newest Cubs superstar to follow his Rookie of the Year campaign with the National League most valuable player award?

It seemed hilariously incongruous that Bryant, who has said he never has tried alcohol, offered an answer in a T-shirt that, if wrung out, would fail a sobriety test.

"We play for this right here," Bryant said, gesturing to the division-clinching gyrating in a delirious Cubs clubhouse.

"We don't play for any individual goal or stat. This is what you're going to remember 20 years from now. Obviously, (winning MVP) would be really cool, but every memory I have in baseball is celebrations like this."

What Bryant, 24, is doing isn't easy.

Never mind the skill to judge speed and space to put bat squarely on pitched ball, a process that has produced 39 home runs, 102 RBIs and a .293 batting average. Those numbers made him, along with teammate Anthony Rizzo, an MVP favorite and helped lead the Cubs to the best record in baseball and their mid-September dance party.

It was the first celebration on the way to snapping a century-old World Series drought.

Forget the versatility that has allowed manager Joe Maddon to move Bryant around defensively like a puppet, shifting him from his natural position of third base to wherever his athleticism is needed. Bryant has started games at two infield and two outfield positions, finished games at a different position than he started more than 25 percent of the time and played four positions in a game.

No, what's most impressive is Bryant living up to his considerable hype after the Cubs drafted him second overall out of the University of San Diego in 2013.

Kris Bryant circles the bases after hitting a game-tying home run during the ninth inning of Game 3 of the NLDS. (Anthony Souffle/Chicago Tribune)

That is never easy but is perhaps more difficult in this age of social-media synopsis and rapid-fire analysis. Meeting potential -- or failing to -- is as old a baseball subject as the ivy on the Wrigley Field walls. It's a process that has chewed up and spat out many. See Vitters, Josh for a Cubs example.

And this is where Bryant's character, composure, work ethic and commitment to team get raised consistently and constantly by those who know him best, qualities so universally hailed as cornerstones to his success.

"You hear about a kid who always kept his grades up, who always worked hard, so you expect that you might have someone who has real character," Cubs Chairman Tom Ricketts said. "But then you see the way he works, the way he cares about the game, about his teammates, and you know you have something special."

Bryant's father, Mike, played minor-league baseball for the Red Sox and, along with wife Sue, raised his two sons with the game always nearby. Mike's influence on his youngest son has been well-documented, and it's present again when Bryant is asked where he gets his composure.

"It's just who I am as a person," Bryant said. "I try to be laid back and not get too high or too low. It's just something I've always had. It can be a good thing or a bad thing, but it's just me.

"I don't really care what people think of me -- good or bad. Holding onto that stuff gets to your head. So I don't worry about it."

If this approach sounds like another soft-spoken, serious-minded Cubs icon, so be it. Maybe it isn't coincidence that Bryant had to ditch the No. 23 he wore at Las Vegas' Bonanza High School because it's retired in Chicago.

When Ryne Sandberg first met Bryant, this composure stood out.

"I liked his demeanor right away," Sandberg said. "I liked the way he handles himself. I liked the way he prepares. He has a good way about him. He's very professional, respects the game."

Sandberg won National League MVP honors in 1984 following his third season with the Cubs, also at age 24. He authored his signature breakout game that season in June, twice hitting game-tying home runs off Cardinals closer Bruce Sutter to send announcer Harry Caray into hyperdrive in Caray's already-over-the-top style.

Thirty-two years and four days later, Bryant became the first player in major-league history to hit three home runs and two doubles in the same game, going 5-for-5 with six RBIs in a road victory over the Reds. That Bryant followed with another 5-for-5 outing in an August victory over the Brewers seemed like piling on.

That August game made Bryant just the second player in major-league history with two five-hit, five-RBI games in the same season. He joined former Cub Phil Cavarretta, who accomplished it in 1945 during his NL MVP season.

"I don't know what Kris Bryant's ceiling is, but it's pretty good right now," Sandberg said. "He's just a tremendous athlete with all the tools to play baseball. And he's obviously very versatile to play different positions, which even puts him in another category."

Indeed, Bryant is vying to become the first MVP since Stan Musial in 1946 to start at least 30 games in both the infield and outfield, according to STATS LLC.

And when accomplishments place you in sentences alongside Hall of Famers like Sandberg and Musial, the burden of being a franchise centerpiece

Versatile defensively and capable of playing multiple positions, Kris Bryant scoops up a ground ball during Game 2 of the NLDS. (Brian Cassella/Chicago Tribune)

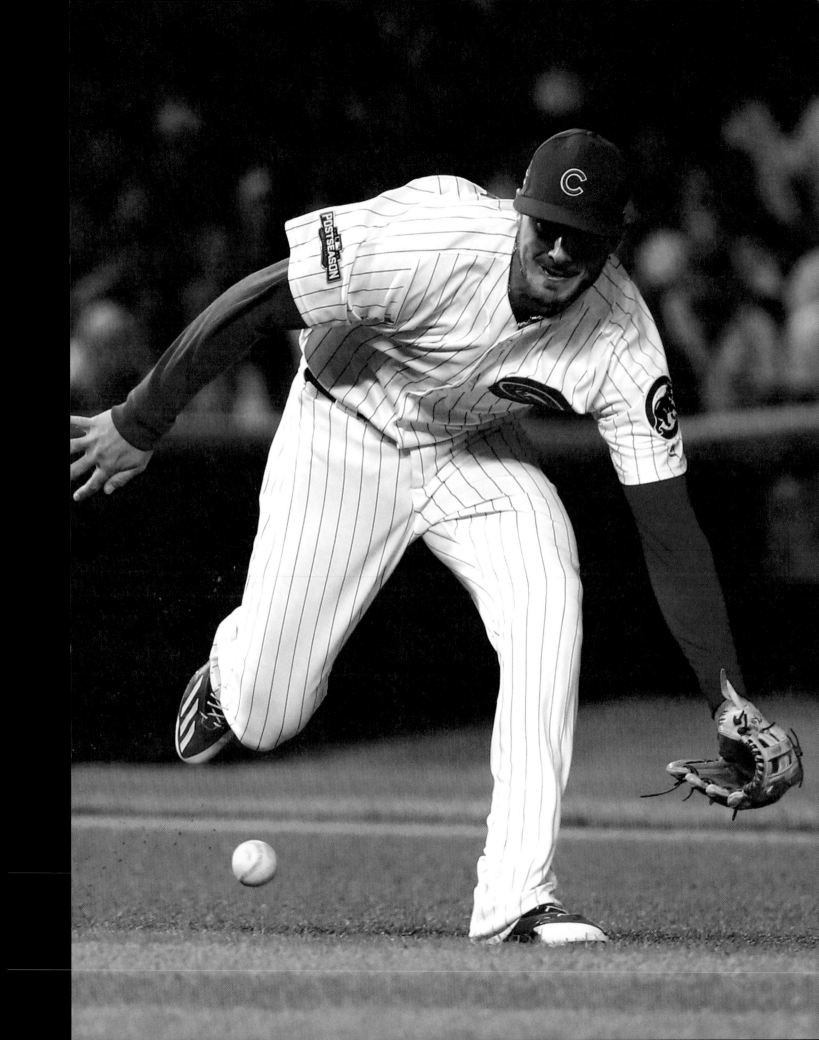

follows close behind. This is where Bryant's even-keeled approach could serve him best.

"Expectations don't always agree with all players," Sandberg said. "But I think he was in the right spot at (the) right time with this team and the talent and all the young players around him. He's not a fish out of water. I think that has helped the Cubs, bringing a lot of guys up at the same time and letting them be a big part of the team.

"Being a (franchise icon) isn't a burden when you have good players around you and you win. This team has a very large window to win. And to be a main player in that, I think that's what any player would want."

David Ross has seen just about everything in his 15 years in the big leagues. He agreed with Sandberg's assessment that having other talented young players surrounding Bryant can be beneficial, citing how Rizzo constantly reminds Bryant, albeit humorously, of the expectations facing him.

Nevertheless, it's a burden Bryant handles in a fashion that makes Ross gush.

"You see it more often than not: Guys come in with all this hype and fail," Ross said. "I'm not sure what's asked of him in terms of playing every day with these expectations, playing different positions a lot, gets enough attention.

"If he and Rizz don't do well, we're probably not going to be a very good team, so that's a lot of pressure on a young guy without a whole lot of time in the league. And he has embraced it as well as anybody can embrace it. This guy lives, eats, breathes baseball and this team and how he can get better. He's constantly working."

Back in the division-clinching clubhouse, Bryant grabbed another fistful of ice cubes and smiled.

"I stink at celebrating," he said.

There you go. The phenom has something on which to work.

Kris Bryant, who recorded 39 home runs and 102 RBIs during the regular season, doubles during Game 1 of the NLDS. (Brian Cassella/ Chicago Tribune)

70

JOE MADDON

Extraordinary Joe

Under Maddon's unusual approach, Cubs stay in the moment

By PAUL SULLIVAN

Joe Maddon has played the roles of philosopher, comedian, zoo director, T-shirt maker and self-help guru in his two years as Cubs manager.

But now that he's the first manager to take the Cubs to a World Series since Charlie Grimm in 1945, his sole task is to outmaneuver Indians counterpart Terry Francona, one of the best in the business.

The pressure is on, and we all know what Maddon thinks about pressure.

"Why would you ever want to run away from that?" Maddon said before a pre-Series workout at Progressive Field. "The alternative right now is I could be in Tampa cooking steaks in my backyard, making sure DirecTV is working properly.

"I'd much prefer this reality, so I plan to enjoy it. I want our guys to enjoy the moment. I want them to take mental snapshots of everything we're doing out here. It's really difficult to get into this position – really difficult.

"This is fortunately my third time I've had a chance to do this, where our players, a lot of them it's the first time. Enjoy it. Enjoy it. Go play your game. It's another game."

Maddon was a coach on the 2002 Angels team that beat the Giants in a seven-game World Series, and he managed the Rays to the 2008 World Series, where they lost to the Phillies in five games.

Ben Zobrist, who played under Maddon with the Rays, said there's no difference between the old model and the 2016 version.

"It's the same, except a little bit more moves because of the National League, the double-switching and that," Zobrist said. "Same guy, same stuff."

Maddon interviewed for the Red Sox managerial opening in the winter of 2003. Theo Epstein, then the Red Sox general manager, liked what he heard, even if he didn't hire Maddon.

"I saw just how different he was than anyone else we ever interviewed – his offbeat sense of humor and the use of the language and the way his mind worked," Epstein said. "Everything about him was different

Fun-loving while making deft, out-of-the box moves, Joe Maddon is the perfect manager for the Cubs. (Armando L. Sanchez/Chicago Tribune)

than what you'd expect from a manager, and it was refreshing."

Epstein believed Maddon was ready but thought Boston was the wrong market for him at the time. So he hired Francona, who went on to win two World Series rings with the Red Sox, ending the "Curse of the Bambino" in 2004.

"In the end we loved (Maddon) but thought taking over a veteran team in a big market, there would've been some risk involved because he's so unique," Epstein said. "He could go to Tampa, which was a Petri dish at the time, try some things out, grow into it with young players and blossom.

"And for us, having (Francona), who had already managed in the big leagues (with the Phillies), I think it turned out great for both."

But Epstein didn't forget about Maddon. And when an out clause in Maddon's Rays contract made him available after 2014, Epstein jumped, even though Rick Renteria had two years left on his deal.

Maddon hit the road running with his "shot-and-a-beer" news conference at the Cubby Bear, where he said he would be "talking playoffs" in 2015. The Cubs indeed made it, losing in the NL Championship Series, then began talking World Series in the spring.

That's when Maddon dressed up like a hippie and drove onto the field in a 1976 Dodge van he called a "shaggin' wagon," some of the daily spring wackiness that is vintage Maddon.

"I think it's part of the formula of who we are," first baseman Anthony Rizzo said. "It's fun, and spring training can get long sometimes. In our camp, it's fun every day. You don't know what to expect."

The lack of rules in the clubhouse makes Maddon a players' manager, and that has helped make this group of diverse personalities such a tight-knit bunch.

"He does a great job of just allowing his players to be themselves," pitcher Jake Arrieta said. "As a young player, I can look back on my first year (with the Orioles) and had a feeling that I kind of was walking on eggshells. I didn't want to do or say the wrong thing to make the wrong person upset.

"That doesn't happen here. Guys can do or say whatever they need to say. You might get yelled at by another guy on the

team, but we do hold ourselves accountable. And it's fun to do it that way. You police yourself, you give guys a lot of freedom. We don't take advantage of it, and that's why it works."

Maddon is so quotable, Epstein once joked the media should help pay part of his salary. We've heard all of his stories about Idaho Falls, Gene Autry Park and the Hazleton-West Hazleton football game a thousand times. He has uttered dialogue from every episode of "The Office" and named-drop his mom, Beanie.

But he has never been rude or condescending. He has never refused to answer a question, no matter how irrelevant.

The journey made Maddon who he is, and the journey is why the Cubs are here now.

"I'm really grateful for the fact it took me so long to become a manager," Maddon said. "Because I think all of the experiences I've had permitted me to think the way I do right now."

Think different.

It's now part of the Cubs Way.

Joe Maddon embraces Javier Baez after the Cubs' series-clinching win over the Giants in the Game 4 of the NLDS. (Brian Cassella/Chicago Tribune). Opposite: Joe Maddon and Dodgers manager Dave Roberts shake hands prior to the start of Game 1 of the NLCS. (Nuccio DiNuzzo/Chicago Tribune)

NATIONAL LEAGUE DIVISION SERIES
3-1 over the Giants

With 2016 being an even-numbered year, there was a sense that the San Francisco Giants — who won the World Series in 2010, 2012 and 2014 — might be the biggest obstacle in the Cubs' path. The series had the feel of a classic right from the start. It began with the Jon Lester-Johnny Cueto 1-0 pitching duel in Game 1, a tense, scoreless affair until the 8th inning, when Javier Baez deposited a home run into the basket in left field. That was the first of several magic moments Baez would conjure on his way to becoming the breakout star of the postseason. It took four tense games, but the Cubs prevailed and moved on to the league championship series for the second straight season. "It felt like a rite of passage almost," Theo Epstein said, "that we had to go through (the Giants) to get there."

Game 1: Cubs 1, Giants 0
Game 2: Cubs 5, Giants 2
Game 3: Giants 6, Cubs 5 (13 innings)
Game 4: Cubs 6, Giants 5

The Cubs celebrate on the field at AT&T Park after defeating the San Francisco Giants in Game 4 to clinch the NLDS. (Brian Cassella/Chicago Tribune)

THE FUN BEGINS

Javier Baez's homer sets confident tone that Cubs can ride through

By DAVID HAUGH

The way Javier Baez brazenly flipped his bat, the ball better have been gone.

The Cubs second baseman paused briefly in the eighth inning of a 1-0 victory over the Giants to watch the home run that seemed to soar as high as it did far into left field. No matter how long Baez lingered at the plate to admire his homer, Cubs fans will spend even longer appreciating what it meant to a team that needed to begin its World Series quest the right way.

Baez emerged from the dugout to take a bow after earning every throaty roar from the Wrigley Field crowd of 42,148. When all is said and done in the National League Division Series, will anybody come through with a bigger hit than Baez's?

"I was waiting for him to make a mistake, and he finally did," Baez said of Giants starter Johnny Cueto. "I thought it was way farther than that. ... I didn't mean to show anybody up."

In a game the Cubs couldn't afford to lose without an epidemic of anxiety spreading through the North Side, Baez provided the antidote by depositing the only mistake Cueto made over the left-field wall.

Statistics say Baez's home run traveled 381 feet, but there's no telling how far the Cubs can ride the confidence gained from surviving such a close call in Game 1 after such a lengthy layoff. The home-run ball, caught in the crosswind, eventually landed in the basket and into Wrigley lore, giving the Cubs a 1-0 lead in the NLDS opener that featured two pitchers defining the word ace.

"It was a classic old-school baseball game," Cubs manager Joe Maddon said.

Cubs starter Jon Lester outdueled Cueto, giving up five hits and economically using his 86 pitches to keep the Giants from scoring. This was the way the Cubs scripted Game 1, with Lester going eight strong innings and closer Aroldis Chapman getting the final three outs. This was the way it seldom has gone for the Cubs of old, but the game should remind everybody that these are not the Cubs of Octobers past.

The defense backed up Lester, who even helped himself by snaring a hard grounder by Buster Posey that appeared to get caught in the webbing of his glove. The only scare came in the fourth, when Angel Pagan hit a sinking liner to left that Ben Zobrist let get under his glove for what was ruled a double.

Zobrist was in left because Maddon chose to play

Jon Lester held the Giants scoreless in Game 1, throwing just 86 pitches over eight innings. (Armando Sanchez/Chicago Tribune)

Baez at second base, Zobrist's position, and keep Kris Bryant at third instead of in left. The decision didn't backfire defensively only because Posey, who runs like he's lugging his catching gear, failed to score from first.

Early on, the growing local legend known as "Grandpa Rossy" nailed baserunners to control the game. In the first, David Ross threw out Gorkys Hernandez trying to steal second. Two innings later, the catcher caught Conor Gillaspie napping at first and picked him off.

Meanwhile, Cueto kept the Cubs guessing by changing speeds and delivery motions, alternating the height of his leg kick and rotation of his body to give up only three hits. Maddon called Cueto a "latter-day Luis Tiant," referring to the former Red Sox hurler from Cuba who used to turn and face center field during his windup. The unorthodox mechanics combined with unhittable stuff to help Cueto cruise.

Despite the fact that only one run crossed the plate all night, nobody in the overflow crowd felt cheated, no matter what they paid for the privilege to watch the Cubs. As the clock approached midnight, fans mingled in the box seats and snapped pictures for posterity. They didn't want the night to end.

Not when it felt like the fun was just beginning. ●

Javier Baez's solo home run in the eighth inning was all the offense the Cubs needed in Game 1. (Brian Cassella/ Chicago Tribune)

NATIONAL LEAGUE DIVISION SERIES: GAME 2
OCTOBER 8, 2016 • CHICAGO, ILLINOIS
CUBS 5, GIANTS 2

UNLIKELY HEROES

Kyle Hendricks and Travis Wood provide offensive spark in 5-2 victory

By Mark Gonzales and David Haugh

The Cubs insisted throughout their 103-win season that they were more than a two-man offense, and pitchers Kyle Hendricks and Travis Wood proved that point again in a 5-2 victory over the Giants in Game 2 of the best-of-five National League Division Series.

Hendricks had a two-run single in the second inning before departing in the fourth with a right forearm bruise. X-rays were negative.

Travis Wood, his replacement, made history when he smacked a home run in addition to pitching 1 1/3 scoreless innings as the Cubs took a 5-2 lead.

Hendricks, who was 9-2 with a 1.32 ERA at Wrigley Field during the regular season, left after an Angel Pagan line drive drilled him on his right forearm with two outs in the fourth and the Cubs owning a 4-2 lead.

But Wood came in and fooled Conor Gillaspie on a called third strike, and then he ripped his homer off Giants reliever George Kontos in the bottom of the inning.

Wood, who has nine career homers, became the first reliever to hit a home run in a playoff game since Rosy Ryan of the New York Giants against the Washington Senators in Game 3 of the 1924 World Series.

Wood joins Rick Sutcliffe (1984) and Kerry Wood (2003) as Cubs pitchers who have hit homers in playoff games.

The Cubs knocked out former teammate Jeff Samardzija after two innings as they surged to a 4-0 lead.

Samardzija hitting 95 mph on the radar gun on his first pitch illustrated how amped the pitcher with the football mentality must have felt facing the team that fulfilled his major-league dream. As a result, Samardzija's sinkers didn't sink and his straight fastballs came with invitations. The last time Samardzija got hit as hard on an autumn Saturday night, he probably was wearing shoulder pads and a helmet for Notre Dame.

"It's fair to say he was a little bit off," Giants manager Bruce Bochy said.

Dexter Fowler, who worked Samardzija for a 13-pitch walk in the first inning of a 5-4 victory on Sept. 1, battled from an 0-2 pitch to smack a double on his ninth pitch and scored on Ben Zobrist's soft single with two out.

Travis Wood takes a curtain call after his fourth inning home run in Game 2. The Cubs' relief pitcher entered the game in the top of the inning after starter Kyle Hendricks left with a right forearm bruise. (Brian Cassella/Chicago Tribune)

The Cubs added three runs in the second. Jason Heyward, who entered the game 2-for-13 lifetime against Samardzija, ripped a double down the left field line. Rookie Willson Contreras poked an opposite-field single to right to load the bases. Javier Baez immediately broke from second base as Hendricks hit his blooper into center and scored after Heyward with a headfirst slide. Kris Bryant capped the rally with an RBI single off the glove of right fielder Hunter Pence.

Bochy owns three World Series rings that give him the benefit of the doubt, but he can expect to be second-guessed for picking Samardzija over lefty Matt Moore, the scheduled Game 4 starter. Especially after Samardzija pitched as poorly as he did Sept. 1 on the same mound, when he endured a three-run, 47-pitch first inning.

Sometimes, you can't go home again.

Spontaneously in the second inning, as the Cubs were building their four-run lead, the revved-up Wrigley crowd of 42,392 stood and started cheering out of unadulterated joy, the type of euphoria at the old ballpark Samardzija once talked of helping create. But twice Samardzija turned the Cubs down; before they traded him to the A's in July 2014, when he rejected a long-term contract offer, and last winter, when he rebuffed a modest one-year deal after meeting with Cubs President Theo Epstein.

The Giants provided Samardzija security in the form of a five-year, $90 million contract. The Cubs moved on and looked forward. Clearly, it was the right direction. ●

Center fielder Dexter Fowler makes a sliding catch to retire the Giants' Angel Pagan in the ninth inning. (Brian Cassella/ Chicago Tribune)

NATIONAL LEAGUE DIVISION SERIES: GAME 3
OCTOBER 10, 2016 • SAN FRANCISCO, CALIFORNIA
GIANTS 6, CUBS 5 (13 INNINGS)

THE CAR BOMB, THE CATCH AND A NIGHT TO REMEMBER

Cubs fail to complete sweep, blowing 3-run lead in 13-inning loss to Giants

By PAUL SULLIVAN

When the ball flew off Kris Bryant's bat in the top of the ninth inning of the heart-stopping 6-5, 13-inning loss to the Giants at AT&T Park, he wasn't sure if Gregor Blanco was going to catch it or not.

"It was tricking me," Bryant said. "I thought he was under it, but the wind is always blowing out there, even with the thick air."

The ball wound up glancing off the top of an ad on the left field wall that features a cartoon dog hanging out the window of a cartoon car that has eyeballs for headlights, and into the left field bleachers for a game-tying two-run home run.

"Why do they have a car out there?" Bryant asked.

Because a game like this needed a ball hitting off the roof of a cartoon car with a cartoon dog hanging out the window. It was mandatory for this kind of theater of the absurd baseball.

Bryant's car bomb was one moment of exhilaration in a manic affair that defied description, an instant classic that will be replayed over and over long after these playoffs are over.

"It feels like it," starter Jake Arrieta said. "Game 1 of the series, and now Game 3, to play out like it did. A tremendous start to the playoffs for us."

Arrieta started it off with his three-run bomb off Madison Bumgarner in the second, ending Bumgarner's postseason scoreless streak at 24 innings and giving the Cubs a quick lead. But the offense shut down after Bryant's two-out single in the fourth. The Cubs went 0-for-14 until Bryant tied it with his blast off Sergio Romo, then went 0-for-13 until Javier Baez's one-out single in the 13th.

With two on, David Ross grounded into an inning-ending double play to end their only extra inning threat. A challenge was made, to no avail. The Cubs wound up 2-for-11 with runners in scoring position, stranding 10 on the night. Anthony Rizzo went 0-for-6 and is 0-for-13 in the NLDS.

"You can't win 'em all, and this is a learning experience and we'll learn from it," Bryant said. "It's good to be in an atmosphere like this in an away city. A lot to take from this game."

Arrieta's home run would've been the play of the game on any other night. He cranked a 377-foot shot on a 1-2 count, saying he just wanted to put a "nice, easy swing on it."

Arrieta pumped his fist as he ran towards first and watched the ball land softly in the bleachers, as road-tripping Cubs fans at AT&T Park pretended they

Aroldis Chapman reacts during the eighth inning of the Cubs' loss to the Giants in Game 3. Chapman entered the game in the eighth inning with the Cubs leading 3-2 and gave up three runs, including a two-run triple to Conor Gillaspie. (Brian Cassella/Chicago Tribune)

were human jack-in-the-boxes. Confidence was high, but the Giants, of course, are the Giants.

The Cubs held on to a one-run lead until Conor Gillaspie's two-run triple past a diving Albert Almora in the eighth, leaving the usually untouchable Aroldis Chapman in position to be the goat. The Giants added another run in the inning, but Justin Grimm helped prevent further damage by getting the final two outs, giving Bryant the opportunity to be a hero.

Mission accomplished.

Almora, who replaced the Gold Glove-winning right-fielder Jason Heyward on a double-switch so Chapman could potentially pitch two innings, saved the Cubs in the ninth with a diving catch in right to rob Buster Posey. After the catch, Almora picked himself up and doubled Brandon Belt off first to end the inning, and the Cubs were alive to fight again.

"I knew the situation at hand, and just wanted to help my team," Almora said.

"An unbelievable play by Almora," left-hander Mike Montgomery said. "It was definitely an emotional rollercoaster, some close calls there and good plays."

"I loved our way," Joe Maddon said after the game. "I thought we played it hard, we played it right, and they beat us." ●

NATIONAL LEAGUE DIVISION SERIES: GAME 4
OCTOBER 11, 2016 • SAN FRANCISCO, CALIFORNIA
CUBS 6, GIANTS 5

COMEBACK FOR THE AGES

Cubs rally in ninth to eliminate Giants 6-5 in NLDS; advance to NLCS

By PAUL SULLIVAN

I took until Game 4 of the National League Division Series for someone to be interviewed outside a ballpark with a goat, setting a modern-day record for the longest goat-free stretch to start a Cubs postseason.

It also took four postseason games for a Cubs player to be asked about the team's reputation as "lovable losers," which prompted Jon Lester to say "the biggest thing is nobody really cares in (our clubhouse) about a curse or a goat or anything else." Lester went even further, suggesting the Cubs were not afraid of "any animals," regardless of the animals' reputation.

After the heart-wrenching, 13-inning loss to the Giants in Game 3, the Cubs entered Game 4 ready to bury all those reminders of the past -- the ghosts of 1984 and 2003 that continue to pop up every time they make it to October.

Another loss would not only create a do-or-cry situation at Wrigley Field in Game 5, it would feed into the narrative of the misery industrial complex, a diverse group of media members devoted to turning every Cubs mistake into some sort of metaphysical mishap.

The Cubs were seemingly on the verge of disaster again in Game 4 of the NLDS before a stunning ninth-inning rally launched them to a 6-5 victory and into their second straight NL Championship Series appearance.

Willson Contreras' two-run single off Will Smith tied it in the ninth and then Javier Baez knocked in Jason Heyward for the game-winner. Aroldis Chapman came on to pitch a scoreless ninth.

The Giants had won 10 straight elimination games, while the Cubs won a major-league-leading 103 games. Something had to give.

The Cubs had been to the postseason five times since 2003, so trying to ignore this seasonal silliness has been an occupational hazard for many of their players and management over the years.

You knew it was just a matter of time before the goat stuff started, and by the seventh inning of Game 4 the TV cameras dutifully showed a fan wearing a goat head in the stands.

This all really began in '03 when a Chicago radio reporter brought up the story of the billy goat curse to Marlins manager Jack McKeon just before the playoffs.

Teammates mob Cubs closer Aroldis Chapman after Chapman pitched a scoreless ninth inning in Game 4. (Anthony Souffle/Chicago Tribune)

McKeon, an eccentric old-timer, had no idea what the reporter was talking about. But when the Marlins came back from a 3-1 deficit to force a Game 7, McKeon brought up the goat himself, suggesting it might be a self-fulfilling prophecy.

"It makes you think a little," he said. "You (media) keep talking, I think it might happen."

It did, though it was the Cubs' fault alone.

This Cubs team, however, is so talented and focused it should be able to shut out any kind of distraction, and Lester said that's exactly what the Cubs have done.

"If we make a mistake, we're not going to blame it on a curse or anything else like that," he said. "We going to blame it on ourselves and be accountable for it and move on to the next play."

In Game 3, Chapman took the blame for coughing up the lead on a two-run, eighth-inning triple to Conor Gillaspie. In Game 4, John Lackey didn't show up, putting the Cubs in a two-run hole and being removed after only four innings.

But the Cubs wouldn't give up, staging another late comeback in a series that was nothing less than an October classic.

"You can't take for granted what we have done this year," Cubs first baseman Anthony Rizzo said. "We have one mission, one goal in mind. That's eight more wins. And we visualized it all year. And we'll keep visualizing it and enjoying it." ●

Jason Heyward scores the go-ahead run in Game 4, completing a stunning 4-run ninth-inning rally.
(Brian Cassella/Chicago Tribune)

NATIONAL LEAGUE CHAMPIONSHIP SERIES
4-2 over the Dodgers

Thanks to Miguel Montero's pinch-hit grand slam, the Cubs were off and running with a dramatic Game 1 victory, but Clayton Kershaw threw up a stop sign in Game 2, throwing seven shutout innings to even the series at a game apiece. The series moved to warm, sunny Los Angeles for Game 3, but the Cubs bats stayed cold as the Dodgers once again held them scoreless. The Cubs' bats came alive in Game 4 and 5, sending the series back to Chicago where a city stood poised to release 71 years of pent-up anxiety. Behind the brilliant pitching of Kyle Hendricks — who outdueled a shaky Kershaw — the Cubs won Game 6 and secured their first World Series berth since 1945. "What a special moment," Ben Zobrist said. "Now it's time to move on to bigger things. The ultimate goal is still out in front of us."

Game 1: Cubs 8, Dodgers 4
Game 2: Dodgers 1, Cubs 0
Game 3: Dodgers 6, Cubs 0
Game 4: Cubs 10, Dodgers 2
Game 5: Cubs 8, Dodgers 4
Game 6: Cubs 5, Dodgers 0

Fans crowd the intersection of Addison St. and Clark St. after the Cubs' win over the Los Angeles Dodgers in Game 1. (Nuccio DiNuzzo/Chicago Tribune)

NATIONAL LEAGUE CHAMPIONSHIP SERIES: GAME 1
OCTOBER 15, 2016 • CHICAGO, ILLINOIS
CUBS 8, DODGERS 4

8TH WONDER

Montero's heroics in decisive inning bail out manager

By David Haugh

Of all the people at Wrigley Field calling Miguel Montero out for a curtain call after his pinch-hit grand slam in the Cubs' 8-4 victory over the Dodgers, the loudest should have been his manager, Joe Maddon.

Montero's 402-foot home run into right field off Dodgers reliever Joe Blanton did more than just give the Cubs a 1-0 lead in the National League Championship Series; it bailed out Maddon for a rare move that backfired.

The biggie from "Miggy" saved the Cubs from losing a game that, until Maddon prematurely pulled starter Jon Lester after six innings, looked like an easy win. And it spared Chicago from spilling angst into the streets that started to build as soon as Maddon pinch-hit for Lester with the toughest nine outs to go.

As Lester walked slowly from the on-deck circle back to the dugout in the sixth inning, his deliberate body language screamed exactly what everyone was thinking.

What are you thinking, Joe Maddon?

The Cubs led 3-1 at the time, but Maddon decided to send Jorge Soler to hit for Lester, ending the night for the Cubs ace who deserved a chance to go deeper. Instead, Maddon pulled Lester after only 77 pitches, six innings, four hits and one run – a wind-aided home run in the left-field basket by Andre Ethier. Lester wasn't as sharp as usual, but he didn't appear to be laboring either. If you think it was hard to see the Cubs unravel two innings later when the Dodgers tied the score, imagine how Lester must have felt watching helplessly.

"I just thought tonight Jon really wasn't at the top of his game," Maddon said. "He didn't have his best stuff."

"Would I have liked to have gone out in the seventh? Absolutely," Lester said.

The seventh inning went smoothly as three Cubs pitchers kept the Dodgers from scoring, but Maddon's move backfired in another unforgettable eighth inning in Cubs playoff lore. With the bases loaded and nobody out, Maddon called on closer Aroldis Chapman. The last time Maddon inserted Chapman to attempt a six-out save – in Game 3 against the Giants – it didn't go well and neither did this experience. After two straight strikeouts, Chapman gave up a two-run, game-tying single to Adrian Gonzalez that stunned the crowd.

Miguel Montero's pinch-hit grand slam propelled the Cubs to a decisive Game 1 victory. (Brian Cassella/Chicago Tribune)

A Dodgers team that had hung around now had been rejuvenated, allowed back in the game by a managerial move by the opponent. Ironically, a move in the bottom half of the eighth by Maddon's counterpart, Dodgers manager Dave Roberts, set up Montero's heroics.

Roberts wanted to force Maddon to pinch-hit for Chapman so, with the pitcher due up next, the Dodgers walked Chris Coghlan to load the bases with score tied at 3-3. Essentially, Roberts chose to face Montero rather than Coghlan and had the numbers to support the decision: Montero was 2-for-11 lifetime against Blanton while Coghlan a robust 8-for-17.

Still, Roberts probably regretted the choice. Montero left no doubt, ripping Blanton's pitch into the seats and assuring everybody that his back was just fine. He had just carried the Cubs to victory, after all.

Despite needing a pinch-hit grand slam to survive their first NLCS victory since 2003, the Cubs proved more than anything that defense wins championships in baseball too. The grass stains covering the front of Dexter Fowler's jersey suggested how busy he was saving runs with diving catches in the outfield. Anthony Rizzo got into the act, too, with a diving stop of Yasiel Puig's grounder.

For a change, Javier Baez didn't make a memorable defensive play, but he did become the first Cubs player to steal home in a playoff game since 1907

Perhaps not since 1908 has a Cubs team looked this complete and worthy of a championship. ●

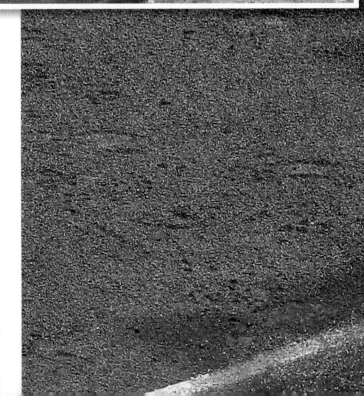

Always an electrifying presence, Javier Baez made his mark in the Cubs' 8-4 win by dodging Carlos Ruiz to steal home. (Brian Cassella/Chicago Tribune)

NATIONAL LEAGUE CHAMPIONSHIP SERIES: GAME 2
OCTOBER 16, 2016 • CHICAGO, ILLINOIS
DODGERS 1, CUBS 0

KER-PLUNK

Cubs can't touch Kershaw as Dodgers even series

By DAVID HAUGH

After Javy Baez's drive to the center-field warning track landed in Joc Pederson's glove to end the seventh inning at Wrigley Field, Dodgers starter Clayton Kershaw smiled like a guy who sensed he had escaped danger.

Like everyone in the ballpark knew he had, based on the crack of the bat.

"We all held our breath a little bit," Dodgers manager Dave Roberts said.

"I thought it was out for sure," Kershaw added.

By the time Kershaw reached the dugout after exhaling, he was still chuckling -- and that's all the Cubs can do now, too, after a 1-0 defeat in Game 2 of the National League Championship Series. Laugh it off. Chalk it up to facing the best pitcher on the planet. Avoid the loss of confidence that can accompany being Kershawed.

Kershaw was Kershaw. Closer Kenley Jansen, who earned a six-out save, was Kenley Jansen. Adrian Gonzalez, whose second-inning home run provided the game-winner, was Adrian Gonzalez. But the Cubs weren't the Cubs, looking overmatched at the plate one night after scoring eight runs in the NLCS opener.

"(Kershaw's) command of his fastball was outstanding," Maddon said. "He didn't strike a lot of guys out (six), and I was taking a lot of solace in that."

Maddon also can find comfort in his team's resilience. The Cubs can overreact to being humbled by

the game's greatest pitcher or practice what their manager preaches and understand a seven-game series is long enough to survive nights like this one, however frustrating. Now is no time to start acknowledging pressure. Anthony Rizzo and Addison Russell, whose slumps are sucking the lifeblood out of the heart of the Cubs order, aren't going to start hitting better by thinking more. Maddon needs to find a way to help everybody relax.

The Cubs must fly to California believing they can avoid seeing Kershaw again if they can win the next three games in Los Angeles -- not a ridiculous notion given the drop-off from the Dodgers ace to the rest of their rotation. This isn't the Giants staff.

Pitching for the fourth time in 10 days, Kershaw looked as fresh as opening day. The lefty retired the first 14 Cubs before Baez singled with two outs in the fifth. A Willson Contreras single followed, and that was as seriously as the Cubs threatened. No Dodger had retired that many in a row in the postseason since Sandy Koufax in the 1963 World Series.

Kershaw's supposedly tired arm lasted seven dominant innings, giving up two measly hits and walking one. He threw 84 masterful pitches, relying more on fastballs and changeups than his deadly curveball, as Maddon noted.

This is what Bulls opponents used to feel like after helplessly watching Michael Jordan drop 35

Javier Baez rounds second base in the fifth inning of Game 2. Baez was the first Cub to reach base against a dominant Clayton Kershaw (Chris Sweda/Chicago Tribune)

in a playoff game. The greatest in the game will have days like this, and baseball has no more elite pitcher than Kershaw.

The aura of Kershaw clouded every at-bat for the Cubs, who looked like they were back in the 2015 NLCS flailing against the Mets. Kershaw reduced Cubs hitters to baseball mannequins, with Contreras even keeping the bat rested on his shoulder for the first pitch of his first at-bat. If Contreras was trying to get in Kershaw's head, he should know the entry is hermetically sealed.

Jansen replaced Kershaw in the eighth after throwing 51 pitches in the NLDS clincher. He looked

well-rested too. With Miguel Montero, Game 1's hero, pinch-hitting again with the Cubs' script ready for Act 2, Jansen blew Montero away with strike three. Jansen's ninth inning included far less drama, easily retiring the first three hitters in the order and jolting Wrigleyville back to reality. ●

NATIONAL LEAGUE CHAMPIONSHIP SERIES: GAME 3
OCTOBER 18, 2016 • LOS ANGELES, CALIFORNIA
DODGERS 6, CUBS 0

OFFENSE IS AWOL

Rearranged lineup no help, Cubs face 2-1 deficit after Hill's gem

By MARK GONZALES

A lineup shake-up didn't help, nor did Jake Arrieta returning to the site of his first no-hitter against a Dodgers team he once dominated.

And for the first time in an otherwise giddy season, the Cubs have approached the vicinity of must-win status.

That's because their offensive funk spread from the middle of their lineup and left Arrieta no margin for error in a 6-0 loss to the Dodgers in Game 3 of the National League Championship Series.

"We couldn't barrel any balls," Miguel Montero said. "We're a pretty young team, but we have experience. We have to learn. That's not an excuse.

"A lot of guys have been in the game for at least two full years. We have to grow. We have to get better. You cannot carry over 'We're a young team, so we're going to get better.' No. We do have to get better, but we have to start now."

Montero's grand slam right before a Dexter Fowler homer in Game 1 represents the Cubs' last runs as their scoreless streak has stretched to 18 innings.

Left-hander Rich Hill continued his renaissance with an array of off-speed pitches and arm angles that confused Cubs hitters for six innings of two-hit ball. And his success came after Anthony Rizzo was dropped from third to fourth in the order and Javier Baez was elevated to fifth.

Making matters more difficult for the Cubs is that they failed to solve their second consecutive left-handed opposing starter, with rookie lefty Julio Urias scheduled to face them in Game 4 and the Dodgers up 2-1 in the best-of-seven series.

"It is different, but I feel like we had the right scouting report on both of them," Kris Bryant said of Game 2 winner Clayton Kershaw and Hill. "We knew how they got us out. They stuck with their game plan, and it worked."

The Cubs' frustration reached a zenith during a 30-pitch second inning in which Hill walked two of the first three batters. But then Addison Russell struck out on a 74-mph curve and Montero grounded to second.

Russell, who was lifted for pinch hitter Jason Heyward in the seventh, is 1-for-24 in the postseason. Rizzo collected a broken-bat single in the eighth, but he's 2-for-26.

Manager Joe Maddon was reluctant to move Baez up but had no other choice because of the lack of hitting in the middle of the order. Jorge Soler also was inserted in an attempt to take advantage of his past success against left-handed pitchers.

In Maddon's perfect world, Soler would have helped the Cubs surge to an early lead as he started in

Kris Bryant and Anthony Rizzo walk away disappointed after failing to capitalize in Game 3. The Cubs' bats were silenced by Dodgers pitching for the second consecutive game. (Nuccio DiNuzzo/Chicago Tribune)

right field, and then Heyward could have taken over in right for defense.

But it never got to that point. First Corey Seager's two-out single scored Andrew Toles in the third to break Arrieta's streak of 18 scoreless innings against the Dodgers. Then the most demoralizing development came in the fourth when Arrieta barely missed on a 2-2 pitch to Yasmani Grandal, who smacked the next offering for a two-run two-out homer to snap a 2-for-20 rut.

Arrieta and Montero said after the game that the 2-2 pitch could have been called a strike, but they weren't upset with plate umpire Gary Cederstrom.

"Grandal did a nice job of getting to the next pitch and putting a nice swing on the next one," Arrieta said. "They fouled off a lot of great pitches in two-strike counts to get to the next pitch." ●

NATIONAL LEAGUE CHAMPIONSHIP SERIES: GAME 4
OCTOBER 19, 2016 • LOS ANGELES, CALIFORNIA
CUBS 10, DODGERS 2

A ROARING RETURN

After consecutive shutouts, Cubs rout it out to pull even in series

By Mark Gonzales

Rookie Willson Contreras nearly threw a ball from behind home plate into the left-field stands before batting practice.

Javier Baez stepped out of the box and took a deep breath before hitting a single into left field in fourth inning.

And Anthony Rizzo was all smiles and fist pumps after breaking out of his postseason slump while using Matt Szczur's bat.

The loose, productive manner that earned the Cubs 103 victories during the regular season returned when they needed it most during their World Series-or-bust mission.

After going scoreless for 21 innings, the Cubs started to break out of their doldrums with Ben Zobrist's bunt single. Rizzo punctuated the offensive renaissance with three hits and three RBIs that enabled the Cubs to coast to a 10-2 victory over the Dodgers and even this best-of-seven National League Championship Series at two games apiece.

"We were due to break out," center fielder Dexter Fowler said. "It was a matter of time."

The only cause for concern for the Cubs occurred when reliever Carl Edwards Jr. left with left hamstring tightness after throwing a pitch to Corey Seager with two out in the seventh.

But any tension stemming from their scoreless streak, their 5-for-57 performance against left-handers in this series and the lack of production from the middle of the order was alleviated.

The most encouraging development was the breakout of Rizzo, who was 2-for-28 before ripping a home run off reliever Pedro Baez to start the fifth.

Rizzo highlighted a five-run sixth when he ripped a line drive into right field for a two-run single and pumped his fist in exultation.

"He doesn't owe me anything," said Szczur, who lent his bat to Rizzo on Tuesday, which resulted in a broken-bat single.

Meanwhile, Zobrist was 4-for-27 before placing his bunt single down the third-base line off 20-year-old left-hander Julio Urias in the fourth.

After missing a chance to score in the second, the Cubs maintained their poise as Baez took a few extra seconds out of the box before moving Zobrist to second with his single.

Contreras showed his defensive prowess in the first when he picked Justin Turner off second base

Starting pitcher John Lackey is energized as his team rediscovers its winning form against the Dodgers. (Brian Cassella/Chicago Tribune)

with Adrian Gonzalez at the plate to end the inning.

With David Ross and Miguel Montero batting a collective 2-for-17 in the postseason, manager Joe Maddon opted for Contreras in Game 4. The move paid off when the rookie singled in Zobrist.

Addison Russell, whom Maddon has been defending despite a 1-for-25 start, smacked a two-run homer to center field to cap the rally and then showed plenty of emotion in a jubilant dugout.

Montgomery allowed a two-run single to Turner that grazed off his glove. The Cubs could have turned a double play had he fielded the ball cleanly or let it roll to Russell.

The Cubs caught a break in the second when plate umpire Angel Hernandez called out Gonzalez trying to score on an Andrew Toles single.

Gonzalez appeared to slide his hand under the tag of Contreras but the call stood upon review.

Despite a 5-0 lead, Maddon pulled starter John Lackey after he walked two batters to start the fifth. Lackey looked at Maddon in disbelief as left-hander Mike Montgomery took over.

Lackey conceded he was "surprised" by the hook but declined to discuss his reaction, preferring instead to poke the media.

"We won a game," Lackey said. "We were terrible yesterday; now all of a sudden we're great. It's amazing this time of year you guys can flip so quick. It's funny." ●

Anthony Rizzo breaks out of his postseason slump with a fifth inning home run in Game 4. (Brian Cassella/Chicago Tribune)

NATIONAL LEAGUE CHAMPIONSHIP SERIES: GAME 5
OCTOBER 20, 2016 • LOS ANGELES, CALIFORNIA
CUBS 8, DODGERS 4

ONE STEP CLOSER

Russell's clutch home run sparks offense, Lester dominates

By MARK GONZALES

The tension turned to relief and heightened anticipation as soon as Addison Russell's drive cleared the center-field wall.

Russell's two-run homer in the sixth inning snapped a 1-1 tie and gave Jon Lester much-deserved run support as the Cubs topped the Dodgers 8-4 in Game 5 of the National League Championship Series at warm Dodger Stadium.

The Cubs own a 3-2 lead in the best-of-seven series with a chance to earn their first NL pennant since 1945 in Game 6 at Wrigley Field.

Lester continued his mastery of the Dodgers with seven innings of five-hit ball. In 28 innings against the Dodgers this season, Lester has allowed only three runs on 16 hits while striking out 25.

Before Russell's homer, the Cubs were 0-for-8 with runners in scoring position and as ineffective as they were in their Game 2 and 3 shutout setbacks.

The Cubs failed to expand a lead in the first after Dexter Fowler singled and scored on Anthony Rizzo's double off starter Kenta Maeda as Javier Baez and Jason Heyward struck out to end the threat.

Dodgers manager Dave Roberts was taking no chances, even with the knowledge that ace Clayton Kershaw is starting Game 6. He pulled Maeda with two out and two on in the fourth with Lester up. The move paid off when Josh Fields retired Lester on a fly to left.

But in the sixth, the Cubs were able to get their second timely homer of this series off Blanton, who surrendered a tiebreaking grand slam to Miguel Montero in Game 1. This time it was Russell, who also had a key two-run home run in the Game 4 triumph.

Roberts said before the game that the Dodgers would try to get into Lester's psyche, and emotions ran high from the time Lester walked Enrique Hernandez to open the bottom of the first.

Hernandez took huge leads but didn't attempt to steal, as Lester would counter by holding the ball longer before throwing to the plate or stepping off the mound.

"We've seen just about every trick in the book this year of trying to mess with him," catcher David Ross said. "So when they do it, it kind of fires him up and gets him every more locked in. You saw that tonight. He really dialed it up."

Lester, however, was in no mood for the Dodgers tricks as he fielded a Joc Pederson bunt and threw

Addison Russell is congratulated by Javier Baez after hitting a two-run home run in the sixth inning of Game 5. (Nuccio DiNuzzo/Chicago Tribune)

a one-bouncer to first for the final out of the second before turning to stare at the Dodgers dugout.

Lester was visibly upset after not getting a strike call on two pitches to Corey Seager before fanning him to end the third and then yelling in the direction of home plate umpire Alfonso Marquez.

The inability to hold runners closely finally caught up with Lester in the fourth when Howie Kendrick lined a double to left and stole third with the benefit of a 30-foot lead.

The Cubs brought the infield in and Adrian Gonzalez hit a grounder to first. But Rizzo momentarily bobbled the ball, enabling Kendrick to score the tying run. That was the first run the Dodgers scored off Lester this season that wasn't a home run.

Meanwhile, reserve outfielder Matt Szczur may be the first MVP to not even play in the postseason after telling the Fox broadcasters Russell borrowed his leggings. Anthony Rizzo snapped out of h is slump in Game 4 after borrowing Szczur's bat.

"It's funny, (Zobrist) was like 'Hey, what have you got for me?'" Szczur said. "The same day everything came out, they ended up breaking out of their slumps, and it just happened to be with my stuff. It's good karma."

It was that kind of a night, and that kind of a series. ●

Anthony Rizzo connects for an RBI double against Kenta Maeda in the first inning. (Nuccio DiNuzzo/Chicago Tribune)

NATIONAL LEAGUE CHAMPIONSHIP SERIES: GAME 6
OCTOBER 22, 2016 • CHICAGO, ILLINOIS
CUBS 5, DODGERS 0

HOLY COW!

Cubs carry out Maddon's mission to KO Kershaw, reach Series

By PAUL SULLIVAN

A little bit of faith was all the Cubs asked for and all they really needed.

Forget about all the things that happened to their predecessors and think about all the hard work and preparation that got them to this moment.

When it mattered most, the Cubs were ready, and so was Wrigley Field.

On an electric night at the 102-year-old ballpark, the Cubs beat the Dodgers 5-0 in Game 6 of the National League Championship Series to clinch their first pennant since 1945. Kyle Hendricks turned in another made-for-Maddux outing in the biggest game of his life, shutting out the Dodgers on two hits in 7 1/3 innings and beating Dodgers ace Clayton Kershaw.

"I thought we played one of our best games all year tonight, under these circumstances," manager Joe Maddon said. "The defense, the pitching, the hitting -- that was a complete game of baseball."

The Cubs have had history thrown in their faces all year long, and they know the numbers by heart: 1908 and 1945, 1969 and 2003.

"The history means a lot," Hendricks said. "It puts it in perspective for us. We enjoy it more because we know (what) it means to the fans of this city. At the end of the day, it's about baseball, it's about winning games, and it comes down to making pitches."

A crowd of 42,386 made every pitch a life-and-death experience while thousands of fans congregated outside to share in the glory. It was a day they'd waited for their entire lives and no one was ready to go home.

A 71-year wait for a pennant seemed like a lifetime, and for most of them it was. There were a few near-misses along the way, most notably in 1984 and 2003, but for the most part the franchise seldom came close to getting this far, earning its reputation as a lovable loser.

Hendricks may not be the best pitcher on the planet, but he just might be the smartest. He was lost in Kershaw's shadow in all the pregame hype despite leading the majors in earned-run average.

"Honestly, it's nothing new for me," Hendricks said. "That's kind of how it's been my whole life, my whole career, but you don't think about it. That's all outside forces. When you make good pitches, you're going to get hitters out."

All the pregame anxiety subsided when Dexter

Javier Baez celebrates turning the game-ending double play to eliminate the Dodgers from the playoffs. Baez would be named NLCS MVP alongside teammate Jon Lester. (Brian Cassella/Chicago Tribune)

Fowler led off the game by slicing a ball into right field that bounced into the seats for a ground-rule double Everyone was well aware of the Cubs' mantra surrounding Fowler.

"He goes, we go."

Another double to right by Kris Bryant brought a giant sigh of relief, and when left fielder Andrew Toles botched an Anthony Rizzo fly ball the Cubs were on their way. Fowler's RBI single in the second made it 3-0, and Willson Contreras and Anthony Rizzo cranked solo home runs in the fourth and fifth innings to pile on.

"It's hard to put into words when you see a guy like David Ross on the podium," Jake Arrieta said. "It's been a storybook year, not only for him but for the team."

The storybook might even have a surprise character for the final chapter: Kyle Schwarber's unexpected return from knee surgery was announced in the afternoon, precluding a possible return as DH in the World Series.

But the Cubs players were ready for anything, and nothing seemed to faze them. Series co-MVP Javier Baez got the crowd into it by pumping his chest a few times after starting a double play in the first and stealing a popup from Rizzo in the fifth despite Rizzo waving his arms and calling for it.

Like a couple of kids in Little League, Rizzo pretended to go after Baez.

Maybe that's why this team is as good as it is: The players have never lost the kid in them, even when the stakes were highest. ●

Chicago Cubs players are exuberant after earning a spot in the 2016 World Series. (Chris Sweda/Chicago Tribune)

Chicago Cubs players and coaches gather
to celebrate the organization's first
National League championship since 1945.
(Nuccio DiNuzzo/Chicago Tribune)